# Transport Systems: Safety Modeling, Visions and Strategies

# Transport Systems: Safety Modeling, Visions and Strategies

Editors

**Krzysztof Goniewicz**
**Robert Czerski**
**Marek Kustra**

MDPI • Basel • Beijing • Wuhan • Barcelona • Belgrade • Manchester • Tokyo • Cluj • Tianjin

*Editors*

Krzysztof Goniewicz
Department of Security
Polish Air Force University
Deblin
Poland

Robert Czerski
Faculty of Aviation Safety
Polish Air Force University
Deblin
Poland

Marek Kustra
Faculty of Aviation Safety
Polish Air Force University
Deblin
Poland

*Editorial Office*
MDPI
St. Alban-Anlage 66
4052 Basel, Switzerland

This is a reprint of articles from the Special Issue published online in the open access journal *Infrastructures* (ISSN 2412-3811) (available at: www.mdpi.com/journal/infrastructures/special_issues/Transport_System).

For citation purposes, cite each article independently as indicated on the article page online and as indicated below:

LastName, A.A.; LastName, B.B.; LastName, C.C. Article Title. *Journal Name* **Year**, *Volume Number*, Page Range.

**ISBN 978-3-0365-3726-9 (Hbk)**
**ISBN 978-3-0365-3725-2 (PDF)**

# Contents

*infrastructures* MDPI

*Article*

# Citizens' Perceptions in Relation to Transport Systems and Infrastructures: A Nationwide Study in the Dominican Republic

**Francisco Alonso [1,2], Mireia Faus [1], Boris Cendales [3] and Sergio A. Useche [1,2,*]**

1 DATS (Development and Advising in Traffic Safety) Research Group, INTRAS (Research Institute on Traffic and Road Safety), University of Valencia, 46022 Valencia, Spain; francisco.alonso@uv.es (F.A.); mireia.faus@uv.es (M.F.)
2 Faculty of Psychology, University of Valencia, 46010 Valencia, Spain
3 Faculty of Economic and Administrative Sciences, El Bosque University, Bogota 110121, Colombia; boriscendales@gmail.com
* Correspondence: sergio.useche@uv.es

**Abstract:** One of the challenges currently faced by emerging countries is to get their citizens to decide to use sustainable transport for their regular trips, in order to reduce the current vehicular pollution rates. The objective of this descriptive research is to examine the perceptions of Dominicans regarding the state of the country's transport systems and road infrastructure. For this purpose, a nationwide survey procedure was performed. This cross-sectional research used the data retrieved from a sample of 1260 citizens aged over 18, proportional in gender, age, habitat, and province of the Dominican Republic. The results showed how Dominicans believe that, compared to other road features, pedestrian roads and public transport vehicles remain in a very poor condition. Further, citizens report to be more interested about the improvement of road infrastructures than in the implementation of any other set of measures performed to promote sustainable road mobility, including those related with alternative transport means. Finally, this study claims for the need of fostering educational, communicative and participative actions and measures aimed at increasing the value given to sustainable transportation, and the relevance of integrate potential structural and vehicular improvements with those related to human behavior in mobility.

**Keywords:** perception; mobility; road safety; cities; infrastructures; Dominican Republic

**Citation:** Alonso, F.; Faus, M.; Cendales, B.; Useche, S.A. Citizens' Perceptions in Relation to Transport Systems and Infrastructures: A Nationwide Study in the Dominican Republic. *Infrastructures* **2021**, *6*, 153. https://doi.org/10.3390/infrastructures6110153

Academic Editors: Krzysztof Goniewicz, Robert Czerski and Marek Kustra

Received: 23 September 2021
Accepted: 21 October 2021
Published: 25 October 2021



## 1. Introduction

Given the recently released Sustainable Development Goals (SDGs), many governmental authorities around the world are developing action plans to encourage sustainable transport as an essential part of their regional development plans [1]. In brief, it is a fact that the present and future of cities is bound to be greener [2]. Therefore, it is necessary to reduce the pollution rates produced by the high concentrations of vehicles on the roads [3,4]. One of the main measures in this regard is the implementation of actions to improve mobility in cities and, thus, avoid traffic jams [5,6].

Over the last two decades, transport mobility problems have turned in a particularly concerning phenomenon worldwide, but especially in emerging countries, whose resources and capability remain more limited to face several problems present in many spheres, including those other than mobility [7]. The idiosyncrasies of these countries exacerbate this situation due to several factors [8]. On the one hand, the existing infrastructures are deficient, and there is a lack of technological systems [9,10]. Further, technical reports frequently show how inadequately constructed sidewalks and roads with obstacles hinder the flow of traffic, endangering users' urban trips. In addition, on many occasions, public roads are not prepared or adapted to the needs of city dwellers [11]. Dangerous road scenes occur due to the lack of traffic lights, pedestrian crossings or level crossings in areas with a high concentration of population and frequency of travel. Thus, poor planning of road construction has a direct impact on the road safety of citizens [12]. On the other hand, another aspect that should be emphasized is that the quality of public transport service is not optimal because of the condition of vehicles and the planning of transport routes [13].

All these elements modify the way citizens move around. In fact, many studies indicate that a large number of people do not commute on foot or use a bicycle because their towns and cities do not have an efficient infrastructure for this purpose, even though these would be their preferred modes of transportation [14].

Some recent studies have been systematically showing how, in addition to socioeconomic factors, there are other issues greatly influencing the quality of infrastructure of countries. These factors include, e.g., the region's size, tourism density, the degree of urbanization and motorization, and government strategies [15,16]. In the particular case of the Dominican Republic, the large annual volume of tourists is, in fact, one of the reasons that have allowed the wider development of the road network, as well as the conditions and coverage of public transport services [9].

However, perceptions in these regards may vary among users, especially when compared to objective data. Indeed, users' perceptions of road infrastructures also tend to substantially differ across countries. Azik et al. (2021) found that road systems tend to be positively evaluated in Russia and Estonia, highlighting its adequacy for pedestrians and cyclists, while Turkish citizens stated that the infrastructural adequacy for driving in their country was rather *unsafe* for users [17]. Similarly, a study performed in the UK reported that sidewalk and traffic conditions were commonly perceived barriers to pedestrians and key factors in the choice of travel route [18]. In other research conducted in the United States, citizens perceived an improvement in road conditions compared to two decades ago, even though not to a very extensive extent. Still, most respondents agreed with a moderate tax increase to improve the road infrastructure in their area [19]. Overall, all these studies show how important it is for the population to have adequate and safe road networks in constant development [20].

### 1.1. Study Area

The situation in the Dominican Republic is framed within the aforementioned particularities. The country has 4,842,367 private vehicles registered in its national vehicle fleet as of 2020, representing an increase of 4.5% over the previous year [21]. This number of vehicles, together with the state of the road infrastructure, has an impact on the country's mobility problems and its high accident rate, which is one of the highest in the world [22]. Although the Dominican Republic has multiple means of public transport, the quality of these means that citizens choose to travel by private car or motorcycle [23]. The public transport supply is mainly composed of motorcycles, cabs, and urban buses, although there are also metro and metropolitan buses in the major cities of Santo Domingo and Santiago [24].

Additionally, in recent years national and local authorities have tried to promote sustainable transport through communication campaigns, but they have not been assessed as very effective [25]. Data from 2018 indicate that only 21% travel by foot regularly, 36% by public transport, and less than 1% make regular trips by bicycle [26].

In regard to economic settings, most trade in the Dominican Republic is carried out by land transport, with the country's road network being the main facilitator of the distribution of goods and services [27]. In addition, the existing literature in the field generally agrees on the importance of counting on adequate development and maintenance actions of roads, routes, and public transport vehicles, given that all them constitute potential engines to invigorate many other important dynamics of the country's economy, including tourism and regional development [28].

### 1.2. Objectives

The present study aims to examine the perceptions of the population of the Dominican Republic regarding the state of their road infrastructure, public transport, and the degree to which they believe their cities are prepared for the travel needs of their citizens. In addition, opinions regarding future measures that the government plans to implement were also analyzed, in order to assess the degree of peoples' predisposition to partake in such changes, and to suggest some practical guidelines for transport-related policymakers in the region.

## 2. Materials and Methods

### 2.1. Participants

This study analyzed the information provided by a nationwide sample of $n$ = 1260 Dominican Republic residents from different cities of the country. It was a completely voluntary and anonymous process and corresponded to the main features of the general Dominican population. According to the ONE census (National Statistics Office of Dominican Republic), the sample distribution was proportional to the population by gender, age (over 18), habitat, and province [18] (Table 1 and Figure 1). If we assume a degree of confidence of 99 percent, a maximum margin of error of 5 percent (=0.05), and a beta of 0.20, which allows for an 80 percent power, the minimum sample size should be around $n$ = 680 (Table 1).

**Table 1.** Sociodemographic data of the sample.

| Feature | Category | Total | | Male | | Female | |
|---|---|---|---|---|---|---|---|
| | | $n$ | % | $n$ | % | $n$ | % |
| Age range | 18–24 | 260 | 20.6% | 136 | 21.6% | 124 | 19.7% |
| | 25–34 | 311 | 24.7% | 146 | 23.2% | 165 | 26.2% |
| | 35–49 | 366 | 29.0% | 193 | 30.6% | 173 | 27.5% |
| | 50–64 | 221 | 17.5% | 108 | 17.1% | 113 | 17.9% |
| | >65 | 102 | 8.1% | 57 | 17.1% | 55 | 8.7% |
| | Total | 1260 | 100% | 630 | 100% | 630 | 100% |
| Do you drive a motor vehicle? | Yes | 580 | 46.0% | 458 | 72.7% | 122 | 19.4% |
| | No | 680 | 54.0% | 172 | 27.3% | 508 | 80.6% |
| | Total | 1260 | 100% | 630 | 100% | 630 | 100% |
| Do you have a driver's license? | Yes | 273 | 21.7% | 244 | 38.7% | 29 | 4.6% |
| | No | 987 | 78.7% | 386 | 61.3% | 601 | 95.4% |
| | Total | 1260 | 100% | 630 | 100% | 630 | 100% |
| Do you normally drive? | Yes | 470 | 37.3% | 392 | 62.2% | 78 | 12.4% |
| | No | 790 | 62.7% | 238 | 37.8% | 552 | 87.6% |
| | Total | 1260 | 100% | 630 | 100% | 630 | 100% |
| Type of driver | Professional | 202 | 35.1% | 190 | 41.5% | 12 | 9.8% |
| | Private | 373 | 64.9% | 264 | 57.6% | 109 | 89.3% |
| | Total | 685 | 100% | 454 | 100% | 121 | 100% |

### 2.2. Design, Procedure and Instruments

The data used in this study came from the Dominican Republic's National Survey on Mobility, which was conducted in 2019 [29]. The questionnaire covered topics such as institutional knowledge and traffic rules, public transportation, private transportation, on-foot movements, bike use, ITS systems and measures, and the variables studied in this study. It is a first-of-its-kind questionnaire in Latin America, where such comprehensive instruments had never been used. It was first administered in 2018 to examine the situation in the country and detect changes in the way Dominicans move as a result of INTRANT's different programs.

**Figure 1.** Distribution of the study sample by provinces or regions.

Personal, in-person interviews were used to administer the survey. The sample was collected between 24 November and 7 December of this year. The information was gathered using a CAPI system (Computer Assisted Personal Interviews) on tablets, which recorded and geo-referenced the interviews in order to shorten the interview time and eliminate any recording errors.

In order to achieve the proposed objectives, the following variables were taken into account:

- Sociodemographic variables and driving data: gender, age group, habitat, Do you habitually drive? Are you a professional driver? Do you currently hold have a driving license?
- Perceptions of road infrastructure: aspects such as street lighting, traffic density and speed, the distance of pedestrians from vehicles, safety or the condition of sidewalks are evaluated. In addition, a general evaluation of the degree to which the Dominican Republic is prepared for walking. All on a Likert scale of 0–10.
- Perceptions of public transport: elements such as comfort, pre-fare, accessibility, cleanliness and punctuality, evaluated on a 10-point Likert scale.
- Assessment of possible future measures in the field of transit mobility: various concrete actions such as the construction of bridges and tunnels, the improvement in the prioritization of transport, the improvement of sidewalk and road conditions or the development of road education programs and traffic communication campaigns scored on a Likert scale ranging between 0 and 10.

### 2.3. Data Processing

The goal of this study was to describe and characterize the general memory of the Dominican public on traffic campaigns through descriptive (frequency) analysis. ANOVA tests were also run to see whether there were any statistical correlations with sociodemographic factors. Following the collection of these data, statistical analyses were conducted using IBM SPSS (Statistical Package for Social Sciences), version 23.0.

### 2.4. Ethics

The Ethics Committee of Research in Social Science in Health of the University of Valencia was consulted before the study, and it confirmed that the research met general ethical criteria and was in agreement with the Declaration of Helsinki (IRB approval number: HE0001251019). After the team had given them a detailed description of the research goal and all preceding considerations, participants gave their informed consent to participate in the study. It is important to remark that the administration of personal information was carried out in compliance with current data protection regulations and ethical standards (including their full anonymity and the blinding of any potential identification information, except for generic demographic features), as it was also explained to each one of the participants before starting the survey.

### 3. Results

The general perception of Dominicans is that their country does not have streets sufficiently prepared for walking (M = 5.20; SD = 3.69). Such assessment is determined by the state of the roads and the road infrastructures linked to pedestrian displacements. Figure 2 shows the scores given to various specific aspects of public roads in the Dominican Republic. The perception that there are few places to cross the street (M = 4.78; SD = 3.57), the short green time at traffic lights when pedestrians are crossing (M = 4.67; SD = 3.78), and the lack of separation between pedestrians and other road users, particularly with vehicles on the road (M = 4.98; SD = 3.61) stand out among them. In addition, citizens point out the low level of safety they perceive when walking (M = 4.59; SD = 3.69). This situation has repercussions for pedestrians, who relatively frequently have to avoid certain streets due to the danger they perceive (M = 6.15; SD = 3.94), as well as having to change sidewalks because of parked vehicles or other obstacles in the road (M = 6.38; SD = 3.88).

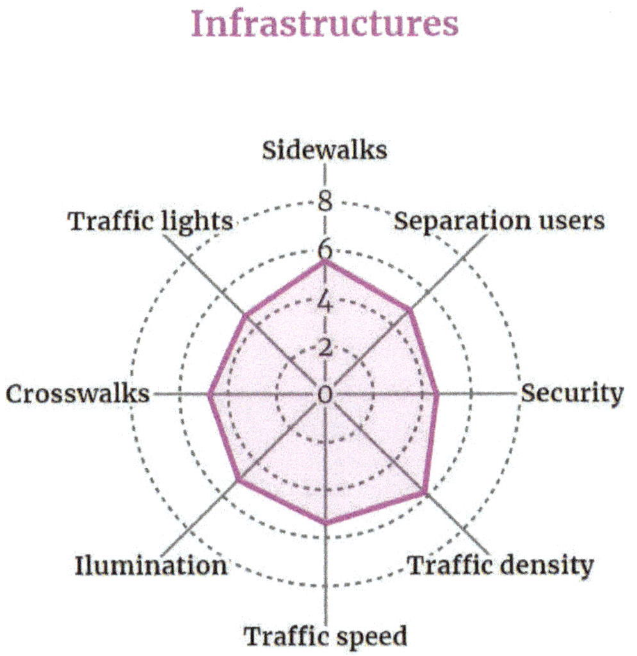


**Figure 2.** Assessment of roadway features by Dominican pedestrians.

The evaluation of public transport is relatively positive, especially in relation to accessibility (M = 7.08; SD = 3.19) and frequency (M = 6.99; SD = 3.08). However, there are some aspects that present insufficient scores. Especially comfort (M = 5.11; SD = 3.56), price (M = 6.27; SD = 3.40), and cleanliness (M = 5.42; SD = 3.67) (see Figure 3).

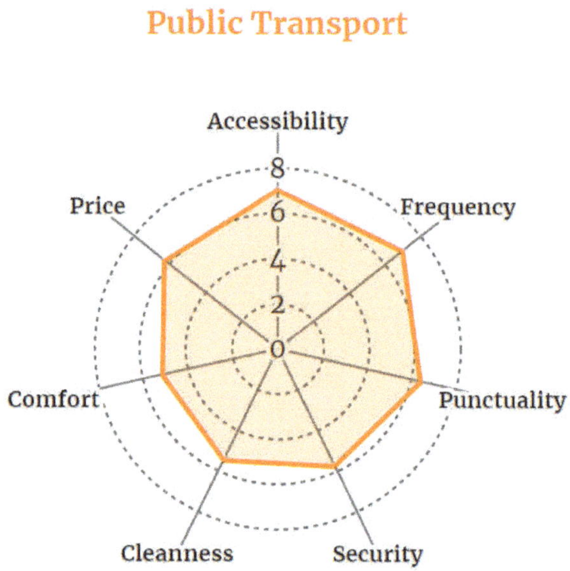


**Figure 3.** Assessment of public transportation conditions in the Dominican Republic.

In general, there was observed a favorable predisposition towards the possible new measures that could be adopted by the Dominican government in terms of road mobility, as none of them were rated, on average, below 7.5 out of 10 possible points (see Figure 4). The improvement of public transport priority (M = 8.93; SD = 2.03), the improvement of sidewalks for pedestrians (M = 8.92; SD = 2.24), and the improvement of roads, highways, and connectors (M = 8.85; SD = 2.24) stand out over the other possible issues presented in relation to transportation system features. In other words, this shows how, overall, there is a perceived priority for improving road conditions and traffic infrastructure over other more educational or transportation planning measures over other relevant issues, such as transport cleanness (especially if the impact of the current COVID-19 pandemic is considered) and transport security.

It should be also noted that most of the measures were more highly rated by women than by men. However, there were only significant differences between these two groups in a total of four items, all of them related to public transport. Therefore, it was determined that females are more willing than males to adopt measures that encourage shared transport, allow greater priority to be given to public transportation, generate specific routes for public transport, and improve modal interchange between different modes of transport. Although there were no significant differences between provinces, there were differences according to habitat. Some measures showed differences between people with a driver's license and those without one. However, given the characteristics of Dominican citizens, it is curious that there were no such significant differences between regular and nonregular drivers. Table 2 presents the mean comparison test scores and significance levels of all the variables analyzed.

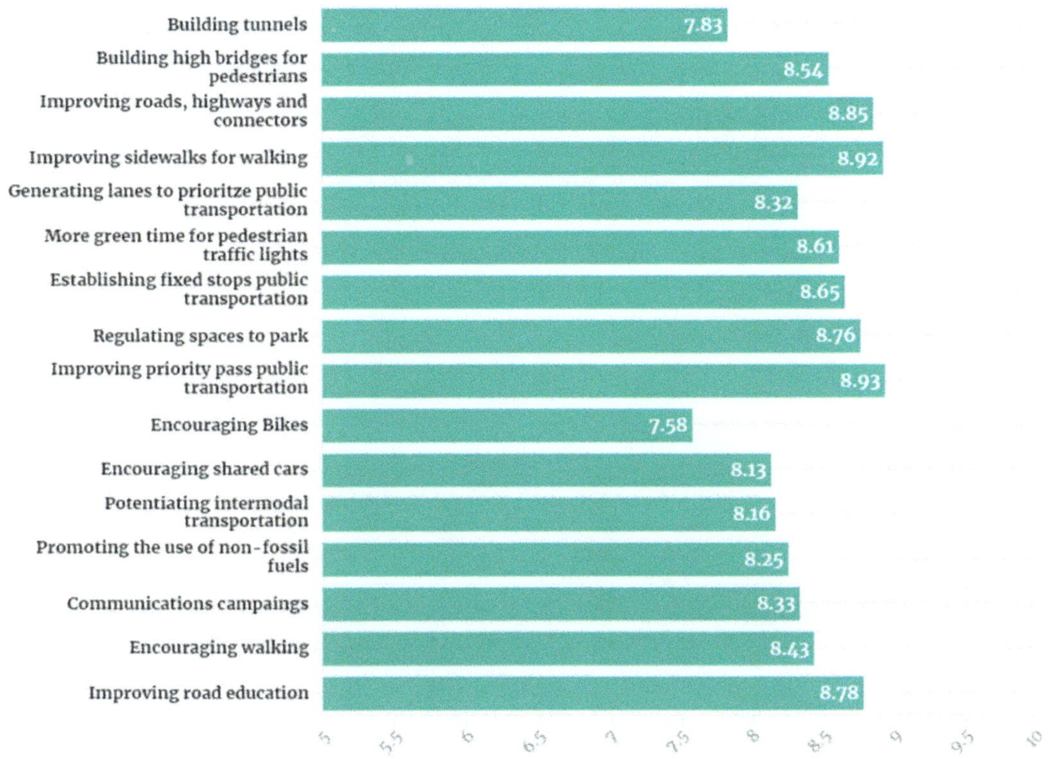


**Figure 4.** Assessment of future mobility measures by Dominican citizens.

**Table 2.** Differences in the assessment of mobility measures according to citizens' genders.

| Mobility Measures and Improvements | Gender | | | | | | ANOVA |
|---|---|---|---|---|---|---|---|
| | Male | | | Female | | | |
| | *n* | M | SD | *n* | M | SD | |
| Generating lanes to prioritize public transportation * | 620 | 8.14 | 2.58 | 614 | 8.51 | 2.30 | $F(1,1233) = 6.924$; $p = 0.009$ |
| Improving priority pass public transportation * | 625 | 8.76 | 2.21 | 626 | 9.10 | 1.82 | $F(1,1250) = 8.832$; $p = 0.003$ |
| Encouraging shared cars * | 604 | 7.95 | 2.67 | 595 | 8.31 | 2.43 | $F(1,1198) = 6.058$; $p = 0.014$ |
| Potentiating intermodal transportation * | 610 | 8.03 | 2.43 | 302 | 8.30 | 2.44 | $F(1,1211) = 3.804$; $p = 0.050$ |
| | **Habitat** | | | | | | **ANOVA** |
| | **Urban** | | | **Rural** | | | |
| | *n* | M | SD | *n* | M | SD | |
| Building tunnels * | 1020 | 8.01 | 3.10 | 226 | 7.04 | 3.50 | $F(1,1245) = 17.423$; $p < 0.01$ |
| Generating lanes to prioritize public transportation * | 1012 | 8.40 | 2.41 | 222 | 7.99 | 2.61 | $F(1,1232) = 5.158$; $p = 0.023$ |
| Establishing fixed stops public transportation * | 1021 | 8.72 | 2.39 | 229 | 8.31 | 2.50 | $F(1,1248) = 5.465$; $p = 0.020$ |
| Regulating spaces to park * | 1023 | 8.83 | 2.23 | 228 | 8.48 | 2.37 | $F(1,1249) = 4.323$; $p = 0.038$ |
| Communications campaigns * | 1021 | 8.41 | 2.52 | 228 | 7.98 | 2.66 | $F(1,1247) = 5.320$; $p = 0.021$ |
| | **Driving License** | | | | | | **ANOVA** |
| | **Yes** | | | **No** | | | |
| | *n* | M | SD | *n* | M | SD | |
| Building tunnels * | 272 | 8.28 | 2.68 | 974 | 7.71 | 3.31 | $F(1,1245) = 6.782$; $p = 0.009$ |
| Regulating spaces to park * | 272 | 9.01 | 1.93 | 979 | 8.69 | 2.34 | $F(1,1249) = 4.187$; $p = 0.041$ |
| Promoting the use of non-fossil fuels * | 269 | 8.57 | 2.21 | 967 | 8.16 | 2.65 | $F(1,1235) = 5.309$; $p = 0.021$ |
| Encouraging walking * | 270 | 8.82 | 2.04 | 977 | 8.32 | 2.77 | $F(1,1245) = 7.623$; $p = 0.006$ |

* All study variable comparisons appended in the table correspond to significant differences ($p < 0.050$).

## 4. Discussion

This manuscript aims to examine the perceptions of the citizens of the Dominican Republic regarding the state of the national road infrastructure and transport vehicles. This is a first approximation of the travel needs of Dominicans, which has direct practical implications for the development of future measures affecting road construction and transportation mobility planning in the country.

There is a general perception that the state of the roads is not entirely adequate. Respondents are clearly dissatisfied with the road conditions, which even forces them to change some of their routes. The proximity to vehicles, the density and speed of traffic, and the obstacles on the sidewalks are some of the problems pedestrians have in their daily lives. Additionally, this is a problem that not only affects mobility and travel, but also has direct repercussions on the road safety of users [30,31]. Factors such as the absence of pedestrian infrastructure [32], poor lighting [33], or the type of street [34] are linked to road accidents. In addition, it has been proven that walking on a street in poor conditions affects pedestrians and makes them more prone to jaywalking or other risky behaviors [35].

This situation undoubtedly makes pedestrians in emerging countries, where pedestrian protection is less developed, particularly vulnerable [36–38]. Data indicate that more than 40% of the annual deaths caused by traffic accidents involve pedestrians in Asia, Africa, and the Caribbean. In comparison, this figure is less than 20% in Europe and the United States [39]. Therefore, it is necessary to develop actions specifically aimed at the protection and safety of pedestrians [40,41]. In fact, one of the measures most highly valued by Dominicans is the improvement of sidewalks as well as roads. In any case, and until an increase in the quality of these road infrastructures is designed and implemented, pedestrians should be aware of the risks of the road and try to protect themselves to the best of their ability [42]. Avoiding being distracted by a phone and being aware of the road circumstances can be crucial to prevent a crash [43].

In this sense, a second group harmed by road conditions is the cyclists. In the Dominican Republic, they are a tremendously reduced road group. In fact, the latest data indicate that only 1% use bicycles on a daily basis [25]. In countries such as Denmark, the United Kingdom, or Australia, infrastructure improvement for cyclists led to a substantial increase in this type of user [44,45]. Therefore, it is very likely that the Dominican Republic would substantially increase its cycling population if appropriate actions are taken.

It is important to promote walking and cycling to reduce pollution rates and increase the sustainability of the country [46]. In addition to this, citizens should also be encouraged to use public transport [47]. The vehicular circumstances and conditions in which the public transport fleet of many emerging countries is in, among other factors, cause citizens to tend not to use them as much as desirable [48]. In these places, public transport tends to have poorer planning and service [49,50]. In particular, the Dominican Republic has several transportation systems but with poorly defined routes that are not adapted to the needs of citizens [51]. In fact, the most commonly used public means of transport are urban buses and motorcycle cabs, which generally do not have established stops but pick up passengers at points of high passenger density that are not defined in the metropolitan bus routes [52]. This leads to some road chaos, traffic jams, and mobility problems [53].

In this sense, it is not surprising that measures focused on improving public transport routes are among the most highly valued. In addition, it should be noted that these types of actions are the ones in which the most significant differences are found according to gender, with females being the ones who prioritize them the most. This is logical given the dynamics of displacement in the country, where there are practically no women drivers [25]. Therefore, they especially demand conditions that are more appropriate to the characteristics of their trips [27].

The lack of safety perceived by users is another element to be mentioned. For both on foot and public transport, security is poorly rated. In these scenarios, robberies, violent actions, or harassment can occur, which also determines the consumption level of public transport services [54,55]. This is undoubtedly an important problem, as it indicates that improving road infrastructure conditions may not be enough to change travel dynamics [56]. Not feeling safe and comfortable is sufficient motivation to avoid traveling in the area or vehicle that causes such insecurity [57].

This context is especially important with women [58]. Figures indicate that public roads, and more specifically, public transport, are areas where harassment situations frequently occur [59–61]. In addition, they have the problem that, even if they do not want to use any particular transport, they are often forced to do so because they have no other travel options [62]. This occurs especially in countries such as the Dominican Republic, where it is very rare to find women drivers [25]. Harassment in transportation is a common phenomenon worldwide, so in recent years specific actions have been developed to reduce the insecurity of female users [63]: from basic measures such as the installation of security cameras [64] or education and social awareness campaigns [65] to major actions such as "pink" vehicles or cars for females only [66], or specific mobile applications [67].

In short, if the authorities intend to change the dynamics of travel of Dominicans in favor of more sustainable mobility, concrete actions must be developed to improve road infrastructure and the conditions of public vehicles [68]. Only this way will it be possible to initiate a change that increases walking, cycling, and public transport in the country [69].

## 5. Conclusions

After analyzing the perceptions of Dominican users regarding the conditions of their country's transportation and infrastructure, the results of this study allow to describe a considerably low valuation of these key transport-related spheres.

On the other hand, citizens tend to support the implementation of new measures to improve these conditions, in order to adapt them to their actual needs. In this regard, these measures should be aimed at improving the public transport fleet, as well as planning routes that meet the needs of the population. In addition, it is necessary to improve the condition of sidewalks and pedestrian walkways, in order to both enhance walkability and active transport, thus fostering sustainable mobility.

The results of this study may be of great use to the authorities of the Dominican Republic and other emerging countries with similar contexts and characteristics [9]. This is the first step before the planning, design, and implementation of concrete actions to improve mobility and, consequently, the pollution levels produced by the large number of trips in private transport.

**Author Contributions:** For this study, F.A., S.A.U. and M.F. conceived and designed the research, and performed the data collection; S.A.U. and M.F. analyzed the data; F.A. and S.A.U. contributed with reagents/materials/analysis tools; M.F., B.C. and S.A.U. wrote and revised the paper. All authors have read and agreed to the published version of the manuscript.

**Funding:** This study was funded by the National Institute of Transit and Land Transportation (INTRANT) and its Permanent Observatory in Road Safety (OPSEVI; public agency of the Dominican Republic)-Grant number: 20170475. Additionally, this work was supported by the research grant ACIF/2020/035 (MF) from "Generalitat Valenciana". Funding entities did not contribute to the study design or data collection, analysis and interpretation, or writing of the manuscript.

**Institutional Review Board Statement:** The study was conducted according to the guidelines of the Declaration of Helsinki, and approved by the Ethics Committee of Research in Social Sciences in Health" from the University Institute on Traffic and Road Safety of the University of Valencia (Spain) (protocol code HE000125101, approved on 25 October 2019).

**Informed Consent Statement:** Informed consent was obtained from all subjects involved in the study.

**Data Availability Statement:** The data will be available upon reasonable request to the corresponding author.

**Acknowledgments:** The authors wish to thank Mayte Duce for the revisions and Arash Javadinejad for the professional edition of the final version of the manuscript.

**Conflicts of Interest:** The authors declare that there are no conflicts of interest or potential disclosures.

## References


1. Sofia, D.; Gioiella, F.; Lotrecchiano, N.; Giuliano, A. Mitigation strategies for reducing air pollution. *Environ. Sci. Pollut. Res.* **2020**, *27*, 19226–19235. [CrossRef]
2. Reisi, M.; Aye, L.; Rajabifard, A.; Ngo, T. Transport sustainability index: Melbourne case study. *Ecol. Indic.* **2014**, *43*, 288–296. [CrossRef]
3. Jacyna, M.; Wasiak, M.; Lewczuk, K.; Karoń, G. Noise and environmental pollution from transport: Decisive problems in developing ecologically efficient transport systems. *J. Vibroeng.* **2017**, *19*, 5639–5655. [CrossRef]
4. Sicard, P.; De Marco, A.; Agathokleous, E.; Feng, Z.; Xu, X.; Paoletti, E.; Diéguemez, J.J.; Calatayud, V. Amplified ozone pollution in cities during the COVID-19 lockdown. *Sci. Total Environ.* **2020**, *735*, 139542. [CrossRef]
5. Mueller, N.; Rojas-Rueda, D.; Khreis, H.; Cirach, M.; Andrés, D.; Ballester, J.; Bartoll, X.; Daher, C.; de Luca, A.; Echav, C.; et al. Changing the urban design of cities for health: The superblock model. *Environ. Int.* **2020**, *134*, 105132. [CrossRef] [PubMed]
6. De Gruyter, C.; Currie, G.; Rose, G. Sustainability measures of urban public transport in cities: A world review and focus on the Asia/Middle East Region. *Sustainability* **2017**, *9*, 43. [CrossRef]
7. Pojani, D.; Stead, D. The urban transport crisis in emerging economies: An introduction. In *The Urban Transport Crisis in Emerging Economies*; Springer: Cham, Switzerland, 2017; pp. 1–10. [CrossRef]
8. Marotti De Mello, A.; Valsecchi Ribeiro De Souza, J.; Marx, R. Public Transport in Emerging Countries: From Old Dilemmas to Opportunities for Transition to Sustainable Mobility Through the Case of Brazil. In *The Robomobility Revolution of Urban Public Transport*; Springer: Cham, Switzerland, 2021; pp. 167–179. [CrossRef]
9. Alonso, F.; Faus, M.; Esteban, C.; Useche, S.A. Is There a Predisposition towards the Use of New Technologies within the Traffic Field of Emerging Countries? The Case of the Dominican Republic. *Electronics* **2021**, *10*, 1208. [CrossRef]
10. Kateja, A. Building infrastructure: Private participation in emerging economies. *Procedia Soc. Behav. Sci.* **2012**, *37*, 368–378. [CrossRef]
11. Silva FN, D. Urban mobility: The challenges of the future. *Cadernos. Metrópole* **2013**, *15*, 377–388. [CrossRef]
12. Gitelman, V.; Balasha, D.; Carmel, R.; Hendel, L.; Pesahov, F. Characterization of pedestrian accidents and an examination of infrastructure measures to improve pedestrian safety in Israel. *Accid. Anal. Prev.* **2012**, *44*, 63–73. [CrossRef]
13. Jaramillo, C.; Lizárraga, C.; Grindlay, A.L. Spatial disparity in transport social needs and public transport provision in Santiago de Cali (Colombia). *J. Transp. Geogr.* **2012**, *24*, 340–357. [CrossRef]
14. Chinchayán, M.J. Política Nacional de Transporte Urbano y Su Impacto en El Uso de la Bicicleta Como Transporte Alternativo en Chiclayo. 2020. Available online: https://hdl.handle.net/20.500.12692/47375 (accessed on 10 September 2021).
15. Statistical Office of the European Communities. *EUROSTAT: Road Safety Statistics at Regional Level*; Eurostat: Luxembourg, 2017. Available online: http://ec.europa.eu/eurostat/statistics-explained/index.php/Road_safety_statistics_at_regional_level (accessed on 8 July 2021).
16. World Health Organization. Key Facts: Road Traffic Injuries. 2018. Available online: http://www.who.int/news-room/fact-sheets/detail/road-traffic-injuries (accessed on 8 July 2021).
17. Azık, D.; Solmazer, G.; Ersan, Ö.; Kaçan, B.; Fındık, G.; Üzümcüoğlu, Y.; Özkan, T.; Lajunen, T.; Öz, B.; Pashkevich, A.; et al. Road users' evaluations and perceptions of road infrastructure, trip characteristics, and daily trip experiences across countries. *Transp. Res. Interdiscip. Perspect.* **2021**, *11*, 100412. [CrossRef]
18. Anciaes, P.R.; Stockton, J.; Ortegon, A.; Scholes, S. Perceptions of road traffic conditions along with their reported impacts on walking are associated with wellbeing. *Travel Behav. Soc.* **2019**, *15*, 88–101. [CrossRef]
19. Fogg, L.M.; Hamilton, L.C.; Bell, E.S. Views of the Highway: Infrastructure Reality, Perceptions, and Politics. *SAGE Open* **2020**, *10*. [CrossRef]
20. Blom, C.M.; Guthrie, P.M. Surveying customer perceptions of road infrastructure comfort. Infrastruct. *Asset Manag.* **2015**, *2*, 173–185. [CrossRef]
21. DGII. *Boletín Estadístico. Parque Vehicuar 2020*; Dirección General de Impuestos Internos: Santo Domingo, Dominican Republic, 2020.
22. Nazif, J.I.; Pérez, G. Revisión del Desempeño de la Seguridad vial en la República Dominicana. 2018. Available online: http://hdl.handle.net/11362/44211 (accessed on 8 September 2021).
23. Mazzucco, E.J.F.; Eusebio, M.P.; Vidal, E.; Mejía, V.B. Manejo de lesiones del talón infantil por rayos de motocicleta en República Dominicana. Serie de casos. *Rev. Mex. Ortop. Ped.* **2020**, *22*, 36–43. [CrossRef]
24. Simmons, D. Structural violence as social practice: Haitian agricultural workers, anti-Haitianism, and health in the Dominican Republic. *Hum. Organ.* **2010**, *69*, 10–18. [CrossRef]
25. Alonso, F.; Faus, M.; Fernández, C.; Useche, S.A. "Where Have I Heard It?" Assessing the Recall of Traffic Safety Campaigns in the Dominican Republic. *Energies* **2021**, *14*, 5792. [CrossRef]
26. INTRANT (Instituto Nacional de Tránsito y Transporte Terrestre). *National Mobility Survey of the Dominican Republic. Results Report 2018*; INTRANT: Santo Domingo, Dominican Republic, 2019.
27. Del Rosario Brito, A.A. Plan de Mantenimiento para Infraestructuras Viales en República Dominicana. Aplicación a la Carretera El Seibo-Hato Mayor. 2018. Available online: https://riunet.upv.es/handle/10251/103062 (accessed on 8 September 2021).
28. Agüera, F.O. Geografía turística de Republica Dominicana: Comportamientos de la demanda, gestión sostenible y propuesta de estudio. *Cuad. Geográficos Univ. Granada* **2019**, *58*, 141–156.

29. INTRANT (Instituto Nacional de Tránsito y Transporte Terrestre). *National Mobility Survey of the Dominican Republic. Results Report 2019*; INTRANT: Santo Domingo, Dominican Republic, 2020.
30. Mukherjee, D.; Mitra, S. Impact of road infrastructure land use and traffic operational characteristics on pedestrian fatality risk: A case study of Kolkata, India. *Int. J. Transp. Econ.* **2019**, *5*, 1–9. [CrossRef]
31. Useche, S.A.; Alonso, F.; Montoro, L. Validation of the walking behavior questionnaire (WBQ): A tool for measuring risky and safe walking under a behavioral perspective. *J. Transp. Health* **2020**, *18*, 100899. [CrossRef]
32. Yasmin, S.; Eluru, N.; Ukkusuri, S.V. Alternative ordered response frameworks for examining pedestrian injury severity in New York City. *J. Transp. Saf.* **2014**, *6*, 275–300. [CrossRef]
33. Loukaitou-Sideris, A.; Liggett, R.; Sung, H.G. Death on the crosswalk: A study of pedestrian-automobile collisions in Los Angeles. *J. Plan. Educ. Res.* **2007**, *26*, 338–351. [CrossRef]
34. Morency, P.; Cloutier, M.S. From targeted "black spots" to area-wide pedestrian safety. *Inj. Prev.* **2006**, *12*, 360–364. [CrossRef] [PubMed]
35. Adinarayana, B.; Mir, M.S. Development of pedestrian safety index models for safety of pedestrian flow at un-signalized junctions on urban roads under mixed traffic conditions using MLR. *Innov. Infrastruct. Solut.* **2021**, *6*, 54. [CrossRef]
36. Zegeer, C.V.; Bushell, M. Pedestrian crash trends and potential countermeasures from around the world. *Accid. Anal. Prev.* **2012**, *44*, 3–11. [CrossRef] [PubMed]
37. Amoh-Gyimah, R.; Aidoo, E.N.; Akaateba, M.A.; Appiah, S.K. The effect of natural and built environmental characteristics on pedestrian-vehicle crash severity in Ghana. *Int. J. Inj. Control Saf. Promot.* **2017**, *24*, 459–468. [CrossRef] [PubMed]
38. Tulu, G.S.; Washington, S.; Haque, M.M.; King, M.J. Investigation of pedestrian crashes on two-way two-lane rural roads in Ethiopia. *Accid. Anal. Prev.* **2015**, *78*, 118–126. [CrossRef] [PubMed]
39. Ribbens, H. Strategies to promote the safety of vulnerable road users in developing and emerging countries: South African experience. *Transp. Res. Rec.* **2003**, *1846*, 26–30. [CrossRef]
40. Lam, W.W.; Yao, S.; Loo, B.P. Pedestrian exposure measures: A time-space framework. *Travel Behav. Soc.* **2014**, *1*, 22–30. [CrossRef]
41. Damsere-Derry, J.; Ebel, B.E.; Mock, C.N.; Afukaar, F.; Donkor, P.; Kalowole, T.O. Evaluation of the effectiveness of traffic calming measures on vehicle speeds and pedestrian injury severity in Ghana. *Traffic Inj. Prev.* **2019**, *20*, 336–342. [CrossRef] [PubMed]
42. Pinna, F.; Murrau, R. Age factor and pedestrian speed on sidewalks. *Sustainability* **2018**, *10*, 4084. [CrossRef]
43. Schwebel, D.C.; Stavrinos, D.; Byington, K.W.; Davis, T.; O'Neal, E.E.; De Jong, D. Distraction and pedestrian safety: How talking on the phone, texting, and listening to music impact crossing the street. *Accid. Anal. Prev.* **2012**, *45*, 266–271. [CrossRef]
44. Pucher, J.; Dill, J.; Handy, S. Infrastructure, programs, and policies to increase bicycling: An international review. *Prev. Med.* **2010**, *50*, S106–S125. [CrossRef]
45. Félix, R.; Moura, F.; Clifton, K.J. Maturing urban cycling: Comparing barriers and motivators to bicycle of cyclists and non-cyclists in Lisbon, Portugal. *J. Transp. Health* **2019**, *15*, 100628. [CrossRef]
46. Russo, F.; Comi, A. City characteristics and urban goods movements: A way to environmental transportation system in a sustainable city. *Procedia Soc. Behav. Sci.* **2012**, *39*, 61–73. [CrossRef]
47. Ma, Z.; Koutsopoulos, H.N.; Liu, T.; Basu, A.A. Behavioral response to promotion-based public transport demand management: Longitudinal analysis and implications for optimal promotion design. *Transp. Res. Part A Policy Pract.* **2020**, *141*, 356–372. [CrossRef]
48. Willoughby, C. How much can public private partnership really do for urban transport in developing countries? *Res. Transp. Econ.* **2013**, *40*, 34–55. [CrossRef]
49. Sietchiping, R.; Permezel, M.J.; Ngomsi, C. Transport and mobility in sub-Saharan African cities: An overview of practices, lessons and options for improvements. *Cities* **2012**, *29*, 183–189. [CrossRef]
50. Hickman, R.; Hall, P.; Banister, D. Planning more for sustainable mobility. *J. Transp. Geogr.* **2013**, *33*, 210–219. [CrossRef]
51. Montañez, M.R. Un nuevo modelo de transporte para el gran Santo Domingo. *Cienc. Soc.* **2016**, *41*, 337–359. Available online: https://www.redalyc.org/pdf/870/87046120005.pdf (accessed on 9 September 2021). [CrossRef]
52. González, P.D. Propuesta para la Mejora del Transporte Público en el Distrito Nacional, Santo Domingo. Ph.D. Thesis, University of Cartagena, Cartagena, Spain, 2015. Available online: https://repositorio.upct.es/handle/10317/5101 (accessed on 11 September 2021).
53. Santana, E.A.; Marte, J.C. Propuesta Estratégica para la Mejora en la Calidad del Servicio de Transporte Público: Caso Transporte Expreso Tarea, Ruta Santo Domingo-Bonao, República Dominicana. Ph.D. Thesis, University of Madre y Maestra, Santiago de los Caballeros, Dominican Republic, 2017. Available online: http://investigare.pucmm.edu.do:8080/xmlui/handle/20.500.12060/1861 (accessed on 12 September 2021).
54. Neupane, G.; Chesney-Lind, M. Violence against women on public transport in Nepal: Sexual harassment and the spatial expression of male privilege. *Int. J. Comp. Appl. Crim. Justice* **2014**, *38*, 23–38. [CrossRef]
55. Tripathi, K.; Borrion, H.; Belur, J. Sexual harassment of students on public transport: An exploratory study in Lucknow, India. *Crime Prev. Community Saf.* **2017**, *19*, 240–250. [CrossRef]
56. Lubitow, A.; Abelson, M.J.; Carpenter, E. Transforming mobility justice: Gendered harassment and violence on transit. *J. Transp. Geogr.* **2020**, *82*, 102601. [CrossRef]
57. Gardner, N.; Cui, J.; Coiacetto, E. Harassment on public transport and its impacts on women's travel behaviour. *Aust. Plan* **2017**, *54*, 8–15. [CrossRef]

58. Alonso, F.; Useche, S.A.; Faus, M.; Esteban, C. Does urban security modulate transportation choices and travel behavior of citizens? A national study in the Dominican Republic. *Front. Sustain. Cities* **2020**, *2*, 42. [CrossRef]
59. Mazumder, H.; Pokharel, B. Sexual violence on public transportation: A threat to women's mobility in Bangladesh. *J. Aggress. Maltreat. Trauma* **2019**, *28*, 1017–1019. [CrossRef]
60. Quinones, L.M. Sexual harassment in public transport in Bogotá. *Transp. Res. Part A Policy Pract.* **2020**, *139*, 54–69. [CrossRef]
61. Lubitow, A.; Carathers, J.; Kelly, M.; Abelson, M. Transmobilities: Mobility, harassment, and violence experienced by transgender and gender nonconforming public transit riders in Portland, Oregon. *Gend. Place Cult.* **2017**, *24*, 1398–1418. [CrossRef]
62. Gekoski, A.; Gray, J.M.; Adler, J.R.; Horvath, M.A. The prevalence and nature of sexual harassment and assault against women and girls on public transport: An international review. *J. Criminol. Res. Policy Pract.* **2017**. [CrossRef]
63. Ceccato, V. Women's transit safety: Making connections and defining future directions in research and practice. *Crime Prev. Community Saf.* **2017**, *19*, 276–287. [CrossRef]
64. Orozco-Fontalvo, M.; Soto, J.; Arévalo, A.; Oviedo-Trespalacios, O. Women's perceived risk of sexual harassment in a Bus Rapid Transit (BRT) system: The case of Barranquilla, Colombia. *J. Transp. Health* **2019**, *14*, 100598. [CrossRef]
65. Naik, M.N. Ensuring Safety for Women at Public Space: Need and Approaches. In *Building Sustainable Communities*; Palgrave Macmillan: Singapore, 2020; pp. 733–746. [CrossRef]
66. Bolaños, I.G.M.; Terán, M.; Paspuezán, R.A.P. Revisión del impacto de la movilidad urbana. *Visión Empresarial* **2019**, *9*, 128–134. [CrossRef]
67. Ruman, M.R.; Badhon, J.K.; Saha, S. Safety assistant and harassment prevention for women. In Proceedings of the 2019 5th International Conference on Advances in Electrical Engineering (ICAEE), Dhaka, Bangladesh, 26–28 September 2019; pp. 346–350. [CrossRef]
68. Abufares, L.; Awadallah, F. Sustainable Civil Infrastructures Utilization and Regulations of Innovative Technology to Improve Road Safety via Drivers' Warnings and Enforcement. In Proceedings of the Civil Infrastructures Confronting Severe Weathers and Climate Changes Conference, Nanchang, China, 19–21 July 2021; Springer: Cham, Switzerland, 2021; pp. 110–126. [CrossRef]
69. Useche, S.A.; Alonso, F.; Sanmartin, J.; Montoro, L.V.; Cendales, B. Well-being, behavioral patterns and cycling crashes of different age groups in Latin America: Are aging adults the safest cyclists? *PLoS ONE* **2019**, *14*, e0221864. [CrossRef]

*infrastructures* MDPI

*Article*

# A Scoping Study on Driver's Perspective of Distracting Factors

**Taleb M. Al-Rousan [1,*], Abdullahi A. Umar [2], Aslam A. Al-Omari [3,4], Yahia A. Khalaylah [1], Hamza M. Alkuime [1] and Ayoub H. Al-Rousan [5]**

1 Department of Civil Engineering, Faculty of Engineering, The Hashemite University, Zarqa 13133, Jordan; yahia@hu.edu.jo (Y.A.K.); alkuime@hu.edu.jo (H.M.A.)
2 Department of Civil Engineering and Quantity Surveying, Military Technological College, Al Matar Street, Muscat 111, Oman; Abdullah.Umar@mtc.edu.om
3 Civil Engineering Department, Jordan University of Science and Technology, Irbid 22110, Jordan; aaalomari3@just.edu.jo
4 Department of Civil Engineering, Applied Science Private University, Amman 11931, Jordan
5 Department of Child Education, Queen Rania Faculty for Childhood, The Hashemite University, Zarqa 13133, Jordan; AyoubH@hu.edu.jo
* Correspondence: taleb@hu.edu.jo; Tel.: +962-5-3903333 (ext. 4383); Fax: +962-5-3826348

**Abstract:** Distracting activities while driving are common and can result in errors that threaten road users' safety. The main objectives of this study were to investigate drivers' perspectives of the factors contributing to distraction, determine the relative rank of types of distractions, recognize the road factors and environmental effects that make distractions more dangerous, and identify the most effective measures to reduce driver distractions. A survey was conducted to assess Jordanian drivers' experiences with distracted driving, and what solutions they believed could be implemented to solve the problems. The study's outcomes revealed that drivers perceive visual distractions as the most dangerous, followed by cognitive, manual, and auditory distractions, respectively. It was also found that "mobile phone texting or dialing" was ranked the top most dangerous visual and manual distracting factor. "Baby is crying or kids are fighting in the back seat" was perceived by all demographic groups as the riskiest auditory factor. Regarding cognitive distraction, four factors were perceived as the most serious, of which "Baby is crying", "Driving while angry or sad or agitated", "Talking on a cell phone—even a hands-free one" and "Conversing with passengers" were determined to be the top four distracting factors. The results also revealed that drivers believe that "laws and enforcement" is the most effective measure to reduce distractions while driving.

**Keywords:** attention; COVID-19; driver's distraction; mobile phone; perspectives; traffic safety

**Citation:** Al-Rousan, T.M.; Umar, A.A.; Al-Omari, A.A.; Khalaylah, Y.A.; Alkuime, H.M.; Al-Rousan, A.H. A Scoping Study on Driver's Perspective of Distracting Factors. *Infrastructures* **2021**, *6*, 139. https://doi.org/10.3390/infrastructures6100139

Academic Editors: Krzysztof Goniewicz, Robert Czerski and Marek Kustra

Received: 26 August 2021
Accepted: 26 September 2021
Published: 30 September 2021

**Publisher's Note:** MDPI stays neutral with regard to jurisdictional claims in published maps and institutional affiliations.



## 1. Introduction

Distracting activities while driving are common and can result in driving errors that threaten road users' safety, as they might result in crashes. This is a crucial factor in the occurrence of traffic accidents, because the safety performance of the driver is reduced [1,2]. It has been reported that over 90% of traffic accidents are the outcome of human error and are caused by visual information acquisition issues [3]. Moreover, drivers are responsible for causing 90% of critical conditions in traffic [4,5].

Particular activities or events can distract the driver while driving. The distraction can be minimal or have no influence on the attention and driving performance of the driver, or it might be so extensive that the driver is not able to provide the required attention to the driving task, which greatly reduces his/her driving performance [6]. Hanowski et al. [7] described a distraction as occurring in the inattentive event, causing a delay in identifying information that is required for safely performing a driving task. Topolšek et al. [8] emphasized that there is no fundamental definition of driver distraction presently appropriate, but they argue that the most authentic definition would be that of Oviedo-Trespalacios et al. [9] who defined distraction as an occurrence encompassing the diversion of a driver's attention, temporarily focusing on something not related to his driving, which particularly mitigates his awareness, performance, and ability to make driving decisions.

Causes of driving distractions can be associated with any cognitive procedure, such as solving mathematical issues, using information systems in the vehicle, mind-wandering, or daydreaming; all of these can impact a driver's attention that should be directed to the driving process [10]. Drivers are fundamentally flexible and can shift their driving-associated behavior in a manner that enables them to meet an elevated demand for activities not associated with their driving [7]. Kinnear and Stevens [11] categorized driver distractions into four categories, which are not mutually exclusive, and drivers have been known to be involved in more than one type of distraction at the same time.

- Visual: taking the eyes off the road and glancing elsewhere to engage in a secondary activity inside or outside the vehicle.
- Manual: taking one or both hands off the steering wheel to engage in another activity.
- Cognitive: taking one's mind off the driving task.
- Auditory: diverting attention while driving. This type is mostly mutual with other distractions.

Potentially the most common distracting factor is the use of mobile phones, explored in a previous study by Sterkenburg and Jeon [12]. The use of such devices reduces driving precision and causes up to 50% slower responses to risks, thus causing a deterioration in performance [13]. Wood et al. [13] indicated that the use of hands-free systems also induces distracting effects. In-vehicle entertainment systems also influence driving behavior through acts such as adjusting radio volume [14,15].

The use of navigation systems has different impacts on the efficiency of driving, associated with the manner of controlling the device, manually or vocally [16]. Jenness et al. [17] revealed that manually operated devices take more attention from the driver, require a longer time to operate, and cause drivers to take their eyes off the road, compared with voice-operated devices.

Elements of the roadside can also present critical driver distractions as compared to in-vehicle distractions. Although observation of the traffic environment and roadside is an essential activity in driving, some elements outside of the vehicle may draw drivers' attention and present a critical distraction. For instance, roadside billboards and posters, electronic billboards, and landscape heritage sites are considered key distractors to drivers [18–20].

Mind-wandering is another important distraction, which commonly occurs when a driver is 30–50% awake [21,22]. Née et al. [23] reported that half of the drivers acknowledge experiencing some mind-wandering prior to having a traffic accident. Xu et al. [24] examined the correlations and frequency of driver mind-wandering, and found that whilst mind-wandering drivers do not reveal most of the vehicle-control impairments, they barely focus their visual attention on the road. Therefore, mind-wandering is associated with a reduced ability to monitor one's environment. Xu et al. [24] also reported that mind-wandering is positively associated with risky driving, negative emotional or cognitive driving styles, aggressive driving, and driving under the impact of alcohol.

Cognitive distractions and visual distractions are the most important distractions that reduce driving performance, and include visual perception efficiency, steering control, response to hazards, and lane variation [25].

In Jordan, accident statistics show a relatively low level of traffic safety compared to that in developed countries, which causes large socio-economic losses. The Annual Report of Traffic Accidents in Jordan for the year of 2019 [26] presents the following facts about the status of traffic safety in Jordan:

- (161,511) traffic accidents occurred in Jordan (a country of 10 million people), of which (10,857) were accidents that caused human injuries, with (643) deaths and an estimated financial cost of JOD 454 million.

- Jordan was ranked among the top four countries to have (4.3) deaths per (10) thousand vehicles in 2017.
- Human error was responsible for 98.2% of accidents involving human injuries in 2019.
- Driver fault (i.e., not taking the necessary precautions) was completely responsible for a high percentage (i.e., around 40%) of injuries and deaths in 2019.
- In 2019, passengers constituted the highest percentage of the total injuries (41.13%), followed by drivers (33.03%), and pedestrians (25.84%), while passenger deaths scored the highest percentage (41.7%), followed by pedestrians (37%) and then drivers (21%).

Furthermore, the Jordan Traffic Institute's statistics show that distracted driving was responsible for 24.2% of traffic accidents on rural and suburban roads for the years 2014 to 2018.

Several research studies have examined the significance of different driver distractions on traffic accidents. However, none have investigated these distractions from the driver's perspective. It is important to understand how drivers perceive distraction factors, which would help researchers, auto-manufacturers, in-vehicle infotainment system developers, traffic experts, and public authorities identify the most effective measures to reduce driver distractions and teach different driver groups the best practices that fit their driving behaviors and keep them attentive. Therefore, as mentioned before, this study aims to investigate drivers' perspectives of factors contributing to driver distractions, determine the rank and order of distraction types, recognize the road factors and environmental effects that make distractions more dangerous, and identify the most effective measures that must be taken to reduce driver distractions. This study is the first in Jordan and, perhaps worldwide, that attempts to pinpoint and rank the major distraction factors and types from drivers' perspectives.

## 2. Methodology

To achieve the study's objectives, a survey was conducted among Jordanian drivers who are licensed and registered with the Vehicle License Department. The survey, written in the Arabic language, was randomly distributed and collected electronically. A total of 850 drivers responded intentionally and returned their responses within four months (July 2020–October 2020). However, due to incomplete responses to the questions, the final sample size used for the analysis was 826 responses that were relevant to the study's objectives.

The survey questionnaire was designed to collect demographic, behavioral, and perspective data from respondent drivers. The questionnaire was divided into (four) sections. Section A was designed to collect information about the driver's gender, age, education, employment type and the age of their car, driving license type, and the holding period. Sections B and C were to collect information related to the driver's behavior during driving and the driver's perspective about distraction types and factors. Section D collected information related to road factors and environmental effects that might increase distraction risks and consequences.

Furthermore, respondents were asked to rank (i.e., give weight or order) each factor of each type of distraction on a scale from 1 to 10 (i.e., 10 for highest danger and 1 for lowest danger) for visual, manual, and cognitive distraction types, and from 1 to 5 for auditory distraction. Moreover, respondents were asked to rank the distraction types from 1 to 4 according to their danger as perceived by drivers, with higher values indicating higher danger (section C). In addition, they were asked to select the most effective measure, in their opinion, to reduce the driver's distractions (section D).

The collected survey data were analyzed using both Microsoft Excel and SPSS software. Descriptive statistics were presented in the form of frequencies and percentages, and rating questions as means and medians. In addition, rankings, which were based on average weights provided by respondent drivers, were used to identify the types of distractions, and the most important distracting road and environmental factors for drivers.

## 3. Results

The analysis of the collected survey data is presented in the following subsections.

### 3.1. Demographic and Driving Characteristics

The demographic characteristics of respondents are summarized in Table 1. Male respondents constituted 68% of the respondents while 32% were female drivers. Out of 826 drivers, 38% of the drivers were aged 24–40 years, 35% 41–60 years, and 19% 18–23 years. Forty-four percent of the participants had a bachelor's degree, 28% had a master's degree, and 18% had a high school certificate. Table 1 clearly shows that the respondents were a rich reflection of the basic profile of both the population of Jordan, and of Jordanian licensed drivers. The respondents cut across different age groups, genders, and education levels.

**Table 1.** Demographic profile of respondents.

| Factor | Frequency | Percent |
|---|---|---|
| Gender | | |
| Male | 558 | 68 |
| Female | 268 | 32 |
| Age (years) | | |
| 18–23 | 160 | 19 |
| 24–40 | 314 | 38 |
| 41–60 | 286 | 35 |
| >60 | 66 | 08 |
| Education | | |
| High school | 152 | 18 |
| Diploma | 78 | 09 |
| Bachelor degree | 366 | 44 |
| Master's degree and above | 230 | 28 |
| Employment | | |
| Full-time | 440 | 53 |
| Part-time | 76 | 09 |
| Retired | 76 | 09 |
| Student | 130 | 16 |
| Home maker/others | 104 | 13 |

The driving characteristics of participants are presented in Table 2. The majority of the participants had a privately owned vehicle (76.0%). About fifty-two percent (51.6%) had driven vehicles manufactured in the last 10 years. About 44.3% of drivers always wore seat belts and a similar percentage (44.3%) had never been involved in a crash. Fifty-four percent (54.0%) of the respondents occasionally sent text messages, whereas (28.6%) of the drivers kept their mobile phones close and within reach. Mobile phones were used by (61.7%) as a means for navigation when car navigation was not available and (48.2%) of the drivers used only one hand to hold the steering wheel except when passing by the police, or during heavy traffic or bad weather. About forty-one percent (41.4%) of drivers used the radio knob to adjust the volume or change the channel, whereas (53.5%) of the drivers occasionally listened to very loud music. In addition, (58.8%) of the drivers occasionally ate, drank, or smoked while driving.

### 3.2. Drivers' Perceptions of Distraction Factors and Types

As stated earlier, respondents were asked to rank (i.e., give weight to) each of the distracting factors for each type of distraction on a scale from 1 to 10 (i.e., 10 for highest danger and 1 for lowest danger) for visual, manual, and cognitive distraction types, and from 1 to 5 for auditory distraction. Respondents were also asked to rank the distraction types from 1 to 4 according to their danger level as they perceived them, with higher values indicating higher danger.

**Table 2.** Driving characteristics of respondents.

| Factor | Observations | Percent |
|---|---|---|
| Number of years having a driver's license | | |
| <2 | 118 | 14.3 |
| 2–5 | 116 | 14.0 |
| 5–10 | 118 | 14.3 |
| >10 | 474 | 57.4 |
| Type of driving license | | |
| Private (Type 3) | 704 | 85.2 |
| Public (Type 4) | 64 | 7.7 |
| Two axles bus and truck < 7.5 ton (Type 5) | 36 | 4.4 |
| All vehicle (Type 6) | 22 | 2.7 |
| Vehicle type | | |
| Private/owned | 628 | 76.0 |
| Private/rented | 18 | 2.2 |
| Private/work | 28 | 3.4 |
| Private/borrowed | 70 | 8.5 |
| Public/car | 48 | 5.8 |
| Public/bus | 34 | 4.1 |
| Vehicle age (year) | | |
| <10 | 426 | 51.6 |
| 10–20 | 262 | 31.7 |
| >20 | 138 | 16.7 |
| Wearing seat belt | | |
| Always | 366 | 44.3 |
| Occasionally | 332 | 40.2 |
| Never | 128 | 15.5 |
| Crash involvement and cause | | |
| Never | 366 | 44.3 |
| Speeding | 94 | 11.4 |
| Close following (tailgating) | 122 | 14.8 |
| Distracted | 138 | 16.7 |
| Others | 106 | 12.8 |
| Text messaging while driving | | |
| Always | 66 | 8.0 |
| Occasionally | 446 | 54.0 |
| Never | 314 | 38.0 |
| Mobile phone position in vehicle | | |
| Never use phone while driving | 110 | 13.3 |
| In hand | 210 | 25.4 |
| Fixed on dashboard | 102 | 12.3 |
| Close so it can be reached easily | 236 | 28.6 |
| Use of blue tooth | 168 | 20.3 |
| Navigation system Used | | |
| Car navigation system | 58 | 7.0 |
| Mobile phone because car navigation has no local maps identified | 166 | 20.1 |
| Mobile phone because car navigation is not available | 510 | 61.7 |
| Mobile phone even if the car has navigation system | 92 | 11.1 |
| Holding steering wheel | | |
| Both hands all the time | 106 | 12.8 |
| One hand all the time | 64 | 7.7 |
| Both hands most of time | 258 | 31.2 |
| One hand most of time except when passing police or in bad weather or heavy traffic | 398 | 48.2 |
| Adjust volume or change channel by: | | |
| Radio knob | 342 | 41.4 |
| Steering wheel control (if available) | 340 | 41.2 |
| Radio knob even if steering wheel control available | 144 | 17.4 |
| Turning the volume to very loud when listening to favorite music | | |
| Always | 130 | 15.7 |
| Occasionally | 442 | 53.5 |
| Never | 254 | 30.8 |
| Eating, drinking, or smoking while driving | | |
| Always | 144 | 17.4 |
| Occasionally | 486 | 58.8 |
| Never | 196 | 23.7 |

Table 3 presents the ranking of distraction factors by type as reported by all respondents. The average value of all the ranks (weights) was used as the basis for ranking the distraction factors and types in Table 3. According to respondents, the visual distraction type was perceived as the most dangerous type of distraction (i.e., ranked 4/4). The second riskiest distraction type was the cognitive distraction, followed by manual distraction, while the auditory distraction was perceived as the least dangerous type.

**Table 3.** Ranking of distraction factors by type as reported by all respondents.

| Distraction Type | Factors | Average of Weights | * Rank Based on Average Weight | Median of Weights |
|---|---|---|---|---|
| **Visual (Overall)** | | 3.338 | 4/4 | 4 |
| | Mobile phone texting or dialing | 8.184 | 10/10 | 10 |
| | Outside person, object, event | 6.842 | 9/10 | 8 |
| | Rubbernecking | 6.406 | 7/10 | 6 |
| | Smoking, looking for a cigarette or lighter | 5.016 | 2/10 | 4 |
| | Programming the navigation (GPS) | 5.332 | 3/10 | 6 |
| | Searching for or changing radio station or car controls | 3.801 | 1/10 | 2 |
| | Looking for something in car or in purse | 5.830 | 5/10 | 6 |
| | Distracting events (spilled packages or drinks or dropped cigarette) | 6.653 | 8/10 | 6 |
| | Moving persons/objects in the vehicle (kids, pets, equipment, things) | 6.213 | 6/10 | 6 |
| | Fixing clothes or putting on makeup (grooming) | 5.447 | 4/10 | 6 |
| **Cognitive (Overall)** | | 2.791 | 3/4 | 3 |
| | Talking on a cell phone—even a hands-free one—or running in-vehicle voice command systems | 6.518 | 10/10 | 6 |
| | Conversing with passengers | 5.656 | 6/10 | 6 |
| | Thinking about a problem that needs solving | 5.215 | 4/10 | 6 |
| | Focusing on an engaging news report | 4.029 | 1/10 | 4 |
| | Engine is making a weird noise | 5.297 | 5/10 | 6 |
| | Music is loud | 5.113 | 2/10 | 4 |
| | Baby is crying | 6.440 | 7/10 | 6 |
| | Reprimanding children (kids are fighting in the back seat) | 6.518 | 10/10 | 6 |
| | Driving while holding a full bladder | 5.147 | 3/10 | 4 |
| | Driving while angry or sad or agitated | 6.484 | 8/10 | 6 |
| **Manual (Overall)** | | 2.622 | 2/4 | 3 |
| | Using phone (texting, dialing, charging) | 8.343 | 10/10 | 10 |
| | Changing the radio station or volume | 4.387 | 3/10 | 4 |
| | Checking navigation (GPS) programming (no voice operated GPS system) | 6.314 | 7/10 | 6 |
| | Adjusting car climate control | 4.038 | 1/10 | 4 |
| | Adjusting mirror, seats, or opening window | 4.135 | 2/10 | 4 |
| | Reaching for a sandwich or drink | 5.443 | 3/10 | 6 |
| | Smoking; reaching for a cigarette or lighter | 5.452 | 4/10 | |
| | Looking for something in car or in purse | 6.803 | 9/10 | 8 |
| | Moving objects in the vehicle (kids, pets, equipment, things) | 6.610 | 8/10 | 6 |
| | Fixing clothes or putting on makeup (grooming) | 5.966 | 6/10 | 6 |
| **Auditory (overall)** | | 2.266 | 1/4 | 2 |
| | Mobile phone ringing | 2.481 | 2/5 | 2 |
| | Engine is making a weird noise | 3.019 | 4/5 | 3 |
| | Music is loud | 2.886 | 3/5 | 3 |
| | Baby is crying or kids are fighting in the back seat | 3.566 | 5/5 | 4 |
| | Audible vehicle warning (seat belt warning or lane departure warning) | 2.438 | 1/5 | 2 |

* Higher values reflect higher danger and lower values reflect lower danger.

Among the visual and cognitive factors, "mobile phone texting or dialing" and "talking on a cell phone" or "dealing with vehicle voice command systems" were the factors that most distracted the respondents from the surrounding traffic environment. Moreover, "outside person, object or event", "distracting events", "rubbernecking", "moving objects in the vehicle", and "looking for something in the car" were other visual factors that distracted the attention of Jordanian drivers. Likewise, "driving while angry, sad or agitated", "crying baby", "conversing with passengers", and "weird engine noise" were other cognitive factors that distracted their attention (Table 3).

In terms of manual factors, "use of phone", "looking for something in the car or in a purse", "moving objects in the vehicle", and "checking the navigation programming" were the factors distracting drivers' attention. In terms of auditory factors, "children making noises", "fighting or crying", and "engine making a weird noise" were some of the factors that distracted attention, according to respondents.

The median of weights was also used as another way to rank the distracting factors for each type of distraction as shown in Table 3. For visual distraction, the median value of (10) suggests that "Mobile phone texting or dialing" was perceived as the highest risk distraction factor in this type. Moreover, the median of weights was equal for a number of factors together, thus putting them in the same risk level. For example, in the case of cognitive distraction, the median values for all the factors were four or six, thus making it hard to order these factors according to risk. It is believed that using the average weights was much more helpful in ranking the factors based on how risky the respondents believe the consequences to be.

In order to investigate how each demographic group perceives distraction types, Table 4 was extracted from the collected data based on the average weight value of respondents' rankings. Table 4 lists the ranks of distraction types as perceived by each demographic group, the top ranked distraction factor among each distraction type, and the most effective measure to reduce distraction. Table 4 clearly shows that almost all demographic groups see that visual distraction is the most dangerous type, followed by cognitive distraction, with manual and auditory distractions coming last. Only educated people with master's degrees and above ranked manual distraction in second place and cognitive in third place, while visual and auditory shared the same ranking with other groups. To make Table 4 more informative, the percentage of drivers in each group who selected each factor as the most distracting one was presented.

Table 4 also shows that "mobile phone texting or dialing" was ranked the top most dangerous visual distraction factor by almost all demographic groups. Only the age group 18–23 and drivers with high school education believed that "Outside person, object, or event" was the most dangerous visual distraction factor. Among all manual distraction factors, "Using phone (texting, dialing, charging)" was perceived as the most distracting factor by all groups. Similarly, "Baby is crying or kids are fighting in the back seat" was perceived by all as the riskiest auditory factor.

Regarding the cognitive distraction type, four different factors were perceived as the most distracting by different demographic groups. "Baby is crying" was perceived as the most dangerous by females, drivers who had had their driving license for 5–10-years, and home makers. "Driving while angry or sad or agitated" was perceived as the most dangerous factor by males, age groups 24–40, and 41–60, people who had had their driving license for >10 years, full-time employees, and drivers with a bachelor's degree or higher. The "Talking on a cell phone—even a hands-free one" cognitive factor was perceived as most dangerous by drivers with part-time employment, retirees, students, people with high school and diploma certificates, people with 0–5 years driving experience, and drivers more than 60. Only one group (18–23 years young people) considered "Conversing with passengers" as the most dangerous cognitive distracting factor.

**Table 4.** Rank of distraction types and top ranked distraction factors as perceived by demographic groups.

| Demographic Variable | | Distraction Type Rank | | | | Top Ranked Visual Factor ** (%) | Top Ranked Manual Factor ** (%) | Top Ranked Cognitive Factor ** (%) | Top Ranked Auditory Factor ** (%) | Most Effective Measure in Reducing Driver Distraction ** (%) |
|---|---|---|---|---|---|---|---|---|---|---|
| | | Visual | Manual | Cognitive | Auditory | | | | | |
| Gender | Females | 4 | 2 | 3 | 1 | Mobile phone texting or dialing (27%) | Using phone (texting, dialing, charging) (31%) | Baby is crying (22%) | Baby is crying or kids are fighting in the back seat (18%) | Laws and enforcement (19%) |
| | Males | 4 | 2 | 3 | 1 | Mobile phone texting or dialing (57%) | Using phone (texting, dialing, charging) (66%) | Driving while angry or sad or agitated (25%) | Baby is crying or kids are fighting in the back seat (26%) | Laws and enforcement (38%) |
| Age | 18–23 | 4 | 2 | 3 | 1 | Outside person, object, or event (48%) | Using phone (texting, dialing, charging) (65%) | Conversing with passengers (41%) | Baby is crying or kids are fighting in the back seat (39%) | Laws and enforcement (43%) |
| | 24–40 | 4 | 2 | 3 | 1 | Mobile phone texting or dialing (57%) | Using phone (texting, dialing, charging) (56%) | Driving while angry or sad or agitated (28%) | Baby is crying or kids are fighting in the back seat (29%) | Laws and enforcement, Education and training (29%) |
| | 41–60 | 4 | 2 | 3 | 1 | Mobile phone texting or dialing (62%) | Using phone (texting, dialing, charging) (66%) | Driving while angry or sad or agitated (20%) | Baby is crying or kids are fighting in the back seat (21%) | Laws and enforcement (41%) |
| | >60 | 4 | 2 | 3 | 1 | Mobile phone texting or dialing (67%) | Using phone (texting, dialing, charging) (94%) | Talking on a cell phone—even a hands-free one (61%) | Baby is crying or kids are fighting in the back sea (46%) | Laws and enforcement (49%) |
| Driving Experience (Number of years having driving license) | <2 | 4 | 2 | 3 | 1 | Mobile phone texting or dialing (46%) | Using phone (texting, dialing, charging) (58%) | Talking on a cell phone—even a hands-free one (39%) | Baby is crying or kids are fighting in the back seat (32%) | Laws and enforcement (46%) |
| | 2–5 | 4 | 2 | 3 | 1 | Mobile phone texting or dialing (48%) | Using phone (texting, dialing, charging) (64%) | Talking on a cell phone—even a hands-free one (41%) | Baby is crying or kids are fighting in the back seat (43%) | Laws and enforcement (33%) |
| | 5–10 | 4 | 2 | 3 | 1 | Mobile phone texting or dialing (46%) | Using phone (texting, dialing, charging) (63%) | Baby is crying (17%) | Baby is crying or kids are fighting in the back seat (25%) | Laws and enforcement (25%) |
| | >10 | 4 | 2 | 3 | 1 | Mobile phone texting or dialing (63%) | Using phone (texting, dialing, charging) (67%) | Driving while angry or sad or agitated (24%) | Baby is crying or kids are fighting in the back seat (26%) | Laws and enforcement (40%) |

**Table 4.** *Cont.*

| Demographic Variable | | Distraction Type Rank | | | | Top Ranked Visual Factor ** (%) | Top Ranked Manual Factor ** (%) | Top Ranked Cognitive Factor ** (%) | Top Ranked Auditory Factor ** (%) | Most Effective Measure in Reducing Driver Distraction ** (%) |
|---|---|---|---|---|---|---|---|---|---|---|
| | | Visual | Manual | Cognitive | Auditory | | | | | |
| Education | High School | 4 | 2 | 3 | 1 | Outside person, object, or event (76%) | Using phone (texting, dialing, charging) (86%) | Talking on a cell phone—even a hands-free one (66%) | Baby is crying or kids are fighting in the back seat (49%) | Laws and enforcement (46%) |
| | Diploma | 4 | 2 | 3 | 1 | Mobile phone texting or dialing (54%) | Using phone (texting, dialing, charging) (72%) | Talking on a cell phone and baby is crying (59%) | Baby is crying or kids are fighting in the back seat (44%) | Laws and enforcement (49%) |
| | Bachelor degree | 4 | 2 | 3 | 1 | Mobile phone texting or dialing (56%) | Using phone (texting, dialing, charging) (54%) | Driving while angry or sad or agitated (31%) | Baby is crying or kids are fighting in the back seat (32%) | Laws and enforcement (31%) |
| | Master's degree and above | 4 | 3 | 2 | 1 | Mobile phone texting or dialing (63%) | Using phone (texting, dialing, charging) (64%) | Driving while angry or sad or agitated (23%) | Baby is crying or kids are fighting in the back seat (22%) | Laws and enforcement (39%) |
| Employment | Full-time | 4 | 2 | 3 | 1 | Mobile phone texting or dialing (56%) | Using phone (texting, dialing, charging) (60%) | Driving while angry or sad or agitated (25%) | Baby is crying or kids are fighting in the back seat (21%) | Laws and enforcement (36%) |
| | Part-time | 4 | 2 | 3 | 1 | Mobile phone texting or dialing (40%) | Using phone (texting, dialing, charging) (66%) | Talking on a cell phone—even a hands-free one (32%) | Baby is crying or kids are fighting in the back seat (37%) | Laws and enforcement (34%) |
| | Retired | 4 | 2 | 3 | 1 | Mobile phone texting or dialing (63%) | Using phone (texting, dialing, charging) (95%) | Talking on a cell phone—even a hands-free one (47%) | Baby is crying or kids are fighting in the back seat (40%) | Laws and enforcement (47%) |
| | Student | 4 | 2 | 3 | 1 | Mobile phone texting or dialing( 43%) | Using phone (texting, dialing, charging) (62%) | Talking on a cell phone—even a hands-free one (40%) | Baby is crying or kids are fighting in the back seat (37%) | Laws and enforcement, Technical approaches to restrict distraction (66%) |
| | Home Maker | 4 | 2 | 3 | 1 | Mobile phone texting or dialing (52%) | Using phone (texting, dialing, charging). (65%) | Baby is crying (23%) | Baby is crying or kids are fighting in the back seat (40%) | Laws and enforcement (46%) |

** (%) percentage of drivers in each group who selected this as the most distracting factor.

Table 4 also conveys an interesting finding on how drivers in Jordan think about corrective measures to reduce distractions. Most demographic groups believe that "laws and enforcement" is the most effective measure to reduce distraction on the road. This reflects the belief of Jordanian drivers, who daily witness and commit many traffic violations, that the only way to succeed in reducing such violations is by enforcing traffic laws and showing no tolerance to careless driving.

### *3.3. Drivers' Perceptions Regarding Effect of Environment, Vehicle Type, and Road Factors*

Table 5 presents drivers' perceptions of environmental and vehicle type factors on distraction. From the findings, (61.3%) of the participants indicated that both "non-daylight" and "adverse weather conditions" had a similar effect on distraction while driving. However, (64.6%) indicated that driving a non-passenger car was more distracting, while (30.3%) believed that driving a passenger car or a non-passenger car had a similar effect.

**Table 5.** Drivers' perceptions of environmental and vehicle type factors on distraction.

| Effect | Frequency | Percent |
|---|---|---|
| Environmental | | |
| Non-day light | 98 | 11.8 |
| Adverse weather conditions | 222 | 26.9 |
| Both will have similar effect | 506 | 61.3 |
| Vehicle Type | | |
| Passenger car | 42 | 5.1 |
| Non-passenger car (SUVs, pickup trucks, vans) | 534 | 64.6 |
| Both will have similar effect | 250 | 30.3 |

Drivers were also asked if wearing a face mask while driving as a precaution against COVID-19 might cause them any kind of distraction and affect their driving. Of the respondents, 284 (34.4%) agreed that it had an effect, while 266 (32.2%) disagreed with such a statement, and the remaining (33.4%) had a neutral perception of the mask's effect on distracting drivers and adversely affecting their driving skills. Table 6 shows the ranking of road factors that influence drivers' distractions based on the average weight given by respondents. According to the responses, intersections were perceived as the most dangerous road element to distracted drivers, followed by high-speed roads >70 km/h, non-level grade, and roadways with more than two lanes.

**Table 6.** Ranking of road factors' effect on distracting drivers as reported by all respondents.

| Road Factor | Intersections | Roadways with More than 2 Lanes | Non Level Grade | High Speed Roads > 70 km/h |
|---|---|---|---|---|
| Average of Weight | 3.208 | 2.254 | 2.617 | 2.695 |
| * Rank based on Average Weight | (4) | (1) | (2) | (3) |
| Median of Weights | 4 | 2 | 3 | 3 |

* Rank: higher value reflects higher danger and lower value reflects lower danger.

### *3.4. Drivers' Perception of Measures to Reduce Drivers' Distraction*

One of the core objectives of this study was to emphasize the measures that can be used to reduce distraction. Figure 1 shows drivers' responses to the questions related to the aforementioned objective. They reveal that laws and enforcement is the drivers' preferred choice to reduce distraction, followed by measuring and understanding the effect of distraction on safety, and then by education and training.

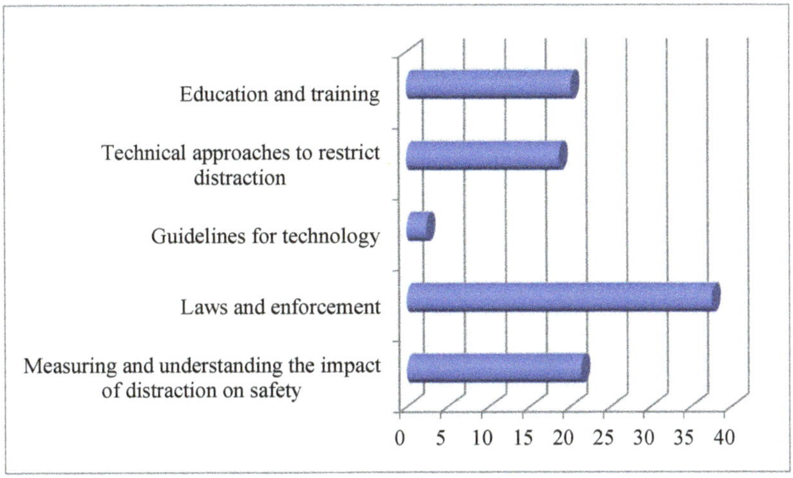


**Figure 1.** Drivers' choices of measures to reduce driver's distraction.

## 4. Discussion

The main goal of this study was to rank the major distraction factors and distraction types from drivers' perspectives. The methods often used in studies of driver distraction are not always effective or feasible in certain conditions. To achieve the purpose of the current research, a naturalistic method was followed to evaluate drivers' distractions in Jordan. Observational studies are considered the most feasible, effective, and appropriate for the recording of continuous data, with the core advantage being the fact that driving is very close to natural reality. Therefore, a high degree of validity and reliability can be associated with the findings.

As introduced earlier, Jordan suffers from a high rate of accidents, resulting in a large socio-economic loss. In fact, it has been ranked among the top four countries in traffic deaths for the year of 2017 [26]. In 2019, traffic accidents in Jordan resulted in 10,857 human injuries and 643 deaths at a financial cost estimated at JOD 454 million. Several factors have been confirmed to cause traffic accidents, mostly related to vehicle, road, or human error. Among these factors, driver fault ("Not taking the necessary precautions") was reported as the cause of a high percentage (around 40%) of injuries and deaths in 2019 [26].

The analysis above showed that Jordanian drivers perceive visual distraction as the most dangerous distraction type, followed by cognitive distraction, manual distraction, and auditory distraction, in this order. It could be observed that drivers of all demographic groups are well aware of the effects of visual distraction on driving, as it involves taking the eyes off the road and glancing elsewhere to engage in a secondary activity inside or outside the vehicle. Such an action may negatively interfere with the driver's performance, causing a prolonged period of reaction time, poor response to road signals, and difficulty keeping to the appropriate lane, or to an appropriate tracking distance. Similar effects can be observed with cognitive distractions, as the drivers' attention is taken away from what is happening during driving. This finding is consistent with Alizadeh and Dehzangi [25] who found that cognitive and visual distractions are the most important noted distractions that negatively influence performance, including visual perception efficiency, steering control, response to hazards, and lane variation.

In addition, it was observed that the use of a mobile phone is one of the most distracting risk factors. Responses indicated that drivers practice risky acts by using their mobile phones while driving, without paying attention to its consequences. For example, it was noticed that the extent of mobile phone usage for activities other than talking was alarming. More than 50% of respondents occasionally sent a text message, and more than 90% of respondents used mobile phones for navigation. These practices cause the drivers to take their eyes off the road, their attention away from the task of driving, and their hands off the wheel, which would increase crash risks. This finding is also consistent with Sterkenburg and Jeon [12], and Niu et al. [27], who highlighted the very negative impact of mobile phones on performance.

Furthermore, the results showed that respondents perceived the use of wireless technologies and hand-free systems as a cause for distraction, which is consistent with earlier findings by Wood et al. and Jenness et al. [13,17]. Wood et al. indicated that the use of hands-free systems led to multiple distractions. Jenness et al. [17] revealed that manually operated navigation systems are a major source of distraction because they take even more attention from the driver and a longer time to operate.

Moreover, the acts of eating, drinking, or smoking were observed by more than half of the drivers as a cause of distraction, despite the fact that these factors are not commonly emphasized by safe driving campaigns. Theses campaigns tend to focus instead on mobile phone use, despite the numerous other distractions which have unfavorable effects on driving. These findings are consistent with others by Huemer and Vollrath [28], who revealed that drivers were predisposed to agree that secondary task involvement can be generally hazardous. However, a majorly mitigated ratio in the same study agreed that they were distracted on particular occasions in which they were involved in secondary activities; an even smaller ratio acquiesced that being involved in such factors put themselves at risk of crashing.

Additionally, drivers' responses revealed that more than 60% believed that both "non-daylight" and "adverse weather conditions" had a similar effect on distraction while "driving a non-passenger car" was more distracting than driving a passenger one. A similar finding was reported by Stutts et al. [29], where distractions were more likely to occur while driving during non-daylight hours, and while driving a pickup truck, van, or sport utility vehicle.

Drivers' perceptions of road factors also showed that intersections were perceived as the most dangerous road component to distracted drivers, followed by high-speed roads of >70 km/h, non-level grade, and roadways with more than two lanes. Drivers' awareness of the most dangerous sections of the roadway may cause them to be more alert and attentive when going through these sections. This interpretation supports Stutts et al. [29], who found that those who were distracted at the time of crashes were less likely to be traveling on multilane roadways and less likely to have crashed at an intersection or other road junction.

In addition, it was observed that most Jordanian drivers did not follow driving instructions or use safety features. A considerable percentage of them did not wear seatbelts, held the steering wheel with one hand, ate or smoked while driving, and listened to very loud music while driving.

Based on the previous discussion, generally a good agreement can be observed between the analyzed perceptions of Jordanian drivers and findings in the literature regarding distractions rankings, the impact of using mobile phones, wireless technologies and hand-free systems, eating, drinking, or smoking, and road and environmental factors [12,13,17,25,27–29].

Similarly, a good agreement can be observed between the opinions of Jordanian drivers, and the real causes of traffic accidents related to drivers' faults in Jordan. Al-Rousan et al. [30] examined the characteristics of traffic accidents caused by distracted driving on rural and suburban roadways in Jordan. The study analyzed 10,200 accidents on nine road segments in Amman, Jordan's capital city, from 2014 through to 2018. It was found that 73% of reported accidents were related to the drivers' faults. Among these, 25.95% were related to distracted driving, while 9.6%, 2.63%, 2.44%, and 1.63% were related to traffic rules violations, reckless driving, loss of control, and ignoring road signs, respectively.

Furthermore, Albdour and Marafi [31] analyzed data of traffic accidents that were caused by the fault of the driver in Jordan from 2009 to 2012. It was observed that these faults were the leading cause of traffic accidents in Jordan. Moreover, it was found that "Tail gating", "Not taking the necessary precautions while driving", "Using Incorrect Lane", "Priorities false", and "Reversing Incorrect" were the main factors related to traffic accidents. The authors recommended enhancing driver training before licensing them to drive on the road, increasing traffic education campaigns in schools and universities, and strengthening the written and practical driving tests to reduce accidents caused by driver faults.

In addition, Al-Omari and Obaidat [32] analyzed the pedestrian accidents in one Jordanian city (i.e., Irbid city) for the period of 1999–2001. The study data showed that 37% and 0.57% of pedestrian accidents related to the driver's fault were caused by "Not Giving Priority to Pedestrians" and "Failing to Comply with Obligatory Traffic Signs", respectively.

As indicated earlier, the analysis revealed that Jordanian drivers did not follow traffic laws or safe driving instructions and did not use the safety features in their cars. A considerable percentage of drivers did not wear seatbelts, consumed food and drink or smoked while driving, and used mobile phones while driving. Although drivers were aware of laws banning such acts, they still engaged in them.

Responses demonstrated that the majority of Jordanian drivers considered traffic laws and their enforcement as the most effective measure to reduce distraction. Traffic laws in Jordan are very strict regarding behaviors which are distracting to drivers. Fines are applied for distracting behaviors such as smoking and eating while driving and for installing any devices or gadgets inside the vehicle that contribute to the driver's distraction. For example, a JOD 15 (USD 21) fine is issued for drivers caught holding their mobiles in their hands to make a call or use its applications [33].

These laws have been legislated and must be well enforced, as a lot of traffic violations have been reported. For example, 20,493 fines were issued during a two-day traffic campaign in mid-June 2018 [34]. Moreover, around 217,000 traffic violations were recorded by 42 cameras across Amman during the third quarter of 2018 [35]. Additionally, 553,616 traffic violations were reported in 2016 [36]. In 2015 and 2016, the total value of traffic fines was estimated to be around JOD 88.5 million (USD 125 million) [37]. Due to a large number of violations, including frequent phone use, there is a will to modify traffic laws in Jordan by increasing the penalties for violations that lead to hazardous situations and/or cause accidents [33].

Currently, several other strategies are applied to reduce the numbers and consequences of traffic accidents in Jordan. Traffic surveillance and traffic awareness are among the strategies of the Jordanian Central Traffic Department (JCTD). Traffic surveillance of different forms (i.e., exposed, hidden, or modern (using cameras)) is used to cover most of the roadway networks and inhibit traffic violations [33].

Furthermore, the level of traffic awareness among drivers, pedestrians, and cyclists at the national level is one of the main goals of the Public Security Directorate's (PSD) work plans. Several approaches are used to enhance awareness levels, including traffic awareness brochures and booklets, traffic awareness lectures given in universities and schools, sending traffic awareness messages via Short Message Service (SMS), the publishing of a traffic news magazine, producing videos covering traffic violations and their consequences and broadcasting them through the national TV Station, and developing an effective communication channel with the public to obtain feedback and to receive suggestions and complaints [33].

In addition, education and awareness campaigns are held to increase awareness on the dangers of phone use while driving, urging people to respect traffic laws, and helping to promote the culture of safe driving by evading dangerous traffic violations [33]. These campaigns are performed regularly and increase during the activation of seasonal surveillance plans in the summer, during the fasting month of Ramadan when traffic greatly increases, especially during the late afternoon hours, schools opening, and winter emergency plans. They are held in coordination with the participation of other parties such as the Ministry of Public Works and Housing, municipalities, the Royal Automobile Club, and several civil society organizations (unions, associations, and clubs). These companies are held at the national level and can sometimes target specific locations or categories such as one city/town, or only the youth, depending on the traffic situations and risks.

However, the current implemented approaches (e.g., law enforcement, education and awareness campaigns) have a limited effect in most cases [38]. For example, drivers can hide their phones to avoid police surveillance. So, certain inventive methods may be essential to reduce distraction risks. Oviedo-Trespalacios et al. [39] suggested the use of mobile phone applications which would reduce distractions while driving. These applications limit interactions with the mobile device (for example, block text messaging and/or browsing) while the vehicle is in motion. Nguyen-Phuoc et al. [40] proposed reducing distractions through custom-made interventions involving a variety of players (legislators, police enforcement, psychological health specialists, advocacy groups and the extensive community) in order to increase awareness, adjust attitudes and improve risk perceptions related to the use of mobile phones during driving. They suggested educational tools and road safety campaigns that include customizing road safety programs for individuals and groups affected by problematic mobile phone use through targeted advertising.

A limitation of this study is that the findings are based on an analysis of Jordanian drivers' perspectives, which may have unique social, demographic, cultural, and other, conditions. Therefore, the findings may not be extendable to other countries. The authors recommend following an approach similar to the one in the current study to explore intercultural differences and to get a deeper understanding of drivers' faults that contribute to distraction. Another limitation of the present study is that it relied on self-assessment of general driving experiences, as compared to an external objective assessment. Thereby, the study proposes that similar research be conducted with an objective measuring of cognitive and visual distractions, while eliciting drivers' perceptions of changes in their traffic environment.

## 5. Conclusions

Jordan has suffered from a high rate of traffic accidents, resulting in a large socio-economic loss. Human error was responsible for 98.2% of accidents involving human injuries in the year of 2019. Among these errors, driver fault ("Not taking the necessary precautions") has been confirmed as the most recurrent cause responsible for a high percentage of injuries and deaths [26]. This study aimed to investigate and rank the major distraction factors and distraction types causing accidents from the drivers' perspectives. Based on the findings of this study, the following can be concluded:

1. Visual distraction was perceived as the most dangerous type, followed by cognitive distraction, and then manual distraction, while auditory distraction came last.
2. Among visual and manual distraction types, "mobile phone" was one of the highest risk factors that distracted drivers; therefore, more campaigns should be launched to elucidate its risks and enforce the banning of its use in driving.
3. "Crying babies" and "fighting kids in the back seat" were the riskiest auditory factors.
4. Regarding cognitive distractions, four factors were perceived as the most distracting by different demographic groups. They are the following: "Baby is crying", "Driving while angry or sad or agitated", "Talking on a cell phone—even a hands-free one", and "Conversing with passengers".
5. Laws and their enforcement were perceived as the most effective measure to reduce distraction on the road. Therefore, legislated laws that ban handheld phones and careless driving should be well enforced. In addition, phone applications that can reduce distractions should be considered.
6. Educational tools and road safety awareness campaigns to encourage and enforce personal responsibility for driving safely should focus on individuals and groups with problematic driving behaviors, such as using mobile phones while driving, not putting on seatbelts, holding steering wheel with one hand, and eating, drinking or smoking while driving.

7. Navigation systems with voice commands can be a better choice and a safer alternative for using mobile phones for navigation.

**Author Contributions:** Conceptualization, T.M.A.-R., Y.A.K., A.H.A.-R.; methodology, T.M.A.-R., A.A.U., A.A.A.-O., Y.A.K., H.M.A., A.H.A.-R.; formal analysis, T.M.A.-R., A.A.U.; resources, T.M.A.-R., A.A.U., A.A.A.-O., Y.A.K., H.M.A., A.H.A.-R.; data curation, T.M.A.-R., A.A.U., A.A.A.-O., Y.A.K., H.M.A., A.H.A.-R.; writing—original draft, T.M.A.-R., A.A.U., Y.A.K.; writing—review and editing, A.A.A.-O., H.M.A., A.H.A.-R.; supervision, T.M.A.-R.; project administration, T.M.A.-R. All authors have read and agreed to the published version of the manuscript.

**Funding:** This research did not receive any specific grant from any funding agencies.

**Institutional Review Board Statement:** The study was conducted according to the guidelines of the Declaration of Helsinki, and approved by the Institutional Review Board of the Hashemite University on 4/6/2020 No. 4/6/2019/2020.

**Informed Consent Statement:** Informed consent was obtained from all subjects involved in the study.

**Data Availability Statement:** All data of this research were presented in the article.

**Conflicts of Interest:** The authors declare no conflict of interest.

## References

1. Jannat, M.; Hurwitz, D.S.; Monsere, C.; Funk II, K.H. The role of driver's situational awareness on right-hook bicycle-motor vehicle crashes. *Saf. Sci.* **2018**, *110*, 92–101. [CrossRef]
2. Parnell, K.J.; Stanton, N.A.; Plant, K. Where are we on driver distraction? Methods, approaches and recommendations. *Theor. Issues Ergon. Sci.* **2018**, *19*, 578–605. [CrossRef]
3. Louw, T.; Madigan, R.; Carsten, O.; Merat, N. Were they in the loop during automated driving? Links between visual attention and crash potential. *Inj. Prev.* **2017**, *23*, 281–286. [CrossRef] [PubMed]
4. Dingus, T.A.; Guo, F.; Lee, S.; Antin, J.F.; Perez, M.; Buchanan-King, M.; Hankey, J. Driver crash risk factors and prevalence evaluation using naturalistic driving data. *Proc. Natl. Acad. Sci. USA* **2016**, *113*, 2636–2641. [CrossRef] [PubMed]
5. Singh, S. Critical Reasons for Crashes Investigated in the National Motor Vehicle Crash Causation Survey (No. DOT HS 812 506). Traffic Safety Facts Crash. Stats Series. National Highway Traffic Safety Administration. 2018. Available online: https://crashstats.nhtsa.dot.gov/Api/Public/ViewPublication/812506 (accessed on 25 December 2020).
6. Papantoniou, P.; Papadimitriou, E.; Yannis, G. Review of driving performance parameters critical for distracted driving research. *Transp. Res. Procedia* **2017**, *25*, 1796–1805. [CrossRef]
7. Hanowski, R.J.; Olson, R.L.; Hickman, J.S.; Bocanegra, J. Driver distraction in commercial motor vehicle operations. In *Driver Distraction and Inattention*; CRC Press: Boca Raton, FL, USA, 2017; pp. 141–156. [CrossRef]
8. Topolšek, D.; Areh, I.; Cvahte, T. Examination of driver detection of roadside traffic signs and advertisements using eye tracking. *Transp. Res. Part F Traffic Psychol. Behav.* **2016**, *43*, 212–224. [CrossRef]
9. Oviedo-Trespalacios, O.; Williamson, A.; King, M. User preferences and design recommendations for voluntary smartphone applications to prevent distracted driving. *Transp. Res. Part F Traffic Psychol. Behav.* **2019**, *64*, 47–57. [CrossRef]
10. Yusoff, N.M.; Ahmad, R.F.; Guillet, C.; Malik, A.S.; Saad, N.M.; Mérienne, F. Selection of measurement method for detection of driver visual cognitive distraction: A review. *IEEE Access* **2017**, *5*, 22844–22854. [CrossRef]
11. Kinnear, N.; Stevens, A. The Battle for Attention: Driver Distraction—A Review of Recent Research and Knowledge. The IAM (Institute of Advanced Motorists) Driver Distraction Report. 2015. Available online: https://www.iamroadsmart.com/docs/default-source/research-reports/report---the-battle-for-attentionv3pdf?sfvrsn=136ce750_6 (accessed on 22 December 2020).
12. Sterkenburg, J.; Jeon, M. Impacts of anger on driving performance: A comparison to texting and conversation while driving. *Int. J. Ind. Ergon.* **2020**, *80*, 102999. [CrossRef]
13. Wood, G.; Hartley, G.; Furley, P.A.; Wilson, M.R. Working memory capacity, visual attention and hazard perception in driving. *J. Appl. Res. Mem. Cogn.* **2016**, *5*, 454–462. [CrossRef]
14. Braun, M.; Broy, N.; Pfleging, B.; Alt, F. Visualizing natural language interaction for conversational in-vehicle information systems to minimize driver distraction. *J. Multimodal User Interfaces* **2019**, *13*, 71–88. [CrossRef]
15. Parnell, K.J.; Stanton, N.A.; Plant, K.L. What's the law got to do with it? Legislation regarding invehicle technology use and its impact on driver distraction. *Accid. Anal. Prev.* **2017**, *100*, 1–14. [CrossRef] [PubMed]
16. Ojsteršek, T.C.; Topolšek, D. Influence of drivers' visual and cognitive attention on their perception of changes in the traffic environment. *Eur. Transp. Res. Rev.* **2019**, *11*, 1–9. [CrossRef]
17. Jenness, J.; Boyle, L.N.; Lee, J.D.; Miller, E.; Yahoodik, S.; Huey, R.; Petraglia, E. In-vehicle voice control interface evaluation: Preliminary driver workload and risk analysis (Report No. DOT HS 812 813). Washington, DC: National Highway Traffic Safety Administration. 2020. Available online: https://www.nhtsa.gov/sites/nhtsa.gov/files/documents/8122314_in_vehvoicecntrlitrfaceperformeval.pdf (accessed on 22 December 2020).

18. Soares, S.; Ferreira, S.; Couto, A. Driving simulator experiments to study drowsiness: A systematic review. *Traffic Inj. Prev.* **2020**, *21*, 29–37. [CrossRef] [PubMed]
19. Sheykhfard, A.; Haghighi, F. Driver distraction by digital billboards? Structural equation modeling based on naturalistic driving study data: A case study of Iran. *J. Saf. Res.* **2020**, *72*, 1–8. [CrossRef] [PubMed]
20. Wörle, J.; Metz, B.; Thiele, C.; Weller, G. Detecting sleep in drivers during highly automated driving: The potential of physiological parameters. *IET Intell. Transp. Syst.* **2019**, *13*, 1241–1248. [CrossRef]
21. Geden, M.; Staicu, A.M.; Feng, J. The impacts of perceptual load and driving duration on mind wandering in driving. *Transp. Res. Part F Traffic Psychol. Behav.* **2018**, *57*, 75–83. [CrossRef]
22. Smith, G.K.; Mills, C.; Paxton, A.; Christoff, K. Mind-wandering rates fluctuate across the day: Evidence from an experience-sampling study. *Cogn. Res. Princ. Implic.* **2018**, *3*, 54. [CrossRef]
23. Née, M.; Contrand, B.; Orriols, L.; Gil-Jardiné, C.; Galéra, C.; Lagarde, E. Road safety and distraction, results from a responsibility case-control study among a sample of road users interviewed at the emergency room. *Accid. Anal. Prev.* **2019**, *122*, 19–24. [CrossRef]
24. Xu, J.; Liu, J.; Sun, X.; Zhang, K.; Qu, W.; Ge, Y. The relationship between driving skill and driving behavior: Psychometric adaptation of the Driver Skill Inventory in China. *Accid. Anal. Prev.* **2018**, *120*, 92–100. [CrossRef]
25. Alizadeh, V.; Dehzangi, O. The impact of secondary tasks on drivers during naturalistic driving: Analysis of EEG dynamics. In Proceedings of the 2016 IEEE 19th International Conference on Intelligent Transportation Systems (ITSC), Rio de Janeiro, Brazil, 1–4 November 2016; pp. 2493–2499. [CrossRef]
26. Directorate of General Security. The Annual Report of Traffic Accidents in Jordan for the Year 2019 AD.; Amman Jordan. 2019. Available online: https://www.psd.gov.jo/images/docs/TrafficRep2019.pdf (accessed on 23 December 2020). (In Arabic)
27. Niu, J.; Wang, X.; Liu, X.; Wang, D.; Qin, H.; Zhang, Y. Effects of mobile phone use on driving performance in a multiresource workload scenario. *Traffic Inj. Prev.* **2019**, *20*, 37–44. [CrossRef]
28. Huemer, A.K.; Vollrath, M. Driver secondary tasks in Germany: Using interviews to estimate prevalence. *Accid. Anal. Prev.* **2011**, *43*, 1703–1712. [CrossRef] [PubMed]
29. Stutts, J.C.; Reinfurt, D.W.; Staplin, L.; Rodgman, E.A. The role of driver distraction in traffic crashes. Available online: https://www.forces-nl.org/download/distraction.pdf (accessed on 22 December 2020).
30. Al-Rousan, T.M.; Umar, A.A.; Al-Omari, A.A. Characteristics of crashes caused by distracted driving on rural and suburban roadways in Jordan. *Infrastruct* **2021**, *6*, 107. [CrossRef]
31. Albdouro, N.; Marafi, M. Study of driver faults and type of intersection contributing to traffic accident in Jordan. *Contemp. Eng. Sci.* **2015**, *8*, 427–440. [CrossRef]
32. Al-Omari, B.H.; Obaidat, E. Analysis of Pedestrian Accidents in Irbid City, Jordan. *Open Transp. J.* **2013**, *7*, 1–6. [CrossRef]
33. Central Traffic Department. Jordan Experience in Traffic Safety. Available online: https://www.psd.gov.jo/images/traffic/docs/reduceTraafic.pdf (accessed on 13 September 2021).
34. Ammonnews. Mobile Phone Fines Generate 614 Thousand Dinars for "CTD" in Two Days. Available online: https://www.ammonnews.net/article/385057 (accessed on 13 September 2021). (In Arabic)
35. Roya News. 217,000 Traffic Violations Committed during Third Quarter of 2018 in Amman. Available online: https://en.royanews.tv/news/15420/217-000-Traffic-violations-committed-during-third-quarter-of-2018-in-Amman (accessed on 13 September 2021). (In Arabic)
36. Ammonnews. Traffic Fines. Available online: https://www.ammonnews.net/article/305194 (accessed on 13 September 2021). (In Arabic)
37. Sarayanews. Traffic Violations Amounted to (88) Million and a Half in Two Years. Available online: https://www.sarayanews.com/article/429583 (accessed on 13 September 2021). (In Arabic)
38. Oviedo-Trespalacios, O. Getting away with texting: Behavioural adaptation of drivers engaging in visual manual tasks while driving. *Transp. Res. Part A Policy Pract.* **2018**, *116*, 112–121. [CrossRef]
39. Oviedo-Trespalacios, O.; King, M.; Vaezipur, A.; Truelove, V. Can our phones keep us safe? A content analysis of smartphone applications to prevent mobile phone distracted driving. *Transp. Res. Part F Traffic Psychol. Behav.* **2019**, *60*, 657–668. [CrossRef]
40. Nguyen-Phuoc, D.Q.; Oviedo-Trespalacios, O.; Su, D.N.; De Gruyter, C.; Nguyen, T. Mobile phone use among car drivers and motorcycle riders: The effect of problematic mobile phone use, attitudes, beliefs and perceived risk. *Accid. Anal. Prev.* **2020**, *143*, 105592. [CrossRef]

*infrastructures* MDPI

*Article*

# Assessment of Traffic Sign Comprehension Levels among Drivers in the Emirate of Abu Dhabi, UAE

**Taleb M. Al-Rousan [1,*] and Abdullahi A. Umar [2]**

1 Department of Civil Engineering, The Hashemite University, Zarqa 13133, Jordan
2 Department of Civil Engineering and Quantity Surveying, Military Technological College, Al Matart Street, Muscat 111, Oman; Abdullah.Umar@mtc.edu.om
* Correspondence: taleb@hu.edu.jo; Tel.: +962-5-3903333 (ext. 4383); Fax: +962-5-3826348

**Abstract:** Road traffic signs are part of the road infrastructure components meant to ensure the safe use of roads by motorists and pedestrians alike. A good knowledge and comprehension of road signs helps ensure smooth flow of traffic, improves safety for other motorists and provides drivers with good reaction time to comply with the message dictated by the signs. Abu Dhabi, being the capital of the UAE, brings together people from all over the world for work, business or tourism. Abu Dhabi has quality roads and traffic signage together with an efficient police force that enforces adherence to traffic rules. Despite all these and the reduced fatalities in absolute terms, traffic violations have been increasing exponentially, resulting in five million traffic fines in 2019 for a population of about 2.9 million inhabitants. This study sought to assess motorists' comprehension of the various traffic signs used across the UAE. The results of the survey (N = 200) revealed that the drivers were able to correctly identify 77% of the road signs in the survey. It was also found that the respondents failed to correctly identify traffic signs within the specific category referred to as "advance warning signs". Respondents' education, nationality, gender, and marital status did not have any statistically significant effects on the results compared to earlier studies. It is recommended that more attention be focused on driver education and training.

**Keywords:** Abu Dhabi; comprehension; driving behaviors; traffic signs; traffic safety

**Citation:** Al-Rousan, T.M.; Umar, A.A. Assessment of Traffic Sign Comprehension Levels among Drivers in the Emirate of Abu Dhabi, UAE. *Infrastructures* **2021**, *6*, 122. https://doi.org/10.3390/ cinfrastructures6090122

Academic Editors: Krzysztof Goniewicz, Robert Czerski and Marek Kustra

Received: 30 July 2021
Accepted: 30 August 2021
Published: 31 August 2021

**Publisher's Note:** MDPI stays neutral with regard to jurisdictional claims in published maps and institutional affiliations.



## 1. Introduction

Road transport is the most common transportation form globally. Road transportation provides benefits both to nations and to individuals by facilitating the movement of goods and people. It enables increased access to jobs, economic markets, education, recreation, and health care, which in turn have direct and indirect positive impacts on the health of populations [1]. However, driving on roads is a complex task that involves extensive interactions between road users and the other components of the transport system, such as the driver, the vehicle, and the road traffic environment [2]. This interaction, if well-coordinated with appropriate road signs, effective drivers' road sign education and comprehension, can result in smooth flow of traffic, enhanced road safety and a general reduction in traffic violations and accidents [3]. However, it has been reported that over 1.2 million deaths and about 50 million non-fatal injuries result from road accidents globally on an annual basis [1]. The global cost of road accidents has been estimated to cost the world economy USD 1.8 trillion between 2015–2030 or 0.12% of global Gross Domestic Product [4]. In a bid to reduce this number of deaths, governments around the world are taking different measures depending on the local domestic characteristics and driving behaviors they wish to stop or encourage. Researchers have also undertaken assisting governments by assessing the relationships between various factors and driving safety on roads. Governments respond to bad driving behaviors mostly through punitive measures such as fines to curb bad driving practices. Others have suggested the standardization of traffic signs internationally to enhance the ability of tourists to drive without further host-country training [5].

The roads in the United Arab Emirates (UAE) are some of the best in the world in terms of quality, as evidenced by their ranking in the road quality index. The UAE roads were ranked ahead of more developed countries such as Germany, USA, UK and France in the 2019 report of the World Economic Forum [6]. Oil wealth has led to the rapid growth and development of Abu Dhabi and its sister Emirates within the UAE arrangement. This rapid economic growth has attracted people from different regions of the world to the UAE with its attendant need for smooth and efficient means of transportation. A large volume of tourists also frequents the UAE annually, reaching over 15 million tourists in 2018 [7]. Some of these tourists prefer to rent cars and drive around on their own in order to get a better feel of the country. While the Emirate of Dubai has introduced the Dubai metro in addition to other modes of public transportation, the Emirate of Abu Dhabi only relies on public buses, taxis, rental cars and private cars for the movement of people. This has led to pressure on residents to own a personal car to ease movements from point to point. With so many drivers from diverse backgrounds and driving educations, the situation is ripe for traffic violations and accidents.

The police in Abu Dhabi issued five million fines against drivers in 2019 [8], with a population of about 2.9 million (2016 estimates from Statistics Centre of Abu Dhabi (SCAD)); this translates to 1.7 fines for every resident. Despite the increased volume of fines against drivers, it has been found that road traffic injuries in the UAE remained stable from 2012 to 2016 [9]. Another alarming factor in the road injuries and fatalities is the overrepresentation of UAE nationals among the fatalities and the injured [10]. One study of five countries within the Gulf Co-operation Council (GCC) found that the drivers correctly comprehended only 56% of the traffic signs they were presented [11]. The authors also found that for the UAE in particular, the respondents (N-861) correctly comprehend only 62% of the traffic signs presented to them. They attribute the poor performance to the manner in which drivers are licensed and the laxity of the assessments. Similar studies carried out in the United States by Ward et al. [12] also found that drivers could not comprehend a large percentage of the international road signs they were presented. In Turkey, Yakut [13] found that on average, participants correctly identified 81% of the signs presented. In Kano city, Nigeria, it was found that the average traffic sign comprehension level was as high as 79%, with the least comprehension being 54.7% on the "Park and Ride" sign. However, they found that truck drivers had a lower understanding level than all other classes of road users [14]. A study of drivers' sign comprehension across four countries (Poland, Finland, Canada and Israel) found that on average the drivers identified 58.5% of the signs correctly [5]. This goes to show that the problem is not limited to developing countries only, developed countries are also struggling.

A recent study of road crashes in Abu Dhabi between 2012 and 2017 revealed that there were 1.26 million crashes, 9327 injuries, and 1305 fatalities during the period covered. The study went on to reveal that the crashes tended to be fatal when collisions occurred between 22:00 and 5:59 o'clock, occurred under adverse weather conditions, involved pedestrians or drunk drivers, occurred on higher speed limit highways, as well as when drivers were male, minors and/or Emiratis [10]. The economic costs of these accidents to the GCC have been estimated to be around $7.5 billion annually [15]. While the police attempt to use fines to correct poor driving behaviors, governments, on the other hand, focus on road improvement projects. Little attention has been paid by governments in assessing drivers' knowledge and comprehension of traffic signs, which facilitates and enhances safety and better road use compliance. The situation is further compounded due to today's travel culture where people are often licensed in one country and then drive without any further training or assessments in another country [5]. This happens to be the case across the GCC where Americans and Europeans seldom undergo any assessments but are issued licenses upon presenting their home-country drivers' licenses. A good understanding of traffic signs assists drivers in proper use of roads, contributes to the smooth flow of traffic and enhances safety. Therefore, this study seeks to assess the level of road traffic signs comprehension among drivers in the Emirate of Abu Dhabi.

## 2. Literature Review

Road traffic signs help regulate traffic, provide crucial visual guidance, can alert drivers to potential hazards on the road and give drivers important preview time during night-time conditions [16]. In addition, well placed and maintained traffic signs provide drivers with clear guidance that enables them to act in a timely manner in accordance with the displayed instruction. Poorly maintained and illegible road signs can cause travelling delays and increase the potential for accidents for road users, especially drivers using such roads for the first time. Poorly maintained road signs are a growing problem even in developed countries. For instance, European Union Road Federation (ERF) [16] reported that 33% of Germany's 25 million road signs are considered non-readable, while another 25% are older than 15 years. Traffic signs come in both text and symbols, while in some instances may be text alone or a symbol alone. Researchers have assessed which option is more effective in delivering the required message to drivers. While it was found that text signs were difficult to comprehend by tourist respondents in Thailand [17], in Israel, a combination of text and symbols was found to be more acceptable and reduced driver comprehension time [18].

Past studies have also found that personal and social factors significantly affect drivers' comprehension of road signs [5,11,17,19,20]. In the case of Al-Madani and Al-Janahi [11], in their comparison of the countries within the GCC, they found that the drivers' education level, income range and nationality affected their ability to correctly identify traffic signs. Interestingly, they also found that males had a better comprehension than females and western drivers performed better than their Arab counterparts did. In Thailand, Choocharukul and Sriroongvikrai [17] assessed tourists in the country and found that drivers' age, experience in a foreign land and their nationality had a significant impact on ability to comprehend and translate road traffic signs. In the case of Shinar et al. [5] who assessed comprehension across four countries (Canada, Finland, Israel and Poland), they found that the age, gender and country (nationality) all had a significant impact on the comprehension levels of the respondents.

Taamneh and Alkheder [20], in their study of Jordanian drivers, found that only 61% of the drivers comprehended regulatory signs, 66% of drivers comprehended warning signs and 75% of drivers comprehended guidance traffic signs. They also found higher comprehension levels among drivers holding a commercial driving license and drivers with driving experience of more than 11 years.

Kirmizioglu and Tuydes-Yaman [21], in their study in Ankara-Turkey, found that out of 39 signs, only 12 were recognized correctly by almost 70% of the participants. They further found that over 10% of the drivers comprehended five of the signs oppositely, and they argued that the implication of this was riskier than not knowing at all. In Iraq, Ismail [19] found that drivers' comprehension of traffic signs increased with increasing education levels, the urbanization level of his residence and daily driving practice. Males and private car drivers were found to have a higher comprehension than females and other driver categories, respectively. He also found that marital status had no significant effect on the comprehension level of drivers. Ou and Liu [3] studied the influence of sign design features and training on the comprehension of 65 selected Taiwanese traffic signs on Taiwanese and Vietnamese drivers. They found that training outcome was positive in both user groups. The average comprehension improved from 0.63 and 0.41 pre-training to 0.98 and 0.89 post-training for Taiwanese and Vietnamese drivers, respectively. More importantly, comprehension scores measured after one month remained higher than pre-training.

Traffic signs are a simple and cost-effective intervention that can yield impressive rates of return in terms of road safety, and thus reducing the socio-economic consequences [16]. The European Union Roads Federation's review revealed that having good signage reduced fatalities by up to 87% in the UK. In Norway, the value derived from improved traffic signs was found to outweigh the costs by a factor of 3.5:1 [22]. While in Australia, its National Black Spot program was estimated to have reduced fatal and casualty crashes at the treated sites by 30%; the report went on to reveal that traffic sign interventions had the best cost-benefit ratio, ranging between 15:1 and 20:1 depending on the financial hypothesis made on the project [23].

## 3. Methodology

This study was conducted in the Emirate of Abu Dhabi in the United Arab Emirates (UAE). A review of relevant past literature was undertaken to understand the state of research in the area of traffic sign comprehension levels among motorists. Traffic comprehension studies at the global, regional and country level were explored. The UAE is a melting pot of people from across the globe working or visiting for tourism. Despite the efficient public transportation, residents often opt to own and drive their own cars, resulting in a highly diverse respondent population within the survey sample. A Likert-based questionnaire was designed based on similar ones used for past studies by Al-Madani and Al-Janahi [11]. The questionnaire was composed of two parts. Part one intended to collect information about drivers' age, gender, nationality, marital status, education level, number of years having a driving license and whether they have multiple ones, the number of fines and number of accidents they have had. Part two of the questionnaire was designed to present to the respondent a list of 18 traffic signs (including regulatory, warning, and guide sign types) with a multiple-choice query so they could pick the meaning of the traffic sign from the offered choices.

Purposive sampling technique [24] was adopted for the administration of the questionnaires. The respondents were chosen among visitors to three major shopping malls within Abu Dhabi, including Marina mall, Al Wahda mall and Abu Dhabi Mall. Due to the often high temperatures, these are the places many residents like to visit and stay during the day, engaging in shopping, dining and amusement activities for children. The parking managers at the three malls were used to distribute the questionnaires to drivers on their way in and they dropped off the questionnaires on their way out. About 203 questionnaires were returned out of the 300 that were distributed. However, only 200 were used for the analysis; three questionnaires were removed for incomplete information. The number of respondents was comparable with previous studies that reported 32 respondents, 59 respondents and 53 respondents used by Alnuaimi and Al Mohsin [25], Ruqaishi and Bashir [26] and Oyegoke and Al Kiyumi [27], respectively. The response rate of about 67% can be regarded as good considering the low responses to surveys within the GCC, knowing that the average response rate for survey data collection from organizations was 35.7% [28].

## 4. Results

The analyses involved 200 respondents who owned a UAE drivers' license as a minimum requirement to be eligible to complete the questionnaire. The respondent's educational profile showed that there were five respondents with a PhD., 10 respondents with a Master's degree, 85 respondents with a B.Sc. degree, 36 with a Diploma certificate and 64 respondents with a high school certificate. In terms of marriage status, there were 88 married and 112 single respondents within the sample. The respondents were a rich reflection of the basic profile of Abu Dhabi's residents, with 20 respondents from Europe, 10 Americans, 42 Asians, 19 Africans and 109 Middle Easterners, as shown in Table 1 below.

**Table 1.** Crosstab marital status vs. region of respondents.

| Marital Status | European | American | Middle Eastern | Asian | African | Total |
|---|---|---|---|---|---|---|
| Married | 10 | 8 | 42 | 22 | 6 | 88 |
| Single | 10 | 2 | 67 | 20 | 13 | 112 |
| Total | 20 | 10 | 109 | 42 | 19 | 200 |

A further analysis of the respondents' profile, shown in Table 2, revealed that respondents with only one country's drivers' license constituted 50.5%, while respondents with over three countries' drivers' license constituted only 4% of the total respondents. The respondents' profile also showed that 170 respondents drove their private cars, 12 were taxi drivers, 7 drove a bus or a lorry, while 11 rode motorcycles.

**Table 2.** Crosstab of vehicle type vs. number of drivers' licenses.

| No. of Licenses | Private Car | Taxi | Bus or Truck | Motorcycle | Total |
|---|---|---|---|---|---|
| 1 | 84 | 6 | 4 | 7 | 101 |
| 2 | 61 | 5 | 1 | 2 | 69 |
| 3 | 18 | 1 | 2 | 1 | 22 |
| Over 3 | 7 | 0 | 0 | 1 | 8 |
| Total | 170 | 12 | 7 | 11 | 200 |

A normality test was conducted on the data to determine the distribution and decide whether parametric or non-parametric procedures would be used in the analysis. Both Kolmogorov-Smirnov and Shapiro-Wilk tests, presented in Table 3, revealed that the data violates normality assumptions, hence non-parametric procedures were employed in analyzing the data [29].

**Table 3.** Tests of normality.

| | Kolmogorov-Smirnov [a] | | | Shapiro-Wilk | | |
|---|---|---|---|---|---|---|
| | Statistic | df | Sig. | Statistic | df | Sig. |
| Mean18 | 0.159 | 200 | 0.000 | 0.973 | 200 | 0.001 |

[a] Lilliefors Significance Correction.

There are two variables within the data set that qualify for analysis using the Mann-Whitney U test for independent samples: they are the gender and marital status variables, while the Kruskal-Wallis H test was used for independent samples with more than two categories. The Mann-Whitney U test to determine whether there exists a statistically significant difference in responses between the genders (males and females) and respondents' marital status returned non-significant results, indicating that these independent variables did not affect road sign comprehension in any way, as shown in Table 4 below.

**Table 4.** Mann-Whitney U test.

| Independent Variable | | Median | N | Mann-Whitney U | Z | Assymp. Sig. (2-Tailed) |
|---|---|---|---|---|---|---|
| Gender (Male/Female) | M | 2.0556 | 146 | 3400 | −1.505 | 0.132 |
| | F | 2.0556 | 54 | | | |
| Marriage Status (Married/Single) | M | 2.0556 | 88 | 4221 | −1.758 | 0.079 |
| | S | 2.0556 | 112 | | | |

Kruskal-Wallis H test was conducted on the independent variables of age, academic qualifications, type of vehicle driven, and the region of origin of the respondents. The results shown in Table 5 reveal that there was no statistically significant difference across the respondents based on age of respondents ($p$-value = 0.184); academic qualification ($p$-value = 0.217); type of vehicle driven ($p$-value = 0.541); and region of respondents ($p$-value = 0.390). The implication of this result is that road sign comprehension capacity is not affected by a driver's age, academic qualification, type of vehicle or the geographical region from which the driver originates. This last result is especially important given the fact that non-citizen residents in the UAE are treated based on their country of origin when seeking to convert their home-country drivers' licenses to a UAE drivers' license. However, the test revealed that there was a statistically significant difference based on respondents' number of licenses.

**Table 5.** Kruskal Wallis H test results.

| Independent Variable | Z-Score | df | Assymp. Sig. |
|---|---|---|---|
| Age of Respondents | 4.834 | 3 | 0.184 |
| Academic Qualification | 5.775 | 4 | 0.217 |
| Type of Vehicle | 2.157 | 3 | 0.541 |
| Number of Licenses | 19.913 | 3 | 0.000 |
| Nationality (Region) | 4.122 | 4 | 0.390 |

To investigate further and determine which group was responsible for the difference, a Kruskal-Wallis one-way ANOVA was conducted, and the results are shown in Table 6 below. This test compares the median of the distribution to determine which group differs from the others [29]. The group with more than three licenses was responsible for the difference, even though the number of cases in this group was very small (8). However, due to their very small number, it would be unwise to generalize the results of this research endeavor.

**Table 6.** Kruskal-Wallis One-Way ANOVA test.

| No. of Licenses | N | Median |
|---|---|---|
| One | 101 | 2.0556 |
| Two | 69 | 2.1111 |
| Three | 22 | 2.0833 |
| Over Three | 8 | 1.9167 |
| Total | 200 | 2.0556 |

The overall average performance of the study sample was 77% across all 200 respondents in terms of their ability to correctly recognize the road traffic signs presented to them. This is an improvement on the earlier study which found a 56% average performance in the comprehension of traffic signs [11]. The performance of the sample is shown in Table 7. The performance of the respondents was below 90% on 8 out of the 18 road signs that were presented. Good comprehension of road signs reduces driving mistakes on the road, and consequently a reduction of accidents on the roads. However, the government relies on punitive measures such as fines to ensure adherence and compliance. As the results above reveal, there are a couple of areas where more sensitizations will be required, especially because all the signs used in the questionnaire were taken from the UAE's Emirates Driving Institutes' (EDI) Guidance chart for road signs, road markings and traffic signals.

A further breakdown of the performance of the respondents according to gender (see Table 8) reveals a very interesting trend. A higher percentage of males failed to correctly name each of the "advance warning signs" they were presented compared to their female counterparts. This finding is contrary to the earlier GCC-wide study by Al-Madani and Al-Janahi [11] who found that male drivers performed better than females.

Interestingly, all the road signs where the respondents failed to pick the correct answer were contained in the "advance warning signs" section of the EDI Guidance chart. Therefore, it has become pertinent that training instructors and police driving assessment officers pay more attention to these areas when training or assessing potential drivers, respectively. Furthermore, the government should consider a traffic sign retest exam for all drivers when they apply for their driving license renewal. While the importance of driver education is recommended [20] and aggressive campaigns have been suggested [21], it has also been empirically proven that driver training [3] holds the most potent potential for enhancing safety on our roads.

**Table 7.** Road sign comprehension performance.

| S/No. | Road Signs | | Sign Type | % Correct |
|---|---|---|---|---|
| 1 | Maximum Speed |  | Regulatory | 92% |
| 2 | Petrol Filling Station |  | Guide | 96% |
| 3 | Hospital |  | Guide | 79% |
| 4 | Restaurants |  | Guide | 89% |
| 5 | Parking |  | Guide | 100% |
| 6 | One-Way Traffic |  | Regulatory | 90% |
| 7 | Hazard Ahead |  | Warning | 77% |
| 8 | Dual-Carriage Way Ends |  | Warning | 17% |
| 9 | Traffic Merges From Left |  | Warning | 18% |
| 10 | Pedestrian Crossing |  | Warning | 95% |
| 11 | Children Crossing |  | Warning | 75% |
| 12 | Hump |  | Warning | 95% |
| 13 | Minimum Speed |  | Regulatory | 33% |
| 14 | Left Only |  | Regulatory | 93% |
| 15 | Turning Left Or Right |  | Regulatory | 90% |
| 16 | U-Turn |  | Regulatory | 90% |
| 17 | Round-About |  | Regulatory | 95% |
| 18 | Shared Track For Pedestrians And Bicycles |  | Regulatory | 67% |

**Table 8.** Percentage of the seven road sign comprehension failures by gender.

| Signs with Comprehension Issues | Males 146 | Females 54 |
|---|---|---|
| Hospital Sign | 24% | 15% |
| Hazard Ahead | 27% | 13% |
| Dual Carriage Ends | 84% | 80% |
| Traffic Merges From Left | 84% | 78% |
| Children Crossing | 28% | 19% |
| Minimum Speed | 64% | 78% |
| Shared Track for Pedestrians and Bicycles | 39% | 19% |

## 5. Discussion

As indicated earlier, the respondents were a rich reflection of the basic profile of Abu Dhabi's residents, which makes the study results more realistic and reflects the real prevailing situation of sign comprehension of drivers in the Emirate of Abu Dhabi.

The results revealed that there was no statistically significant difference in responses between the genders (males and females) and respondents' marital status, indicating that these independent variables did not affect road sign comprehension in any way. Both results tend to be an improvement on an earlier study conducted by Al-Madani and Al-Janahi [11] across the GCC countries. However, the majority of earlier studies have consistently found that differences exist between the genders when it comes to traffic-related issues and accidents [30–33]. Cordellieri et al. [30] and McKenna et al. [32], however, found that these differences do not exist in terms of driving risk perception, while the SIRC [33] argued that these differences can best be explained by virture of fundamental evolutionary differences in behavior and psychology rather than levels of competence and driving skills. In a related study, Massie and Campbell [31] found that the differences witnessed between male and female drivers disappear by the age of 60 and onwards. The results from this study may, however, have been impacted by the low number of female respondents, which was about 27%. Another possible explanation could be the large number of under 40 respondents (76%), since it has been found that age tends to mediate the observed difference [31,34].

Moreover, several earlier studies on gender revealed that males were in general better than females regarding traffic sign comprehension [19,35]. Al-Madani and Al-Janahi [36] indicated that posted signs were comprehended better by male drivers than females in Arab, European and American countries. Similarly, Hawkins Jr et al. [37] reported that men better recognized one fifth of the warning signs correctly. When education background is controlled for, the differences between males and females may become less remarkable [35]. Gender was found to have no statistically significant impact in a study that considered male and female European and American drivers having at least undergraduate degrees [11]. Likewise, Ng and Chan [38] indicated that there was no significant difference for traffic sign guessability between males and females of similar education levels. In regards to marital status, the findings of this study were in line with the finding of Ismail [19], who also found that marital status had no significant effect on the comprehension level of drivers.

The results revealed that there was no statistically significant difference across the respondents based on age, academic qualifications, type of vehicle driven and region of respondents. The implication of this result is that road sign comprehension capacity is not affected by a driver's age, academic qualification, type of vehicle and the geographical region from which the driver originates. These results disagree with Al-Madani and Al-Janahi [11], who found that the driver's education level, income range and nationality impacted ability to correctly identify traffic signs in countries within the GCC. However, this could be interpreted as an improvement in the training and testing methods in Abu Dhabi. Previous studies in general indicated that drivers' comprehension of traffic signs increased with increasing education levels [19,35,38].

As presented in the Results section, the overall average performance of the study sample was 77%, reflecting respondents' ability to correctly recognize the road traffic signs presented to them. This result can be considered as an improvement on the earlier study which found a 56% average performance in the comprehension of traffic signs, and 62% for the UAE in particular [11]. Similar studies showed that drivers could not comprehend a large percentage of the road signs presented to them [12]. In Turkey, participants correctly identified 81% of the signs presented [13]. In Kano city, Nigeria, it was found that the average traffic sign comprehension level was as high as 79% [14]. A study of drivers' sign comprehension across four countries (Poland, Finland, Canada and Israel) found that on average the drivers only identified 58.5% of the signs correctly [5]. This goes to show that the problem is not limited to developing countries only, as developed countries are also struggling.

The timeliness and the robustness of traffic sign comprehension while driving is very important to drivers. Safe driving and accident avoidance can be ensured when a timely visual recognition of traffic signs takes place [21,39,40]. Zhang et al. [41] clustered the factors that affect a traffic sign's visual recognizability into three groups: (1) geometric factors of traffic sign, such as sign's size, placement, mounting height, aim, depression angle, occlusion angle, curvature of road and changing road surface [41]; (2) movement factors of vehicle, such as speed, Geometric Field Of View (GFOV), which decreases with speed being increased [42], and height and direction of line of sight which governs whether the traffic sign is contained by the GFOV; and (3) other factors, for example, weather conditions [43], lighting conditions [44], drivers' view reaction time which is affected by drivers' age and sight capabilities [44], and traffic density cognitive burden [45]. Moreover, occlusion may cause interruptions to visual continuity, thus affecting the recognition of the traffic signs [46]. Considering the abovementioned factors that affect the recognizability of the traffic sign in real-life driving practice, it is expected that the level of comprehension of drivers will reduce to an extent that might be significant if the above factors are not considered in the design and placement of these signs.

Traffic Sign Recognition (TSR) systems have recently become common in car manufacturing industries. Road safety enhancement can be achieved using TSR technology by providing timely warnings and dynamically assisting drivers in adhering to posted speed limits [47]. The most basic TSR systems employ vehicle-mounted cameras for identification of traffic signs. Their main function is to notify the driver of near traffic signs in a process that starts with scanning the roadside for signs, then using real-time image processing software to identify and inform the driver by a sound or displaying a symbol on the vehicle's dashboard panel [48]. Zhang et al. [41] indicated that the most current traffic sign detection and classification methods are based on color and shape information within images or videos. These methods use color information to segment the sign candidate area, and then to extract the traffic sign. Challenges to the vision-based TSR systems include variations in lighting and weather conditions, occluded signs and image distortion due to vehicle motion [41,48]. Zhang et al. [41] pointed out that there are different methods for recognition evaluation (simulator and image methods and naturalistic driving experimentation), but each has its own limitations. As indicated earlier, deployment of TSR systems will bring great enhancement to road safety and reduce accident involvement. Meanwhile, limitations to TSR deployment should be addressed, which include fixing conflicts in signage design, cooperation between the vehicle industry and road operators to achieve reliability of the TSR system, and adaptation with continuous development of the TSR technology which is expected to become more accurate and more reliable [48].

The study outcomes clearly show that traffic safety can be enhanced by means of providing well maintained, readable and well-placed signs; driver education and training; inclusion of TSR technology into the transportation system; and consideration of traffic sign retest exams for all drivers when they apply for their driving license renewal.

## 6. Conclusions

Traffic signs are components of road infrastructures that are meant to assist road users in safely navigating to their destinations. This study sought to assess the comprehension level of drivers in the Emirate of Abu Dhabi (UAE). The respondents' overall performance was an improvement on earlier studies, however, there is still much to be improved upon. Although earlier studies found that driver's age, marital status, gender, nationality, level of education and type of vehicle all had a statistically significant impact on road sign comprehension, the data analysis for this study did not support such a conclusion. Furthermore, contrary to earlier studies, a higher percentage of males failed to correctly identify the "advance warning signs" compared to female respondents. One of the most critical findings from this study is the ability to identify the category of road signs that are problematic to drivers in Abu Dhabi. This finding should assist driving instructors and police driving assessment officers in redesigning their teaching materials and assessments, respectively. The fact that despite increased fines driving violations persist points to the need to shine a spotlight on the training of drivers and the assessment methods for issuing licenses, as well as requirements for license renewal.

**Author Contributions:** Conceptualization, T.M.A.-R.; methodology, T.M.A.-R.; formal analysis, T.M.A.-R., A.A.U.; resources, T.M.A.-R., A.A.U.; data curation, T.M.A.-R., A.A.U.; writing—original draft, T.M.A.-R., A.A.U.; writing—review and editing, T.M.A.-R., A.A.U.; supervision, T.M.A.-R.; project administration, T.M.A.-R. All authors have read and agreed to the published version of the manuscript.

**Funding:** This research did not receive any specific grants from any funding agencies.

**Data Availability Statement:** All data of this research were presented in the article.

**Acknowledgments:** The authors would like to thank the following individuals for their help in distributing and collecting the survey questionnaires: Samir Aldraidi, Mahmoud M. Ayman, Abdullah S. Abueidda and Mohammed S. Almansoori.

**Conflicts of Interest:** The authors declare no conflict of interest.

## References

1. WHO. *Global Status Report on Road Safety: Time for Action*; World Health Organisation (WHO): Geneva, Switzerland, 2020; Available online: https://www.afro.who.int/publications/global-status-report-road-safety-time-action (accessed on 20 February 2021).
2. Oviedo-Trespalacios, O.; Truelove, V.; Watson, B.; Hinton, J.A. The impact of road advertising signs on driver behaviour and implications for road safety: A critical systematic review. *Transp. Res. Part A* **2019**, *122*, 85–98. [CrossRef]
3. Ou, Y.-K.; Liu, Y.-C. Effects of sign design features and training on comprehension of traffic signs in Taiwanese and Vietnamese user groups. *Int. J. Ind. Ergon.* **2012**, *42*, 1–7. [CrossRef]
4. Chen, S.; Kuhn, M.; Prettner, K.; Bloom, D.E. The global macroeconomic burden of road injuries: Estimates and projections for 166 countries. *Lancet Planet. Health* **2019**, *3*, 390–398. [CrossRef]
5. Shinar, D.; Dewar, R.; Summala, H.; Zakowska, L.Z. Traffic sign symbol comprehension: A cross-cultural study 2. *Ergonomics* **2004**, *46*, 1549–1565. [CrossRef]
6. WEF, Roads Quality-Country Rankings. 2019. Available online: https://www.theglobaleconomy.com/rankings/roads_quality (accessed on 21 February 2020).
7. Puri-Mirza, A. International Overnight Visitors to Dubai 2010–2018. 2020. Available online: https://www.statista.com/statistics/284636/visitor-arrivals-in-dubai-from-international-destinations (accessed on 21 February 2021).
8. Haza, R. UAE Road Deaths Lowest in Almost a Decade as Drivers Hit with 8 Million Fines. 2020. Available online: https://www.thenationalnews.com/uae/transport/uae-road-deaths-lowest-in-almost-a-decade-as-drivers-hit-with-8-million-fines-1.1045642 (accessed on 21 February 2021).
9. Ankit, A.; Hamidi, S.; Sengoelge, M. Causes and Health-Related Outcomes of Road Traffic Crashes in the United Arab Emirates: Panel Data Analysis of Traffic Fines. *Glob. J. Health Sci.* **2018**, *10*, 165–171. [CrossRef]
10. Albuquerque, F.D.; Awadalla, D.M. Characterization of Road chrashes in the Emirates of Abu Dhabi. *Transp. Res. Procedia* **2020**, *48*, 1095–1110. [CrossRef]
11. Al-Madani, H.; Al-Janahi, A.R. Assessment of Drivers' comprehension of Traffic signs based on their Traffic, Personal and Social Characteristics. *Transp. Res. Part F* **2002**, *5*, 63–76. [CrossRef]

12. Ward, S.; Wogalter, M.; Mercer, A. *Comprehension and Training of International Road Signs;* HFES: New Orleans, LA, USA, 2004; pp. 2104–2108. [CrossRef]
13. Yakut, S. Comprehensibility of Traffic Signs (in Turkish Trafik İşaretlerinin Anlaşılabilirliği). Master's Thesis, Gazi University, Ankara, Turkey, 2006.
14. Umar, I.K.; Bashir, S. Comprehension of Road Traffic Signs by various Road Users in Kano City. *Cumhur. Sci. J.* **2019**, *40*, 197–203. [CrossRef]
15. Farook, L. Traffic Accidents Cost GCC $7.5 Billion Annually. 2001. Available online: https://gulfnews.com/uae/traffic-accidents-cost-gcc-75b-annually-1.414222 (accessed on 24 February 2021).
16. European Union Road Federation (ERF). Improved Signage for Better Roads, Brussels: European Union Road Federation. 2018. Available online: https://erf.be/publications/improved-signage-for-better-roads/ (accessed on 24 February 2021).
17. Choocharukul, K.; Sriroongvikrai, K. Road safety awareness and Comprehension of Road signs from International Tourist' Perspectives: A case study of Thailand. *Transp. Res. Procedia* **2017**, *25*, 4518–4528. [CrossRef]
18. Shinar, D.; Vogelzang, M. Comprehension of traffic signs with symbolic versus text displays. *Transp. Res. Part F Traffic Psychol. Behav.* **2013**, *18*, 72–82. [CrossRef]
19. Ismail, A.A. Comprehension of Posted Highway Traffic Signs in Iraq. *Tikrit J. Eng. Sci.* **2012**, *19*, 62–70. [CrossRef]
20. Taamneh, M.; Alkheder, S. Traffic sign perception among Jordanian drivers: An evaluation study. *Transport. Policy* **2018**, *66*, 17–29. [CrossRef]
21. Kirmizioglu, E.; Tuydes-Yaman, H. Comprehensibility of traffic signs among urban drivers in Turkey. *Accid. Anal. Prev.* **2012**, *45*, 131–141. [CrossRef] [PubMed]
22. ETSC. Cost Effective EU Transport Safety Measures, Brussels: European Transport Safety Council (ETSC). 2003. Available online: https://etsc.eu/cost-effective-eu-transport-safety-measures/ (accessed on 25 February 2021).
23. BITRE. Evaluation of the National Black Spot Program, Canberra: Bureau of Infrastructure, Transport and Regional Economics. 2012. Available online: https://www.bitre.gov.au/publications/2012/report_126 (accessed on 27 February 2021).
24. Dolores, M.; Tongco, C. Purposive Sampling as a Tool for Informant Selection. *Ethnobot. Res. Appl.* **2007**, *5*, 147–158. Available online: https://ethnobotanyjournal.org/index.php/era/article/view/126 (accessed on 27 February 2021).
25. Alnuaimi, A.S.; Al Mohsin, M.A. Causes of Delay in Completion of Construction Projects in Oman. In Proceedings of the International Conference on Innovations in Engineering and Technology (ICIET'2013), Bangkok, Thailand, 25–26 December 2013.
26. Ruqaishi, M.; Bashir, H.A. Causes of Delay in Construction Projects in the Oil and Gas Industry in the Gulf Cooperation Council Countries: A Case Study. *J. Manag. Eng.* **2013**, *31*, 05014017. [CrossRef]
27. Oyegoke, A.S.; Al Kiyumi, N. The causes, impacts and mitigations of delay in megaprojects in the Sultanate of Oman. *J. Financ. Manag. Prop. Constr.* **2017**, *22*, 286–302. [CrossRef]
28. Baruch, Y.; Holtom, B.C. Survey response rate levels and trends in organizational research. *Hum. Relat.* **2008**, *61*, 1139–1160. [CrossRef]
29. Pallant, J. *SPSS Survival Manual: A Step by Step Guide to Data Analysis Using IBM SPSS*, 7th ed.; Open University Press: London, UK, 2020.
30. Cordellieri, P.; Baralla, F.; Ferlazzo, F.; Sgalla, R.; Piccardi, L.; Giannini, A.M. Gender Effects in Young Road Users on Road Safety Attitudes, Behaviors and Risk Perception. *Front. Psychol.* **2016**, *7*, 1412. [CrossRef]
31. Massie, D.L.; Campbell, K.L. *Analysis of Accident Rates by Age, Gender, and Time of Day Based on the 1990 Nationwide Personal' Transportation Survey;* Insurance Institute for Highway Safety: Arlington, VA, USA, 1993.
32. McKenna, F.P.; Waylen, A.E.; Burkes, M.E. *Male and Female Drivers: How Are They Different?* Foundation for Road Safety Research: Basingstoke, UK, 1998.
33. SIRC. *Sex Differences in Driving and Insurance Risk;* The Social Issues Research Centre: Oxford, UK, 2004.
34. Rhodes, N.; Pivik, K. Age and gender differences in risky driving: The roles of positive affect and risk perception. *Accid. Anal. Prev.* **2011**, *43*, 923–931. [CrossRef]
35. Zhang, T.; Chan, A. Traffic Sign Comprehension: A Review of Influential Factors and Future Directions for Research. In Proceedings of the International Multi Conference of Engineers and Computer Scientists 2013 Vol II, IMECS 2013, Hong Kong, China, 13–15 March 2013; Available online: http://www.iaeng.org/publication/IMECS2013/IMECS2013_pp1026-1030.pdf (accessed on 27 August 2021).
36. Al-Madani, H.; Al-Janahi, A. Role of drivers' personal characteristics in understanding traffic sign symbols. *Accid. Anal. Prev.* **2002**, *34*, 185–196. [CrossRef]
37. Hawkins, H., Jr.; Womack, K.; Mounce, J. Driver Comprehension of Regulatory Signs, Warning Signs, and Pavement Markings. *Transp. Res. Rec.* **1993**, *1403*, 67. Available online: http://onlinepubs.trb.org/Onlinepubs/trr/1993/1403/1403-010.pdf (accessed on 27 August 2021).
38. Ng, A.W.Y.; Chan, A.H.S. The guessability of traffic signs: Effects of prospective-user factors and sign design features. *Accid. Anal. Prev.* **2007**, *39*, 1245–1257. [CrossRef] [PubMed]
39. Liu, B.; Wang, Z.; Song, G.; Wu, G. Cognitive processing of traffic signs in immersive virtual reality environment: An ERP study. *Neurosci. Lett.* **2010**, *485*, 43–48. [CrossRef] [PubMed]
40. Ben-Bassat, T.; Shinar, D. The effect of context and drivers' age on highway traffic signs comprehension. *Transp. Res. Part Traffic Psychol. Behav.* **2015**, *33*, 117–127. [CrossRef]

41. Zhang, S.; Wang, C.; Lin, L.; Wen, C.; Yang, C.; Zhang, Z.; Li, J. Automated Visual Recognizability Evaluation of Traffic Sign Based on 3D LiDAR Point Clouds. *Remote Sens.* **2019**, *11*, 1453. [CrossRef]
42. Mourant, R.R.; Ahmad, N.; Jaeger, B.K.; Lin, Y. Optic flow and geometric field of view in a driving simulator display. *Displays* **2007**, *28*, 145–149. [CrossRef]
43. Belaroussi, R.; Gruyer, D. Impact of reduced visibility from fog on traffic sign detection. In Proceedings of the 2014 IEEE Intelligent Vehicles Symposium Proceedings, Dearborn, MI, USA, 8–11 June 2014; pp. 1302–1306.
44. Rogé, J.; Pébayle, T.; Lambilliotte, E.; Spitzenstetter, F.; Giselbrecht, D.; Muzet, A. Influence of age, speed and duration of monotonous driving task in traffic on the driver's useful visual field. *Vis. Res.* **2004**, *44*, 2737–2744. [CrossRef] [PubMed]
45. Costa, M.; Simone, A.; Vignali, V.; Lantieri, C.; Bucchi, A.; Dondi, G. Looking behavior for vertical road signs. *Transp. Res. Part Traffic Psychol. Behav.* **2014**, *23*, 147–155. [CrossRef]
46. Tieri, G.; Tidoni, E.; Pavone, E.; Aglioti, S.M. Mere observation of body discontinuity affects perceived ownership and vicarious agency over a virtual hand. *Exp. Brain Res.* **2015**, *233*, 1247–1259. [CrossRef] [PubMed]
47. Roper, Y.; Rowland, M.; Chakich, Z.; McGIll, W.; Nanayakkara, V.; Young, D.; Whale, R. Implications of Traffic Sign Recognition (TSR) Systems for Road Operators. BN 978-1-925671-71-1 Austroads Project No. CAV6056 Austroads Publication No. AP-R580-18. Austroads Ltd., 2018. Available online: https://austroads.com.au/publications/connected-and-automated-vehicles/ap-r580-18/media/AP-R580-18_-Implications_of_Traffic_Sign_Recognition.pdf (accessed on 27 August 2021).
48. The Clemson University Vehicular Electronics Laboratory CVEL. Traffic Sign Recognition Systems. Available online: https://cecas.clemson.edu/cvel/auto/systems/sign-recognition.html (accessed on 27 August 2021).

infrastructures

MDPI

*Article*

# Characteristics of Crashes Caused by Distracted Driving on Rural and Suburban Roadways in Jordan

**Taleb M. Al-Rousan [1,*], Abdullahi A. Umar [2] and Aslam A. Al-Omari [3,4]**

1 Department of Civil Engineering, The Hashemite University, Zarqa 13133, Jordan
2 Department of Civil Engineering and Quantity Surveying, Military Technological College, Al Matart Street, Muscat 111, Oman; Abdullah.Umar@mtc.edu.om
3 Civil Engineering Department, Jordan University of Science and Technology, Irbid 22110, Jordan; aaalomari3@just.edu.jo
4 Department of Civil Engineering, Applied Science Private University, Amman 11931, Jordan
* Correspondence: taleb@hu.edu.jo; Tel.: +962-5-3903333 (ext. 4383); Fax: +962-5-3826348

**Abstract:** The objective of this study was to identify the most salient driver faults that cause crashes on some Jordanian rural and suburban roadway segments, to examine crashes with distracted driving as the driver's fault, and to investigate the differences between crashes caused by distracted driving. Data for more than 10,200 crashes on nine roadway segments (five rural and four suburban) were accessed from the relevant government agency, but only n = 2472 were used for analysis after controlling for crashes specified as being caused by drivers' distracted driving. IBM SPSS version 22 was used to perform descriptive analysis and independent samples' *t*-tests. The results revealed that distracted driving was the second most common driver fault to cause crashes and the second main cause of fatalities and injuries on both rural and suburban roadways. Distracted driving on rural highways appears to be more fatal, whereas it caused more crashes with severe injuries on suburban roads. The variables at junction, road grade, number of lanes, weather condition, crash type, and number of vehicles involved were found to be statistically significant but with a small effect size. The following categories showed high percentages of distracted driving crashes on rural and suburban roadways: males, drivers 25–39 years old, non-holidays, weekdays, tangent sections, two-way divided roads, not at junction, level roads, two-lane roads, clear weather, dry surface, daylight, and automobile vehicles showed high percentages of distracted driving crashes on rural and suburban roadways. Differences between crashes on rural and suburban roadways caused by distracted driving were found to be small.

**Keywords:** attention; crashes; distraction; drivers' fault; traffic safety

**Citation:** Al-Rousan, T.M.; Umar, A.A.; Al-Omari, A.A. Characteristics of Crashes Caused by Distracted Driving on Rural and Suburban Roadways in Jordan. *Infrastructures* **2021**, *6*, 107. https://doi.org/10.3390/infrastructures6080107

Academic Editors: Krzysztof Goniewicz, Robert Czerski and Marek Kustra

Received: 18 June 2021
Accepted: 22 July 2021
Published: 29 July 2021

**Publisher's Note:** MDPI stays neutral with regard to jurisdictional claims in published maps and institutional affiliations.



## 1. Introduction

Safe driving entails a complex combination of behaviors in which the driver is required to successfully perform a number of complex activities concurrently [1]. Such activities include (but are not limited to) route detection and tracking, speed and lateral position controlling, collision avoiding, road laws obeying, and vehicle systems status monitoring [2]. Drivers are often observed as engaging in activities that will likely divert their attention away from the main crucial activity required for safe driving [1]. Pashler [3] pointed out that humans normally have limited capability to carry out more than two tasks in parallel.

The definitions of distracted driving reported in the literature vary. Distracted driving occurs when the recognition of the information required for safe driving is delayed due to something such as an individual, an event, or an activity inside or outside the vehicle, forcing the driver to divert his attention away from the driving task [4,5]. Distraction can undermine driving performance and impact driver behavior in different ways and to various degrees. Dingus et al. [6] maintained that driver distraction and slips of attention have a significant influence on road crashes and other related road safety issues. Distraction reduces the performance of the driver and is an important factor in the occurrence of traffic accidents [7,8]. Louw et al. [9] indicated that over 90% of reported traffic accidents were the outcome of human error and caused by issues related to the acquisition of visual information. Moreover, drivers can be held responsible for causing 90% of critical traffic conditions [6,10]. Khattak et al. [11] indicated that human factors still contribute to 93% of crashes, whereas recognition errors (including distraction) are found to be the driving error contributing to the highest percentage of crashes.

Regan et al. [12] defined driver inattention as " ... insufficient, or no attention, to activities critical for safe driving". They also listed several forms of driver inattention such as biological factors that block the driver from noticing crucial information for safe driving; misprioritized attention of drivers (i.e., drivers' attention focused on one side of driving while excluding another); and driver distraction, which is considered as one form of driver inattention where a competing or a secondary task (which can be driving-related or non-driving-related) diverts the attention of the drivers away from crucial safe driving tasks.

Goodsell et al. [1] conducted a comprehensive review of studies on driver distraction and listed four major moderating factors that might influence the occurrence of driver distraction. The first moderating factor is driver characteristics (age and driving experience). The second moderating factor is the level of demand of the driving task. Weather, traffic, and road conditions were found to influence the demand of driving tasks [13]. The third moderating factor is the level of demand for attention of the competing activity (i.e., visual–manual vs. auditory–vocal). The fourth moderating factor is the drivers' ability to change their behavior to keep satisfactory driving performance in the face of competing tasks (also known as self-regulation) [14].

Shortfalls of driving performance due to engagement in competing tasks have been found to include the following: poor lane keeping and speed control, increase in reaction time, skipping traffic signals, inadequate headway distances, risky gap acceptances, reduction in situational awareness, and visual scanning of the roadway [15–18]. Many of these shortfalls in driving performance are correlated with a substantial risk of crashes [6]. For example, poor speed control, when examined separately from other causal factors such as driver distraction, might increase crash risk by 12.8 times, and short headway distances can increase crash risk by 13.5 times [6].

Young et al. [13] indicated that driver distraction might be affected by the demand of the driving task, which in turn may be influenced by factors such as weather, traffic, and road conditions. Generally, more demanding tasks impair driving performance more. Accordingly, it is expected that distractions in different areas and road types may vary.

Driving tasks might be affected by road aggressiveness [19]. Spanish drivers' perceptions of aggressive behavior and the most aggressive acts performed when driving were studied by Alonso et al. [19]. Their results show that both infractions and dangerous behaviors correspond to aggressive driving, which definitely becomes a source of distraction. It has also been found that drivers who tend to have several accidents give less importance to elements that can affect the driving task such as distraction.

Xuedong et al. [20] indicated that crash rates in rural sections are regularly lower than those in urban ones. They also indicated that rural areas have lower crash risk when compared to urban places. Additionally, it was found that an increase in traffic volume and section length would increase the frequency of crashes and lower the chances of the occurrence of severe crashes. Research indicates that fatality rates in rural areas are higher than in urban locations [21–23]. Similarly, it is expected that suburban roadways will have similar characteristics of crash potential. Suburban roadways are transitional high-speed roadways between low-speed urban streets and high-speed rural highways. They have the characteristics of both rural (i.e., high-speed) and urban (i.e., with curb and gutter used for drainage) roadways [24]. Territorial variables (built environment and physical severance) can affect the occurrence of accidents, even due to distraction. In their study on traffic crashes on rural roads with older pedestrians, Casado-Sanz et al. [25] indicated that a small number of studies in the literature have discussed territorial variables (built environment and physical severance). Casado-Sanz et al. [25] aimed at determining the significant factors that increase the probability of a fatal outcome in the case of a crash involving at least one seriously injured individual at rural crosstown roads. The results revealed that the physical severance index (territorial variable) was very significant and suggested that the probability of a fatal outcome on a lateral rural crosstown road is almost two times higher than that at the baseline condition of a central rural crosstown road.

In Jordan, the rapid growth in population was accompanied by an increase in vehicle ownership. According to Jordan's Department of Statistics [26], there were about 10.5 million inhabitants in 2019. Additionally, Driver and Vehicle License Department (DVDL) [27] records show that the number of licensed drivers in 2019 exceeded 2.5 million, and that there were around 1.6 million registered vehicles. The majority of Jordan's population (90.33%) live in urban or suburban areas (areas are classified as follows: urban when the population > 10,000 inhabitants, and suburban when the population falls between 5000 and 10,000 inhabitants [28]). Consequently, a rapid growth in population and vehicle ownership has contributed, among other factors, to the increasing number of crashes.

Accident statistics clearly show that when compared to developed countries, Jordan suffers from a relatively low level of traffic safety, which results in great socio-economic losses. The Annual Report of Traffic Accidents in Jordan [29] showed that 161,511 traffic accidents occurred in Jordan in 2019, of which 10,857 were human injury accidents that resulted in 643 fatalities at an estimated financial cost of around USD 454 million. When compared with accidents worldwide, Jordan ranked in the top four countries in the year 2017 in relation to deaths per 10,000 vehicles. In the year 2019, human-related factors were responsible for 98.2% of accidents in Jordan that resulted in human injuries. Driver fault (not taking the necessary precautions) accounted for a high percentage (around 40%) of injuries and deaths in 2019 [26].

Due to the significant impact of distraction on driver performance and the great losses resulting from it, this study aimed to identify the most salient driver faults that cause crashes on nine segments of Jordan's rural and suburban roadways using the available crash data. The study also sought to examine crashes with distracted driving as the driver's fault and to investigate the differences between crashes caused by distracted driving on rural and suburban roadways. Knowing which road factors influence distracted driving on rural and suburban roadways can help researchers, traffic experts, and authorities to identify the most effective measures that may reduce driver distraction and target different driver groups with the best practices that fit their driving behaviors and keep them attentive. Likewise, the best practices can be implemented on different roadway types, under varying weather conditions, and at different times of the year.

## 2. Methodology

### 2.1. Crash Data

The data used in this study were extracted from traffic accident records obtained from the Jordan Traffic Institute for the years 2014 to 2018. The available data provide information about more than 10,200 crashes on nine roadway segments (five rural and four suburban), which connect different areas with Amman (capital city of Jordan). The information includes crash date and time; driver's age, gender, and fault; pavement surface type and condition; lanes' direction, number, horizontal alignment, and grade; weather and lighting conditions; crash type and speed of vehicles involved; severity; and location coordinates. Some of the driver age records were incomplete (missing or mistakenly entered). The retention of cases with outliers (out-of-range values) can distort the results of the analyses; hence, such cases were either corrected or deleted [30]. It is worth mentioning here that distracted driving was listed among drivers' faults, but the records mentioned nothing about what caused the distraction. Therefore, it is assumed that distracted driving may be attributed to any of the known distraction types (visual, manual, cognitive, and auditory) or a combination of them. Although some of the drivers' faults can be interrelated—for example, distraction can lead to degraded lane keeping, speed control problems, missed traffic signal, etc.—the results presented here depend solely on the provided information, and thus, there is no way to find such a link between the driver's faults. Therefore, the total sample size analyzed in this study was restricted to those cases that the police clearly indicated as being caused by distracted driving (n = 2472). Among the 2472 crashes that were caused by distracted driving, 910 (36.8%) occurred in suburban areas, and 1562 (63.8%) took place in rural areas. The details of the collected data and their categories are discussed in the next section.

### 2.2. *Data Analysis*

The IBM SPSS version 22 statistical software package was used to perform independent samples *t*-tests to determine whether there were statistically significant differences between drivers. The analysis conducted in this work consisted of two levels. In the first level, an analysis of drivers' faults was conducted by using descriptive statistics to discover the most common driver faults responsible for causing crashes on rural and suburban roadways. In the second level, on the other hand, an independent samples *t*-test analysis was used to examine the characteristics of distracted driving crashes and investigate the differences between crashes caused by distracted driving on rural and on suburban roadways based on human- and location-related factors.

## 3. Analysis and Results

### 3.1. *Drivers' Faults Analysis*

The analysis of the available accident data for both rural and suburban roadway segments for the years 2014–2018 is shown in Table 1 below. The analysis revealed that three of the drivers' faults listed in Table 1 were responsible for almost 73% of all reported crashes. Lane departure (25.95%), distracted driving (24.19%), and tailgating (22.79%) were the top driver faults causing crashes. In fourth and fifth places came traffic rules violation (9.6%) and wrong-way driving (8.21%). The remaining driver faults, listed in Table 1, were responsible for less than 10% of reported crashes. Moreover, the analysis of the severity of crashes showed that the most frequently occurring driver's faults (lane departure and distracted driving) were the causes of crashes with the highest severity. These driver faults were responsible for almost 81% of the total reported fatalities, 77% of severe injuries, 63% of moderate injuries, 67% of slight injuries, and almost 46% of property damage only (PDO) crashes. Reckless driving was ranked as the third major fault causing fatalities with almost 7%, and control loss and traffic rules violation were also responsible for nearly 7% of reported fatalities.

**Table 1.** Percentage and severity of crashes based on drivers' faults.

| Drivers' Faults | % of All Crashes | Fatal | Severe Injury | Moderate Injury | Slight Injury | PDO |
|---|---|---|---|---|---|---|
| Lane departure | 25.95 | 95 | 202 | 67 | 919 | 2089 |
| Distracted driving | 24.19 | 37 | 85 | 35 | 522 | 1963 |
| Tailgating | 22.79 | 3 | 13 | 10 | 215 | 2211 |
| Traffic rules violation | 9.6 | 5 | 16 | 0 | 164 | 901 |
| Wrong-way driving | 8.21 | 2 | 9 | 2 | 69 | 799 |
| Reckless driving | 2.63 | 8 | 10 | 12 | 65 | 219 |
| Control loss | 2.44 | 6 | 10 | 5 | 68 | 207 |
| Ignoring road signs | 1.63 | 1 | 1 | 0 | 17 | 152 |
| Overtaking | 0.71 | 1 | 14 | 22 | 33 | 60 |
| Commercial vehicle loads | 0.55 | 0 | 0 | 0 | 2 | 55 |
| Speeding | 0.44 | 1 | 7 | 4 | 22 | 31 |
| Red light running | 0.29 | 0 | 2 | 0 | 17 | 24 |
| Improper stopping | 0.28 | 0 | 3 | 2 | 10 | 21 |
| Reckless at curves | 0.24 | 4 | 0 | 3 | 15 | 16 |
| Vehicle defect | 0.03 | 0 | 2 | 0 | 5 | 1 |
| Brake failure | 0.02 | 0 | 0 | 0 | 0 | 2 |

### 3.2. Distracted Driving Analysis

As stated earlier, distracted driving was found to be the second highest ranking drivers' fault responsible for crashes on rural and suburban roads, and it was the second most hazardous cause of fatalities and injuries. Available records show that the number of crashes with distracted driving listed as the driver's fault is 2472, which represents 24.19% of all crashes. Distracted driving as a driver's fault was responsible for 22.7% of fatalities, 22.7% of severe injuries, 21.6% of moderate injuries, 24.4% of slight injuries, and 22.4% of PDO crashes. The characteristics of these crashes are discussed based on statistics acquired from the available data. Differences between crashes on rural and suburban roads caused by distracted driving were investigated based on three different factors: human- and time-related factors, presented in Table 2; road- and environment-related factors, presented in Table 3; and crash-type- and vehicle-related factors, shown in Table 4. Among the 2472 crashes with distracted driving listed as the driver's fault, 910 (36.8%) occurred in suburban areas and 1562 (63.8%) took place in rural areas. The severity of crashes in rural and suburban roads is presented in Figure 1. Distracted driving in rural areas seemed to be more fatal, whereas that on suburban roads led to more severe injuries.

**Table 2.** Distracted driving crashes on rural and suburban roadways according to human- and time-related factors.

| Factor | Category | Percent of Total Distracted Driving Crashes on | | |
|---|---|---|---|---|
| | | **Rural and Suburban** | **Rural** | **Suburban** |
| Gender | Females | 32.81 | 33.93 | 30.77 |
| | Males | 67.19 | 66.07 | 69.23 |
| Age | Below 25 | 5.4 | 5.81 | 4.76 |
| | 25–39 | 64.2 | 64 | 63.11 |
| | 40–54 | 22.7 | 22.61 | 24.46 |
| | Above 60 | 7.7 | 7.58 | 7.67 |
| Holiday | No | 96.04 | 96.29 | 95.6 |
| | Yes | 3.96 | 3.71 | 4.4 |
| Time of the day | Evening | 32.4 | 32.46 | 32.31 |
| | Morning | 13.03 | 12.04 | 14.72 |
| | Midday | 36.93 | 38.35 | 34.51 |
| | Night time | 17.64 | 17.15 | 18.46 |
| Day | Weekday | 75.32 | 75.67 | 74.73 |
| | Weekend | 24.68 | 24.33 | 25.27 |

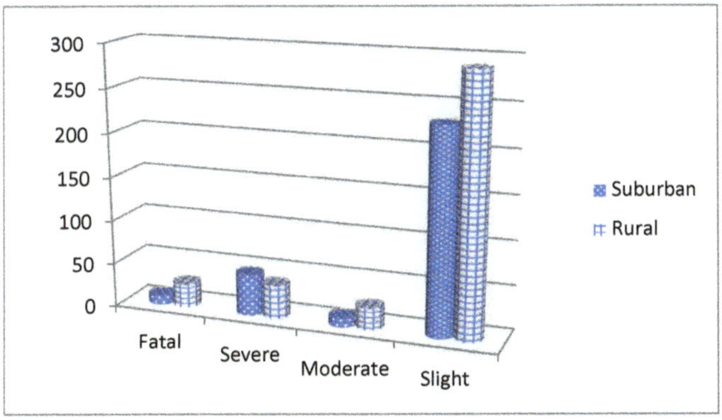


**Figure 1.** Severity of crashes with distracted driving listed as driver's fault on rural and suburban roads.

**Table 3.** Distracted driving crashes according to road- and environment-related factors.

| Factor | Category | Percent of Total Distracted Driving Crashes on Rural and Suburban | Rural | Suburban |
|---|---|---|---|---|
| Alignment | Curve | 1.7 | 1.54 | 1.98 |
| | Tangent | 98.3 | 98.46 | 98.02 |
| Direction | One-way | 6.19 | 8.06 | 2.97 |
| | Two-way divided | 66.07 | 62.04 | 73.07 |
| | Two-way undivided | 27.74 | 29.9 | 23.96 |
| At junction | No | 87.62 | 88.67 | 85.82 |
| | Yes | 12.38 | 11.33 | 14.18 |
| Grade | Ascending | 7.36 | 7.36 | 7.36 |
| | Descending | 4.41 | 3.33 | 6.27 |
| | Level | 88.23 | 89.31 | 86.37 |
| No. of lanes | 1 | 0.65 | 1.02 | 0 |
| | 2 | 87.62 | 98.98 | 68.13 |
| | 3 | 11.73 | 0 | 31.87 |
| Surface | Dry | 95.45 | 94.81 | 95.7 |
| | Wet | 4.55 | 5.19 | 4.3 |
| Weather | Clear | 95.1 | 94.24 | 96.7 |
| | Dust | 0.73 | 1.03 | 0.22 |
| | Fog | 0.57 | 0.7 | 0.33 |
| | Rain | 2.99 | 3.2 | 2.53 |
| | Snow | 0.04 | 0.06 | 0 |
| | Storm wind | 0.57 | 0.77 | 0.22 |
| Lighting | Dark | 2.87 | 3.65 | 1.54 |
| | Daylight | 68.07 | 67.35 | 69.23 |
| | Night with insufficient lighting | 9.07 | 8.52 | 10 |
| | Night with sufficient lighting | 14.24 | 14.6 | 13.62 |
| | Sunrise | 0.57 | 0.83 | 0.22 |
| | Sunset | 5.18 | 5.05 | 5.39 |

**Table 4.** Distracted driving crashes according to crash-type- and vehicle-related factors.

| Factor | Category | Percent of Total Distracted Driving Crashes on Rural and Suburban | Rural | Suburban |
|---|---|---|---|---|
| Crash type | Collision | 83.62 | 89.18 | 74.07 |
| | Pedestrian | 14.24 | 7.87 | 25.16 |
| | ROR | 2.14 | 2.95 | 0.77 |
| Vehicles involved | 1 | 25.81 | 29.58 | 19.34 |
| | 2 | 68.28 | 65.81 | 72.31 |
| | 3 | 5.14 | 3.84 | 7.14 |
| | 4 or more | 0.77 | 0.77 | 1.21 |
| Vehicle speed | <40 | 4.05 | 3.91 | 4.29 |
| | 40–<60 | 35.32 | 26.18 | 50.99 |
| | 60–<80 | 32.36 | 32.52 | 32.09 |
| | 80–100 | 16.46 | 33.87 | 12.63 |
| | >100 | 11.81 | 3.52 | 0 |
| Vehicle type | Automobile | 50.93 | 52.56 | 48.13 |
| | Heavy vehicle | 5.7 | 4.29 | 8.13 |
| | Light vehicle | 32.61 | 27.78 | 40.88 |
| | Medium vehicle | 8.74 | 12.36 | 2.53 |
| | Motorcycle | 0.28 | 0.45 | 0 |
| | Tractor vehicle | 1.74 | 2.56 | 0.33 |

Table 2 shows the characteristics of crashes caused by distracted driving as the drivers' fault according to human- and time-related factors. According to the table, males were responsible for almost two-thirds of the crashes on both rural and suburban roadways. The differences in crash percentages between rural and suburban areas for males and females indicate that females were more distracted on rural roadways than males were, who appeared to be more distracted on suburban roadways where driving tasks are more demanding. Table 2 shows that drivers in the age group of 25–39 years were responsible for 64.2% of crashes, while drivers in the age group of 40–54 years caused only 22.7% of distracted driving crashes on both rural and suburban roadways. The percentages of crashes between age groups for rural and suburban areas show no major difference, except a slight increase in percentage in suburban areas for drivers of the age group 40–54.

The analysis in Table 2 shows that the majority of crashes (96%) occurred on "no holiday" days. The percentages of crashes between "holiday" and "no holiday" show no major differences between rural and suburban roadways. Distracted driving crashes during weekdays are almost three times more frequent than those that occur on weekends. Unlike suburban roadways, rural roadways seem to have slightly more distracted driving crashes during weekdays, although suburban roads show more crashes during weekends. Table 2 also shows that around 69% of distracted driving crashes occurred at midday and evening on both rural and suburban roadways. Morning and night-time crashes caused by distracted driving seem to be slightly more common on suburban roadways. Meanwhile, rural roadways show a higher percentage of crashes due to distracted driving around midday.

The characteristics of crashes caused by distracted driving as the drivers' fault according to road- and environment-related factors are shown in Table 3. More than 98% of these crashes took place on tangent sections on both rural and suburban roads. A higher percentage of crashes caused by distracted driving on two-way divided roads took place on suburban roads, whereas a higher percentage of crashes were seen on one-way and two-way undivided rural roads. The analysis shows that the majority of crashes (87.62%) took place at "no junction" roadway sections in both rural and suburban areas. The percentage of "at junction" crashes was slightly higher on suburban roads.

Table 3 shows that the majority of distracted driving crashes occurred on level grades, under dry surface conditions, in clear weather, and on two-lane roads for both rural and suburban areas. Rural roads witnessed more crashes at level grades, while suburban roadways saw more crashes on descending sections. No major difference was noticed in terms of the surface condition between urban and suburban areas. A higher percentage of crashes with distracted driving was noticed on two-lane rural roadways, while a higher percentage of crashes was seen on three-lane suburban roads. Suburban roads witnessed more crashes with distracted driving noted as the driver's fault during clear weather and daylight hours, whereas more crashes were seen on rural roadways when lighting conditions were dark.

The characteristics of crashes caused by distracted driving as the driver's fault according to crash-type- and vehicle-related factors are shown in Table 4. Collision, with a percentage of 83.62%, was the most often occurring crash type in both rural and suburban areas. Crash types caused by distracted driving seem to occur in different percentages in rural and suburban roadway sections. Collision and run-off-road (ROR) crashes occurred in higher percentages on rural roads, whereas more pedestrian crashes were seen on suburban road sections. Crashes that involved more than one vehicle were seen in higher percentages in suburban road sections.

Distracted driving crashes that occurred at speeds of 40–80 km/h were the most observed among all speed categories. The highest percentage of crashes on suburban roads occurred at speeds of 40–80 km/h, while for rural roads, the highest percentage of crashes occurred at speeds of 60–100 km/h. Crashes at speeds of higher than 100 km/h seemed to occur on rural roads only. Rural roads witnessed a higher percentage of crashes caused by distracted driving involving automobiles, medium vehicles, and tractor vehicles. On the other hand, crashes on suburban roads involved more light and heavy vehicles.

After comparing the differences between crashes resulting from distracted driving on rural and suburban roads based on crash percentages, a statistical analysis was conducted to assess whether these differences are statistically significant. Table 5 shows the results of the independent samples *t*-test for rural and suburban roadways. Six variables were found to be statistically significant: at junction, road grade, number of lanes, weather condition, crash type, and number of vehicles involved. For these variables with statistically significant differences, the effect size was calculated using Eta square and classified using Cohen's [31] guidelines, where 0.01 = small effect, 0.06 = moderate effect, and 0.14 = large effect. From the foregoing, and as shown in the table below, the six variables with statistically significant differences ended up having only a small effect. This indicates that the reported differences do not have a strong effect.

**Table 5.** Independent samples *t*-test: rural vs. suburban roadways.

| Variables | F | t | df | Sig. (2-Tailed) | Effect Size |
|---|---|---|---|---|---|
| Holiday | 2.804 | −0.838 | 2470 | 0.402 | - |
| Time of day | 4.133 | −0.059 | 1830.403 | 0.953 | - |
| Weekday/weekend | 1.098 | 0.527 | 2470 | 0.599 | - |
| Horizontal alignment | 2.680 | 0.819 | 2470 | 0.413 | - |
| Direction | 44.532 | −0.392 | 2196.874 | 0.695 | - |
| At junction | 16.922 | −2.020 | 1756.910 | 0.044 | 0.001 |
| Road grade | 35.640 | 2.821 | 1601.583 | 0.005 | 0.001 |
| No. of lanes | 10,307.452 | 20.620 | 909.000 | 0.000 | 0.01 |
| Surface condition | 7.561 | −1.419 | 2112.542 | 0.156 | - |
| Weather condition | 17.967 | −2.256 | 2203.157 | 0.024 | 0.001 |
| Lighting condition | 0.643 | −0.069 | 2470 | 0.945 | - |
| Crash type | 137.264 | 6.956 | 1770.340 | 0.000 | 0.003 |
| No. of vehicles involved | 31.675 | 5.507 | 2094.276 | 0.000 | 0.002 |

Moreover, the independent samples test was also conducted to explore whether differences exist between genders in terms of distracted driving. The results shown in Table 6 below indicate that differences only exist under three conditions, namely road surface conditions, weather conditions, and lighting conditions. However, the effect size calculations revealed that the differences were very small, as reflected by the fact that no values crossed Cohen's [31] guideline classifications for a small effect size (0.01).

**Table 6.** Independent sample *t*-test: males vs. females.

| Variables | F | t | df | Sig. (2-Tailed) | Effect Size |
|---|---|---|---|---|---|
| Holiday | 9.101 | 1.439 | 1413.70 | 0.150 | - |
| Time of day | 0.136 | −0.245 | 2470 | 0.806 | - |
| Weekday/weekend | 7.885 | 1.396 | 1656.194 | 0.163 | - |
| Horizontal alignment | 1.369 | 0.584 | 2470 | 0.559 | - |
| Direction | 3.639 | −0.529 | 2470 | 0.597 | - |
| At junction | 0.036 | 0.095 | 2470 | 0.924 | - |
| Road grade | 2.244 | 0.731 | 2470 | 0.465 | - |
| No. of lanes | 14.353 | 1.933 | 1755.32 | 0.053 | - |
| Surface condition | 80.096 | 5.155 | 2385.556 | 0.000 | 0.002 |
| Weather condition | 68.251 | 4.812 | 2400.721 | 0.000 | 0.002 |
| Lighting condition | 15.670 | 2.224 | 1774.341 | 0.026 | 0.001 |
| Crash type | 0.044 | 0.104 | 2470 | 0.917 | - |
| No. of vehicles involved | 1.393 | −0.056 | 2470 | 0.956 | - |

## 4. Discussion

The driver fault analysis conducted in this study proves the significant influence of distraction on driver performance and the great losses resulting from it. The analysis revealed that distracted driving was responsible for causing nearly one-fourth of the reported crashes included in this study. Moreover, the analysis of the severity of crashes showed that distracted driving was responsible for 22.7% of all reported fatalities, 22.7% of severe injuries, and 22.4% of PDO crashes. These results are in line with previous findings [6–11] indicating that human error was responsible for a very high percentage of crashes, and distraction had a significant influence on road crashes. These results also prove that humans continue to have limited capability to perform more than two tasks in parallel, as reported by Pashler [3].

The analysis of distracted driving on rural and suburban roads was performed based on three different groups of factors: human- and time-related factors, road- and environment-related factors, and crash-type- and vehicle-related factors. Distracted driving in rural areas seemed to be more fatal, whereas suburban roads witnessed more severe injuries. The higher frequency of fatalities on rural roads could be attributed to the fact that traffic on rural roads runs at higher speeds, resulting in more severe and fatal crashes. This finding is in line with those of Eberhardt et al. [21], Kmet et al. [22], and Gonzalez et al. [23], who indicated that fatality rates in rural areas are higher than those in urban locations.

The analysis of distracted driving based on human factors revealed that males were responsible for almost two-thirds of the crashes on both rural and suburban roadways. This percentage is reasonable considering that the number of licensed male drivers in Jordan is almost twice that of licensed female drivers [23]. The differences between genders in terms of distracted driving were investigated using an independent samples *t*-test. Statistically significant differences with a small effect size were found between male and female drivers under three conditions, namely road surface conditions, weather conditions, and lighting conditions. As reported by Young et al. [13], distractions and road and environmental factors are expected to make the driving task more demanding, thus leading to impaired driving performance.

Differences were noted between drivers' age groups in that younger age groups were causing crashes due to distracted driving almost three times more often than older groups. This finding is in line with that of Regan et al. [12], who suggested that older and/or more experienced drivers are more skillful at conducting multiple activities while driving, unlike younger and/or less experienced drivers. The slight difference in percentages of crashes between age groups for rural and suburban areas can be attributed to the more demanding driving tasks on suburban roads due to higher traffic volumes and extra accessing maneuvers.

Road aggressiveness is one important human factor that was not included in the crash records. Alonso et al. [19] indicated that drivers who tend to have several accidents give less importance to elements that can affect the driving task. The number and types of traffic violations (accident history) of drivers can be used to indicate the road aggressiveness factor. Therefore, the availability of the driver's accident record in the crash report can be very helpful in studying driving behaviors and can contribute to a better understanding of driver distraction for reducing road crashes.

The study of the effect of time-related factors on distracted driving showed that the majority of crashes occur on "no holiday" days and during weekdays, which can be attributed to the higher exposure to risky situations resulting from higher traffic volumes that occur on roads on regular working days. Rural roadways showed a slightly higher occurrence of distracted driving crashes during weekdays, although suburban roads showed more crashes during weekends. Morning and night-time crashes were slightly more frequent on suburban roadways; this could be due to the higher traffic volumes on suburban roadways during these times. Meanwhile, rural roadways showed a higher percentage of crashes due to distracted driving at midday; this could also be attributed to the active movement of traffic on rural roads during this time.

Young et al. [13] indicated that distraction on different areas and road types may vary. Weather, traffic, and road conditions influence the demandingness of the driving task. Therefore, the characteristics of crashes caused by distracted driving according to road- and environment-related factors were investigated. The result of the independent samples *t*-test revealed that four variables were statistically significant with a small effect size: at junction, road grade, number of lanes, and weather condition. The percentage of at-junction crashes was slightly higher on suburban roads, which could be attributed to the higher demandingness level of the driving task due to higher traffic volumes. The majority of distracted driving crashes were seen on level grades, under dry surface conditions, in clear weather, and on two-lane roads for both rural and suburban areas. Suburban roads witnessed more crashes with distracted driving as the drivers' fault during clear weather and daylight times, whereas more crashes were recorded on rural roadways when the lighting conditions were dark. This is consistent with Stutts et al. [32], who found that those who were distracted at the time of their crashes were less likely to be traveling on multi-lane roadways and were less likely to have crashed at an intersection or other road junction.

Casado-Sanz et al. [25] suggested using the physical severance index in future research, which considers the distribution of urban land as a relationship between the difference in the built areas on both sides of the road and the total built area. Territorial variables (built environment and physical severance) can affect the occurrence of accidents. Since the available data provide the coordinates of crashes, it might be possible to consider such territorial variables in future studies.

The analysis of the crashes caused by distracted driving as the drivers' fault according to crash-type- and vehicle-related factors showed that collision was the most common crash type in both rural and suburban areas. The crash types and the number of vehicles involved were statistically significantly different between rural and suburban roads. Collision and run-off-road (ROR) crashes occurred in higher percentages on rural roads, whereas more pedestrian crashes were seen on suburban road sections. The high percentage of pedestrian crashes in suburban areas makes sense, as pedestrians are seen in urban and suburban areas more often and are only occasionally seen on rural roadways. Crashes that involved more than one vehicle were seen in higher percentages in suburban road sections, which could be explained by the existence of traffic-congested sections in suburban areas. The number of distracted driving crashes involving one vehicle was higher in rural areas due to less traffic and higher speeds.

As presented in the previous section, the highest percentages of crashes on suburban roads occurred at speeds of 40–80 km/h, while for rural roads, the highest percentages of crashes occurred at speeds of 60–100 km/h. Crashes at speeds of higher than 100 km/h seemed to occur on rural roads only. This is consistent with earlier findings by Thomason [24], who reported the same result about suburban roadways and rural highways. As for vehicle type, we noticed that both automobiles and light vehicles comprised more than 80% of vehicles involved in the reported crashes. Rural roads witnessed a higher percentage of crashes caused by distracted driving involving automobiles, medium vehicles, and tractor vehicles. A similar finding was reported by Stutts et al. [32], who indicated that distracted drivers were more likely to be driving during non-daylight hours and were more likely to be driving a pickup truck, van, or sport utility vehicles.

One of the major limitations of the present study is that the obtained data lack, in some respects, important details that, if they existed, would deliver more thorough and useful results about distraction. Therefore, it is recommended that accident reports be carefully designed to include all specific details, such as the type of distraction factor (visual, manual, cognitive, and auditory) that caused the driver's distraction. Providing such details in the crash report would help eliminate confusion caused by interrelated information and would deliver complete information that will be significantly helpful to this field of research. It is also suggested that crash reports should include information on the number of accidents that drivers were previously involved in. Having this factor available can help researchers examine the effect of aggressive driving, as recommended by Alonso et al. [19], on all kinds of crashes, including distraction.

## 5. Conclusions

The aim of this study was to highlight the risk of driver distraction, which is one of the major driver's faults, in causing traffic crashes that cost great losses of lives and resources. Most drivers' faults that cause crashes on rural and suburban roadways were identified. Crashes caused by distracted driving were examined, and the differences between crashes on rural and suburban roadways were investigated. Based on the findings of this study, the following can be concluded:

Comprising almost one-fourth of the reported crashes (24.19%), distracted driving was the second most frequent driver fault causing crashes on both rural and suburban roadways.

(1) Distracted driving was the second most hazardous fault causing fatalities and injuries on both rural and suburban roadways, comprising an average of nearly 22% of all reported fatalities and injuries.
(2) Distracted driving on rural highways appeared to be more fatal, whereas suburban roadways witnessed more severe injuries.
(3) Six variables were found to be statistically significant but with small effect size values: at junction, road grade, number of lanes, weather condition, crash type, and number of vehicles involved.
(4) Statistically significant differences between gender groups only exist under three conditions: road surface conditions, weather conditions, and lighting conditions.
(5) High percentages of distracted-driving-related crashes on rural and suburban roadways were noticed among the following categories: males, drivers aged 25–39 years, non-holidays, weekdays, tangent sections, two-way divided roads, not at junction, level roads, two-lane roads, clear weather, dry surface, daylight, and automobile vehicles.
(6) Differences between crashes on rural and suburban roadways caused by distracted driving showed that a higher percentage of crashes occurred on rural roadways when the driver was female, the driver was 25–39 years old, the time was midday, the road was two-way and undivided, it was not at a junction section, there were two lanes, the driving speed was above 80 km/h, and light vehicles were involved.
(7) Differences between crashes on rural and suburban roadways caused by distracted driving showed that a higher percentage of crashes occurred on suburban roadways when the driver was male, the driver was 40–54 years old, the time was morning and night, the road was two-way and divided, it was at a junction, there were three lanes, there was clear weather, the driving speed was 40–60 km/h, and automobiles and medium vehicles were involved.
(8) Collision and ROR crash types were seen on rural roadways in a higher percentage, whereas more pedestrian crashes were observed on suburban roadway sections.

Considering the above-mentioned results, it is recommended that practitioners and policy-makers establish specialized programs and awareness campaigns intended to educate drivers on several factors that affect their driving abilities and emphasize and stimulate mindful driving with a sufficient cognitive and visual emphasis on driving initiatives and the traffic environment. It is also recommended that this same dataset be used in the future for model development to obtain a deeper understanding about factors that contribute to distracted driving and simulate the impact of distracted driving on the injury or crash severity of a given crash.

**Author Contributions:** Conceptualization, T.M.A.-R.; Methodology, T.M.A.-R. and A.A.U.; formal analysis, T.M.A.-R., A.A.U. and A.A.A.-O.; Investigation; T.M.A.-R.; resources, T.M.A.-R.; data curation, T.M.A.-R.; writing—original draft, T.M.A.-R., A.A.U. and A.A.A.-O.; writing—review and editing, T.M.A.-R., A.A.U. and A.A.A.-O., visualization, T.M.A.-R., A.A.U. and A.A.A.-O.;

supervision, T.M.A.-R.; project administration, T.M.A.-R. All authors have read and agreed to the published version of the manuscript.

**Funding:** This research did not receive any specific grant from any funding agencies.

**Data Availability Statement:** The data that support the findings of this study are not publicly available due to privacy/ethical restrictions, but they are available from the corresponding author upon reasonable request.

**Acknowledgments:** Thanks are due to the Jordan Traffic Institute officers for providing the traffic accident data that were used in this study.

**Conflicts of Interest:** The authors declare no conflict of interest.

## References


1. Goodsell, R.; Cunningham, M.; Chevaleir, A. Driver Distraction: A Review of Scientific Literature. National Transportation Commission. ARRB Report. Project No. 013817. 2019. Available online: https://www.ntc.gov.au/sites/default/files/assets/files/Driver%20distraction%20%20A%20review%20of%20scientific%20literature.pdf (accessed on 25 December 2020).
2. Cunningham, M.; Regan, M. Driver distraction and inattention. In *Safe Mobility: Challenges, Methodology and Solutions*; Transport and, Sustainability; Lord, D., Washington, S., Eds.; Emerald Publishing: Bingley, UK, 2018; Volume 11.
3. Pashler, H. Overlapping mental operations in serial performance with preview. *Q. J. Exp. Psychol.* **1994**, *47*, 161–191. [CrossRef] [PubMed]
4. Chand, A.; Bhasi, A.B. Effect of driver distraction contributing factors on accident causations—A review. *AIP Conf. Proc.* **2019**, *2134*, 060004. [CrossRef]
5. Casado-Sanz, N.; Guirao, B.; Attard, M. Analysis of the risk factors affecting the severity of traffic accidents on Spanish crosstown roads: The driver's perspective. *Sustainability* **2020**, *12*, 2237. [CrossRef]
6. Dingus, T.A.; Guo, F.; Lee, S.; Antin, J.F.; Perez, M.; Buchanan-King, M.; Hankey, J. Driver crash risk factors and prevalence evaluation using naturalistic driving data. *Proc. Natl. Acad. Sci. USA* **2016**, *113*, 2636–2641. [CrossRef] [PubMed]
7. Jannat, M.; Hurwitz, D.S.; Monsere, C.; Funk, K.H., II. The role of driver's situational awareness on right-hook bicycle-motor vehicle crashes. *Saf. Sci.* **2018**, *110*, 92–101. [CrossRef]
8. Parnell, K.J.; Stanton, N.A.; Plant, K. Where are we on driver distraction? Methods, approaches and recommendations. *Theor. Issues Ergon. Sci.* **2018**, *19*, 578–605. [CrossRef]
9. Louw, T.; Madigan, R.; Carsten, O.; Merat, N. Were they in the loop during automated driving? Links between visual attention and crash potential. *Inj. Prev.* **2017**, *23*, 281–286. [CrossRef]
10. Singh, S. Critical Reasons for Crashes Investigated in the National Motor Vehicle Crash Causation Survey (No. DOT HS 812 506). Traffic Safety Facts Crash. Stats Series. National Highway Traffic Safety Administration. 2018. Available online: https://crashstats.nhtsa.dot.gov/Api/Public/ViewPublication/812506 (accessed on 25 December 2020).
11. Khattak, A.J.; Ahmad, N.; Wali, B.; Dumbaugh, E. A taxonomy of driving errors and violations: Evidence from the naturalistic driving study. *Accid. Anal. Prev.* **2021**, *151*, 105873. [CrossRef]
12. Regan, M.A.; Hallett, C.; Gordon, C.P. Driver distraction and driver inattention: Definition, relationship and taxonomy. *Accid. Anal. Prev.* **2011**, *43*, 1771–1781. [CrossRef] [PubMed]
13. Young, K.; Regan, M.; Lee, D. Factors moderating the impact of distraction on driving performance and safety. In *Driver Distraction: Theory, Effects, and Mitigation*; Regan, M.A., Lee, D.J., Young, K.L., Eds.; CRC Press Taylor & Francis Group: Boca Raton, FL, USA, 2008.
14. Young, K.; Regan, M. Driver distraction: A review of the literature'. In *Distracted Driving*; Faulks, I.J., Regan, M., Stevenson, M., Brown, J., Porter, A., Irwin, J.D., Eds.; Australasian College of Road Safety: Sydney, NSW, Australia, 2007; pp. 379–405. Available online: https://www.researchgate.net/publication/251312763_Driver_Distraction_A_Review_of_the_Literature (accessed on 29 December 2020).
15. Bayly, M.; Young, K.; Regan, M. Sources of distraction inside the vehicle and their effects on driving performance. In *Driver Distraction: Theory, Effects and Mitigation*; Regan, M.A., Lee, J.D., Young, K.L., Eds.; CRC Press: Boca Raton, FL, USA, 2008.
16. Horberry, T.; Edquist, J. Distractions outside the vehicle. In *Driver Distraction: Theory, Effects, and Mitigation*; Regan, M.A., Lee, J.D., Young, K., Eds.; CRC Press: Boca Raton, FL, USA, 2008; pp. 215–228.
17. Cunningham, M.; Regan, M.; Imberger, K. Understanding driver distraction associated with specific behavioural interactions with in-vehicle and portable technologies. *J. Australas. Coll. Road Saf.* **2017**, *28*, 27–40.
18. Caird, J.K.; Simmons, S.M.; Wiley, K.; Johnston, K.A.; Horrey, W.J. Does talking on a cell phone, with a passenger, or dialing affect driving performance? An updated systematic review and meta-analysis of experimental studies. *Hum. Factors* **2018**, *60*, 101–133. [CrossRef] [PubMed]
19. Alonso, F.; Esteban, C.; Montoro, L.; Serge, A. Conceptualization of aggressive driving behaviors through a Perception of aggressive driving scale (PAD). *Transp. Res. Part F Traffic Psychol. Behav.* **2019**, *60*, 415–426. [CrossRef]
20. Xuedong, Y.; Wang, B.; An, M.; Zhang, C. Distinguishing between Rural and Urban Road Segment Traffic Safety Based on Zero-Inflated Negative Binomial Regression Models. *Discret. Dyn. Nat. Soc.* **2012**, *2012*, 789140. [CrossRef]

21. Eberhardt, M.S.; Ingram, D.D.; Makuc, D.M. *Urban and Rural Health ChartBook Health*; National Center for Health Statistics: Hyattsville, MD, USA, 2001.
22. Kmet, L.; Brasher, P.; Macarthur, C. A small area study of motor vehicle crash fatalities in Alberta, Canada. *Accid. Anal. Prev.* **2003**, *35*, 177–182. [CrossRef]
23. Gonzalez, R.P.; Cummings, G.R.; Phelan, H.A.; Harlin, S.; Mulekar, M.; Rodning, C.B. Increased rural vehicular mortality rates: Roadways with higher speed limits or excessive vehicular speed? *J. Trauma* **2007**, *63*, 1360–1363. [CrossRef]
24. Thomason, C. Roadway Design Manual. Manual Notice 2020-1. Chapter 3. 2020. Available online: http://onlinemanuals.txdot.gov/txdotmanuals/rdw/suburban_roadways.htm (accessed on 13 December 2020).
25. Casado-Sanz, N.; Guirao, B.; Gálvez-Pérez, D. Population ageing and rural road accidents: Analysis of accident severity in traffic crashes with older pedestrians on Spanish crosstown roads. *Res. Transp. Bus. Manag.* **2019**, *30*, 100377. [CrossRef]
26. Department of Statistics/Jordan (DOS). Yearbook for 2019. 2019. Available online: http://dosweb.dos.gov.jo/DataBank/Population_Estimares/PopulationEstimates.pdf (accessed on 23 December 2020). (In Arabic)
27. Driver and Vehicle License Department (DVDL) Records/Jordan. Available online: https://www.dvld.gov.jo/dvldportal/faces/misc/annualReport?_afrLoop=676752790620234&_afrWindowMode=0&_afrWindowId=b7oefx2nz_204#%40%3F_afrWindowId%3Db7oefx2nz_204%26_afrLoop%3D676752790620234%26_afrWindowMode%3D0%26_adf.ctrl-state%3Db7oefx2nz_272 (accessed on 26 December 2020). (In Arabic)
28. Ababsa, M. *Atlas of Jordan: History, Territories and Society*; Presses de l'Ifpo, Institut Français du Proche-Orient: Beirut, Lebanon, 2013.
29. Directorate of General Security. *The Annual Report of Traffic Accidents in Jordan for the Year 2019 AD*; Amman Jordan. 2019. Available online: https://www.psd.gov.jo/images/docs/TrafficRep2019.pdf (accessed on 23 December 2020). (In Arabic)
30. Pallant, J. *SPSS Survival Manual: A Step-by-Step Guide to Data Analysis Using IBM SPSS*, 7th ed.; Open University Press: London, UK, 2020.
31. Cohen, J. *Statistical Power Analysis for the Behavioral Science*; Academic Press: New York, NY, USA, 1988.
32. Stutts, J.C.; Reinfurt, D.W.; Staplin, L.O.R.E.N.; Rodgman, E.A. The Role of Driver Distraction in Traffic Crashes. AAA Foundation for Traffic Safety, USA. 2001. Available online: https://rosap.ntl.bts.gov/view/dot/17717 (accessed on 3 January 2021).

*infrastructures*

*Article*

# Utilizing UAVs Technology on Microscopic Traffic Naturalistic Data Acquirement

**Apostolos Anagnostopoulos and Fotini Kehagia ***

Highway Laboratory, Division of Transportation and Construction Management, School of Civil Engineering, Aristotle University of Thessaloniki, 54124 Thessaloniki, Greece; aposanag@civil.auth.gr
* Correspondence: fkehagia@civil.auth.gr; Tel.: +30-2310-994380

**Abstract:** Research into collecting and measuring reliable, accurate, and naturalistic microscopic traffic data is a fundamental aspect in road network planning scientific literature. The vehicle trajectory is one of the main variables in traffic flow theory that allows to extract information regarding microscopic traffic flow characteristics. Several methods and techniques have been applied regarding the acquisition of vehicle trajectory. The forthcoming applications of intelligent transport systems on vehicles and infrastructure require sufficient and innovative tools to calibrate existing models on more complex situations. Unmanned aerial vehicles (UAVs) are one of the most emerging technologies being used recently in the transportation field to monitor and analyze the traffic flow. The aim of this paper is to examine the use of UAVs as a tool for microscopic traffic data collection and analysis. A comprehensive guiding framework for accurate and cost-effective naturalistic traffic surveys and analysis using UAVs is proposed and presented in detail. Field experiments of acquiring vehicle trajectories on two multilane roundabouts were carried out following the proposed framework. Results of the experiment indicate the usefulness of the UAVs technology on various traffic analysis studies. The results of this study provide a practical guide regarding vehicle trajectory acquirement using UAVs.

**Keywords:** UAVs; naturalistic vehicle trajectories; microscopic traffic data; traffic data collection; guiding framework

**Citation:** Anagnostopoulos, A.; Kehagia, F. Utilizing UAVs Technology on Microscopic Traffic Naturalistic Data Acquirement. *Infrastructures* **2021**, *6*, 89. https://doi.org/10.3390/infrastructures6060089

Academic Editors: Krzysztof Goniewicz, Robert Czerski and Marek Kustra

Received: 16 May 2021
Accepted: 10 June 2021
Published: 16 June 2021



## 1. Introduction

### *1.1. Microscopic Traffic Data Acquirement*

Research into collecting and measuring reliable microscopic traffic data is a fundamental aspect in road network planning scientific literature. Several applications can be implemented by using the acquired dataset in terms of traffic safety, road capacity, and level of service analysis [1–4]. However, as the traffic conditions get more complex, the level of detail and the quality of the collected information is getting higher.

The forthcoming applications of intelligent transport systems on vehicles and infrastructure mean that existing road layouts need to be examined across a wider range of scenarios [5]. As new technologies are applied to transport systems, accurate calibration and validation approaches of microscopic traffic flow models are essential. Driver behavior modelling, especially in complex scenarios and dynamic environments, such as roundabouts, is challenging and depends mainly on the size and the variety of the obtained data [6]. A dataset of accurate and high detailed microscopic traffic data can improve the reliability of models and allow a sufficient traffic analysis.

The vehicle trajectory is one of the main variables in traffic flow theory that allows to extract information regarding microscopic traffic flow characteristics [7–9]. The ability to extract the position of the vehicles over time along the roadway can provide an understanding of the way vehicles move and a comprehensive dataset for implementation in several applications regarding traffic flow and safety analysis [10,11].

Several data collection techniques are used regarding the acquisition of vehicle trajectory [12–17]. Each one is characterized by its potential capabilities and limitations. Thus, the selection of the proper technique for the execution of the survey is strongly related to the level of detail, accuracy and the purpose of the study. The most common methods, as have been identified according to the literature, are summarized in the following: (a) application of global positioning systems (GPS), (b) video processing techniques, (c) applications based on smartphone device technology, and (d) on satellite navigation systems.

However, a main challenge for researchers and traffic engineers is the ability to extract accurate and naturalistic traffic data. Data mining techniques by acquiring accurate traffic data from naturalistic driving behavior is a remarkable and active field of research during last years. Several applications can be found in the scientific literature addressing these issues [18,19]. Nevertheless, it is noted that in most vehicle trajectory studies, collected data lack naturalness, as experiments are conducted under the awareness of the drivers. Thus, the necessary quality of the dataset is weak in terms of representing the actual driving behavior.

In the last years, video image processing techniques are applied more frequently as they represent a low-cost and non-infrastructure-based method for acquiring naturalistic vehicle trajectories [5,20]. Several studies have been developed by extracting traffic data from recorded videos.

In this context, unmanned aerial vehicles (UAVs) are one of the most emerging technologies being used recently in the transportation field to monitor and analyze the traffic flow. UAV image acquisition technologies have been developed and allow to extract and analyze the traffic information in a sufficient way.

### *1.2. UAV Technology for Traffic Surveys and Analysis*

UAVs can be integrated in various applications of the transport engineering sector, such as road safety inspections, traffic analysis and damage assessment for roads [21–25]. The benefits of deploying UAVs for traffic monitoring and analysis have been considered in several studies in the past few years [5,20,26–28]. As the camera is in the air, the drivers' attitude is not distracted by the equipment. According to this, extracted data represent naturalistic driving behavior which is significant for the study of vehicle trajectories. Moreover, UAVs require less experience and training to be controlled while they can handle a wide field of view, covering large areas quickly. These assets result in a time-saving, low-cost, and non-infrastructure-based technique for acquiring individual vehicle trajectories, compared to other methods.

However, as UAVs are rapidly growing in popularity and their technology is improving constantly, the implemented applications on transportation sector have not fully developed yet. Considering this, several limitations can be identified [11,29,30]. There are many factors that influence the performance of this process. Among them, weather conditions (e.g., rain), technical issues (e.g., low battery duration), and regulatory issues (e.g., no-fly zones) are the most critical to be mentioned. Thus, the ability to select and implement UAVs as an efficient traffic survey tool depends on many aspects. Table 1 summarizes the main benefits and limitations of using UAVs for traffic surveys.

**Table 1.** The main benefits and limitations of using UAVs for traffic surveys.

| Benefits | Limitations |
| --- | --- |
| UAVs require little experience | Climate characteristics |
| UAVs provide wide field of view | Technical issues of UAVs |
| UAVs can cover large areas quickly | Time constraints |
| Low cost and saving-time technique | Regulatory issues |
| Non-infrastructure-based technique | Safety issues |
| Monitoring and analysis of naturalistic driving behavior | Automatic process techniques require high expertise |

The aim of this paper is to examine the use of UAVs as a tool for microscopic traffic data collection and analysis. A comprehensive guiding framework for accurate and cost-effective naturalistic traffic surveys using UAVs is proposed and presented in detail. An experiment involving the acquisition of vehicle trajectories on two multilane roundabouts is described. Finally, the utility of UAVs regarding microscopic traffic data acquirement is discussed based on the literature review and the analyzed guiding framework of the study.

## 2. The Framework

An extensive literature review of existing studies and frameworks regarding traffic data acquirement using UAVs was carried out [11,15,26–28,31] to establish and applicate a comprehensive guiding framework in this study. A bibliometric and visualization analysis was conducted by identifying the articles with the most effort on traffic data acquirement using UAVs, to evaluate patterns of the existing literature. This methodology is widely accepted in the literature and in bibliometrics [32,33].

Specifically, a comprehensive database of gathered data from Scopus [34] was developed. Documents that contain the keywords "UAVs" and "traffic data collection" were selected for the evaluation. The software VOS [35] was applied to examine and analyze the distribution of co-occurrent keywords of the most common keywords outlined below articles' abstracts. The presence of 1104 keywords in 105 publications was confirmed. The threshold of 4 occurrences was adopted. The consistency of the database ensured the validation of the analysis to the context of this study. The final analyzed keywords and their node size are illustrated in Figure 1.

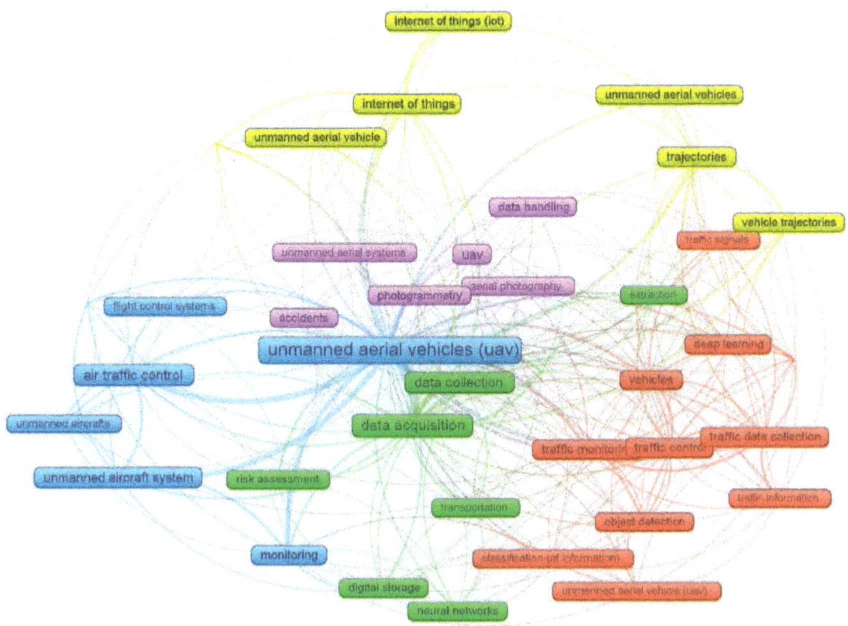


**Figure 1.** Network visualization of authors' keyword occurrence.

According to the analysis, the higher the keyword and the node, the larger number of articles contain the specific keyword. Moreover, thick lines indicate co-occurrence of the keyword in the literature. Five clusters were developed according to the analysis and each one represents a set of related items. The leading keyword of each cluster and its characteristics in terms of total numbers of occurrences and total link strength of co-occurrences are presented in Table 2.

**Table 2.** The top keywords co-occurrence and total link strength.

| Keyword | Cluster | Occurrences | Total Link Strength |
|---|---|---|---|
| unmanned aerial vehicles | blue (1) | 74 | 221 |
| data acquisition | green (2) | 28 | 106 |
| UAV | purple (3) | 12 | 47 |
| traffic data collection | red (4) | 11 | 47 |
| trajectories | yellow (5) | 8 | 36 |

According to the identified keywords, it can be concluded that various methodologies regarding the extraction of the traffic information exist. The vehicles' detection and classification to extract trajectories for operational and safety analysis, is the main issue the existing literature is dealing with.

Findings and methods of the existing literature were considered to establish a comprehensive framework regarding UAV survey execution and microscopic traffic data acquirement, following the discrete steps of Figure 2.

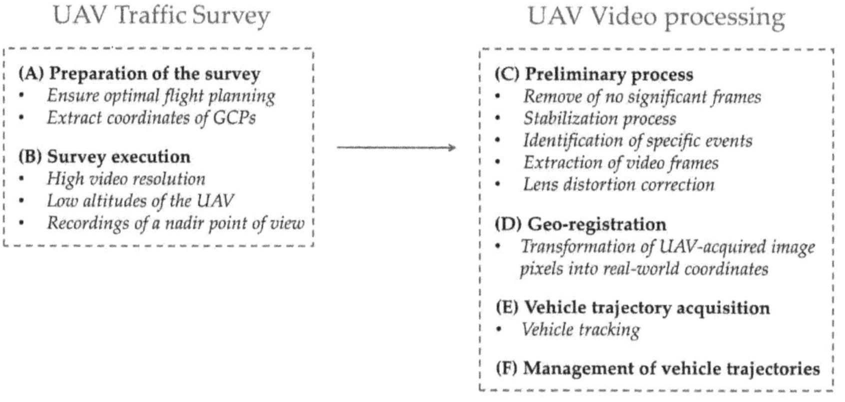


**Figure 2.** The discrete steps to acquire traffic data using UAVs.

The proposed methodology of this paper is structured in such a way to be simply and effectively adopted by researchers and engineers. Detailed naturalistic vehicle trajectories data through UAVs can be extracted following a low-cost method, requiring less demand for high skills or expertise in image processing techniques.

## 2.1. UAV Traffic Survey

### 2.1.1. Preparation of the Survey

UAV flight planning for the collection of the required data depends on several aspects that are critical for ensuring a successful UAV flight operation. According to [26], safety issues (such as prohibited fly zones or need for the existence of sufficient space regarding safety distance from sensitive installments) and climate characteristics (such as the weather conditions) can directly affect the survey execution. Thus, an in-depth flight planning before the execution of the UAV survey is essential.

After the identification of the study area, an appropriate number of ground control points (GCPs) need to be distributed homogenously within the area of interest (Figure 3).

**Figure 3.** The location of GCPs as distributed homogeneously for the survey.

The aim of this task intends to transform the acquired frames on real-world coordinates through the process of georeferencing. GCPs of well-known coordinates significantly increase the absolute accuracy of the analysis as presented in the following steps. In the case of manual or semi-automatic georeferencing process as in the experiment of this study, GCPs are required to be visible in all acquired frames. Their use intends to correct errors due to UAV tilt (wind forces affect) and camera lens distortion issues. It is noted that the use of natural GCPs (such as corners of manholes and tactile pavements, intersections of white pavement markings, etc.) provides the flexibility to conduct surveys over different time periods, skipping time-consuming field measurements of GCPs coordinates per survey. The restraint of UAVs low battery and the requirement for visible GCPs per each survey means that permanent natural ground control points are an efficient choice. A proper tool can provide the coordinates of the selected ground control points in high accuracy. Figure 4 presents an example of natural GCPs, the coordinates of which are measured using a RTK GNSS receiver.

**Figure 4.** Natural ground control points.

#### 2.1.2. Survey Execution

During the UAV survey execution, the safety and legal issues should be addressed. UAV flight can be handled manually via a controller or automatically according to a predefined route. It is mentioned that both the surveyor and the equipment should not be noticed by road users. Any distraction of drivers' attitude affects the naturalness of the collected data.

There are three main aspects that affect the level of detail of the study and the surveyor should consider during a UAV flight: (a) the video resolution, (b) the altitude of the UAV and (c) the viewing angle. More specifically, it is recommended video recordings be saved at the highest possible quality. High-resolution videos and low flight altitudes optimize the required time regarding the video processing and increase the accuracy and the quality of the study. Videos recorded from an angle require a process of pixel transformation to achieve an orthographic view. This is usually carried out using perspective filters. Thus, recordings of a nadir point of view minimize camera errors and are preferable.

Through these main aspects, the ground sample distance (GSD) can be reduced, enhancing the final accuracy of the analysis. With lower GSD, the identification of the appropriate point regarding vehicle tracking analysis, will be much easier. It is noted that the measured pixel size determines the minimum threshold of the final accuracy.

Finally, the location of the UAV should be stable to minimize the bias in the stabilizing process. A gimbal system attached to the camera can stabilize the recorded shots in an efficient way.

### 2.2. *UAV Video Processing*

#### 2.2.1. Preliminary Process

A preliminary process is required to simplify the video processing. This step includes the following operations: Firstly, no significant frames form videos (take-off and landing) are removed. A stabilization process is required to minimize rough bias. Proper filters contribute to smoother videos and the elimination of camera shakiness. In the following step, specific events according to the scope of the analysis are identified (for example, in a speed analysis the time periods of vehicles on free-flow speed conditions are identified). The video frames of the selected time periods are extracted per second. Finally, the lens distortion of the acquired images needs to be corrected. There are several techniques that can be adopted. A common practice is to transform images by adopting the distortion profile of the implemented camera.

#### 2.2.2. Geo-Registration

The transformation of UAV-acquired image pixels into real-world coordinates allows the extraction of vehicle trajectory data into real-world coordinates. The use of a cartesian coordinate system calibrated to a specific scale is a common practice regarding the geo-registration process. However, the use of GCPs in the experiments, except for the high accuracy of the analysis and the correction of image distortion, provides a comprehensive dataset that can be managed by several applications, depending on the purpose of the study.

A reference image of the study area is georeferenced according to the known coordinates of the GCPs. The extracted frames of the identified events are then co-registered to the reference image. This process can be carried out either in a manual way, which provides accurate but time-consuming results, or in an automatic way by using pixel matching algorithms, which promises quicker and less accurate results.

#### 2.2.3. Vehicle Trajectory Acquisition

To acquire microscopic traffic data, the extraction of accurate vehicle trajectories is essential. Several studies carried out recently are dealing with this issue [11,20,26,36–39]. The adopted methodologies can be divided into three main categories: (a) the manual process, (b) the semi-automatic process, and (c) the automatic process technique. The first two methods are more accurate and offer many flexibility advantages, however, they are time-consuming. On the other hand, the third method promises quicker results by using detection techniques and tracking algorithms with minimum manpower involved. Nevertheless, this requires high expertise and knowledge of computer vision techniques, while its accuracy on high spatial data such as vehicle trajectories sometimes requires manual effort for the correction of missed trajectories.

#### 2.2.4. Management of Vehicle Trajectories

Utilizing the vehicle trajectory data, several applications can be carried out and information of great importance can be provided. Thus, it is required that the vehicle location data be organized in detail on a comprehensive dataset along with supplementary information (such as the type of the vehicle). Researchers and engineers can interpret the measured data to understand the way the vehicles move.

## 3. Case Study Experiment

The described methodology was applied on a multilane roundabout layout where the complexity of driving behavior is challenging as the road geometry provides high uncertainty in driving maneuvers. The method was tested for two different lighting conditions: daylight and night. An analysis on vehicle trajectories was carried out to extract microscopic traffic data such as vehicles speeds, travel time measurements, and the spatial distribution of vehicle maneuvers. The selected multilane roundabouts (Figure 5) are in the cities of (a) Larissa and (b) Thessaloniki (Greece).

(a) (b)

**Figure 5.** UAV shot of the examined case studies: (**a**) Larissa and (**b**) Thessaloniki.

### *3.1. Survey Material and Equipment*

Two types of equipment were used to perform the experiment described in this paper to acquire reliable naturalistic vehicle trajectories data of the roundabouts: (a) a quadcopter UAV (Figure 6) and (b) a RTK GNSS receiver. The selected UAV (DJI Phantom 4 Advanced) can capture videos up to C4K analysis with a frame rate of 60 fps and high-resolution images (5472 × 3078). It is a low-cost UAV and requires less experience to be controlled. Its camera is attached to a gimbal, which stabilize shots. Moreover, its weight (1368 g) and size contribute to better maneuverability, while low altitudes flights achieve high spatial resolution. The RTK GNSS receiver that was used provides reliable and high-accuracy data collection. The position of selected GCPs can be determined in centimeter-level accuracy in real world conditions. Specifically, the accuracy of this equipment examined for a survey is 8 mm + 1 ppm (horizontal) and 15 mm + 1 ppm (vertical).

Figure 6. (a) The quadcopter UAV and (b) the captured study area as presented on the controller during the survey.

### 3.2. UAV Survey

Roundabouts' performance was recorded with the use of the Unmanned Aerial Vehicle (UAV) during summer and autumn of 2019. Data regarding the kinematic characteristics of the vehicles were collected in this experiment.

Field measurements were selected to be conducted during of-peak periods to ensure free flow speed conditions. Real vehicle speeds in unobstructed traffic conditions were collected. Weather conditions were stable and did not affect the vehicle movements. Low flight altitudes of a nadir point of view and high-resolution recordings allowed to measure accurate and naturalistic spatiotemporal phenomena of high detail.

### 3.3. Data Processing

Vehicle trajectories were extracted from the UAV videos following specific steps. These steps aimed to: (a) reduce any bias and increase the accuracy and (b) digitize and study vehicle motion paths.

Firstly, no significant frames from videos (take-off and landing) were removed. A stabilization procedure was followed [40]. Proper filters made videos smoother while camera shakiness was eliminated. Specific events were identified (vehicle through movements on free flow speed conditions) and video frames were extracted for each examined video. Lens distortion of each frame was corrected [41]. The acquired images were georeferenced in high accuracy using an open-source GIS software [42]. The selected geographic reference was the "GGRS87/Greek Grid". The ground sample distance was measured to the value of 35.6 mm and the maximum value of the RMSE between the real location and the final georeferenced location per each frame was 0.6.

Finally, a digitization process was carried out to acquire vehicle trajectories. Specifically, the center of the front bumper of each vehicle was identified and the coordinates were extracted. Mathematical interpolation based on the known coordinates was used in CAD software using spline curves so the discrete data could be transformed into continuous functions to further study vehicle maneuvers and microscopic traffic data.

### 3.4. Experiment Results

Several applications regarding microscopic traffic data analysis can be carried out regarding the extracted dataset. Understanding the way road users move in roundabouts is of great importance, since many conflicts occur in this type of intersections [43,44].

Figure 7 presents a heatmap of the spatial distribution of vehicle maneuvers according to the extracted vehicle trajectories of the examined case study roundabout. Various driving behavior patterns for through movements on the multilane roundabout are indicated. Improper and unexpected paths are created and that can probably cause unexpected behavior, and therefore potential danger.

**Figure 7.** Heatmap of the spatial distribution of vehicle maneuvers of Roundabout A.

To calculate vehicle speeds at the entrance of the roundabout, firstly the proper events were identified. Then, the captured distances per 0.2 s were calculated and divided by the corresponding time. Considering the measured value of the ground sample distance (35.6 mm) and the RMS error of 0.6, it is concluded that the maximum error in speed estimation is less than 1 km/h. An indicative calculated speed profile of a vehicle traversing the roundabout is presented in Figure 8.

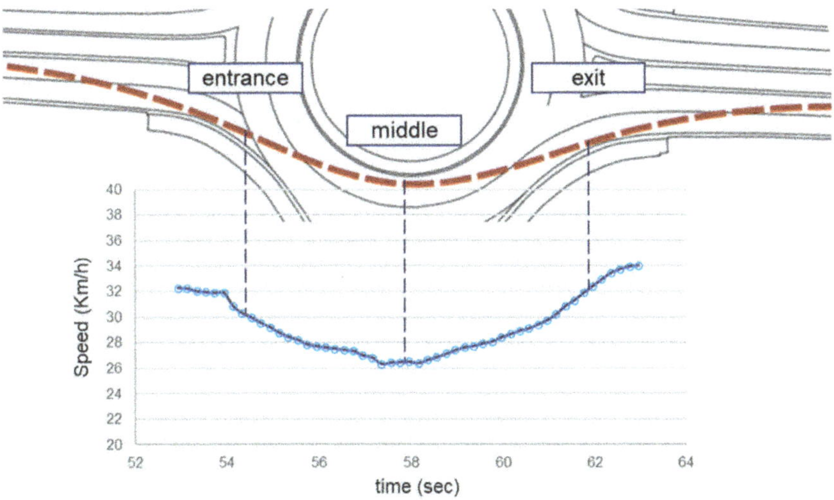


**Figure 8.** A typical vehicle speed profile has been extracted by processing UAV shots.

The vehicle speed profile indicates significant changes in speeds because of the complexity of the road geometry. The driver reduces the vehicle speed along the entry and the center of the roundabout and then accelerates to the exit lane.

With the second case study roundabout, an analysis regarding the travel time of 31 vehicles passing through the roundabout was conducted. An algorithm was developed and applied to the extracted trajectories. Two detection lines were coded at the entrance and the exit of the roundabout to identify the timestamps of each vehicle passing these sections (Figure 9). Results provide information regarding the travel time of vehicles through-movements. The average travel time of through movements under free-flow speed conditions is 5.14 s.

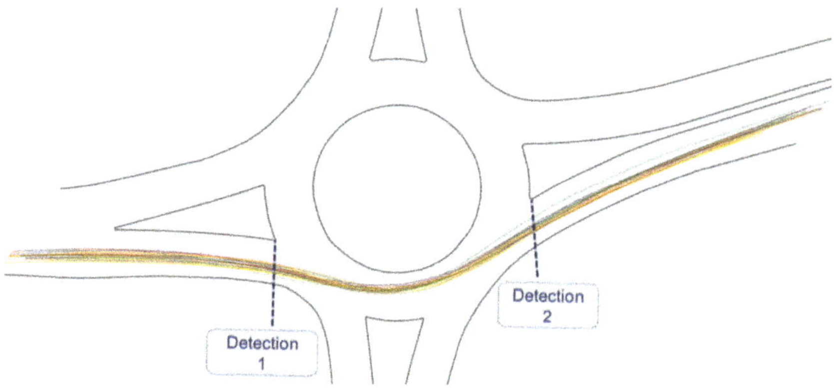


**Figure 9.** Graphical representation of the vehicle trajectories and the location of coded detectors.

## 4. Conclusions

Research into collecting and measuring reliable, accurate, and naturalistic microscopic traffic data is a fundamental aspect in road network planning scientific literature. According to the literature review and the bibliometric and visualization analysis, it can be concluded that UAVs are recently being used in the transportation field to monitor and analyze the traffic flow. The vehicles' detection and classification to extract trajectories for operational and safety analysis is the main issue the existing literature is dealing with.

The proposed methodology of this paper is structured in such a way to be simply and effectively adopted by researchers and engineers. Detailed and naturalistic vehicle trajectories data can be extracted through UAVs in a low-cost way, requiring less demand for high skills or expertise in image processing techniques.

Two experiments were carried out on different light conditions following the presented framework. Results indicate that the accuracy of the extracted microscopic traffic data is high enough as the maximum error in speed estimation is less than 1 km/h. The measured data can be interpreted and applied to several studies. In these experiments, vehicle trajectories were analyzed to extract vehicles speeds, travel time measurements, and the spatial distribution of vehicle maneuvers. The extracted dataset can be utilized and be applied on various traffic studies (gap-acceptance analysis, road safety analysis, study on lane-change behavior, calibration of car-following models, etc.).

The limitations of the study are related mainly to the technical issues of the UAV technology and the climate characteristics of the examined area. More specifically, the restraint of the low battery duration of UAVs and the weather conditions of the study area (rain) resulted in short video recordings and time-consuming field experiments.

## 5. Discussion and Final Remarks

Accurate and high detailed naturalistic microscopic traffic data are essential for reliable traffic analysis and efficient calibration process of traffic models. The forthcoming applications of intelligent transport systems on vehicles and infrastructure require sufficient tools to calibrate existing models on more complex situations.

UAVs are one of the most emerging technologies being used recently in transportation field to monitor and analyze the traffic flow. The increased commercial market share of this technology during the last years and the developed traffic applications entail a promising contribution to the transportation sector.

Several applications and methodologies regarding the acquirement of microscopic traffic data have been tested until now. This paper aims to add value to the existing literature. A comprehensive framework for extracting naturalistic vehicle trajectories recorded by UAVs is proposed. The presented methodology describes a highly accurate and low-cost method to conduct UAV traffic surveys and extract the required information, considering the methods and the limitations reported in previous studies. Researchers and engineers can efficiently apply the structured process as it is simplified and does not require great skills or expertise in automated image processing techniques.

Overall, the benefits of using UAVs on microscopic traffic data collection surveys, as explained in the literature review and highlighted in the presented experiment are great of importance. However, there are still many limitations and issues that need to overcome during the next years to optimize the general process of UAV traffic surveys. Thus, the ability to select and implement UAVs as an efficient traffic survey tool depends on many factors.

Further research is required regarding the acceptability of UAVs on traffic data collection surveys. Specifically, a comprehensive guiding framework under what circumstances this technology should be preferred or discouraged compared to other traditional methods will enhance the overall process of the examined traffic analysis. Finally, due to the forthcoming applications of intelligent transport systems on vehicles and infrastructure, experiments on the capabilities of UAVs regarding real-time traffic data collection techniques and methods of sharing the traffic information to road users are expected to enhance UAVs technology in the transportation engineering sector.

**Author Contributions:** A.A. and F.K., conceptualization; A.A., methodology; A.A., writing; F.K. review, supervision. All authors have read and agreed to the published version of the manuscript.

**Funding:** This research received no external funding.

**Informed Consent Statement:** Not applicable.

**Conflicts of Interest:** The authors declare no conflict of interest.

## References


1. Shen, J.; Yang, G. Crash Risk Assessment for Heterogeneity Traffic and Different Vehicle-Following Patterns Using Microscopic Traffic Flow Data. *Sustainability* **2020**, *12*, 9888. [CrossRef]
2. Michael, P.G.; Leeming, F.C.; Dwyer, W.O. Headway on urban streets: Observational data and an intervention to decrease tailgating. *Transp. Res. Part F Traffic Psych. Behav.* **2000**, *3*, 55–64. [CrossRef]
3. Durrani, U.; Lee, C.; Maoh, H. Calibrating the Wiedemann's vehicle-following model using mixed vehicle-pair interactions. *Transp. Res. Part C Emerg. Technol.* **2016**, *67*, 227–242. [CrossRef]
4. Zafri, N.M.; Rony, A.I.; Adri, N. Analysis of Pedestrian Crossing Speed and Waiting Time at Intersections in Dhaka. *Infrastructures* **2019**, *4*, 39. [CrossRef]
5. Anagnostopoulos, A.; Kehagia, F. CAVs and Roundabouts: Research on traffic impacts and design elements. *Transp. Res. Proc.* **2020**, *49*, 83–94. [CrossRef]
6. García Cuenca, L.; Guindel, C.; Aliane, N.; Armingol, J.M.; Fernández Andrés, J. Dataset Construction from Naturalistic Driving in Roundabouts. *Sensors* **2020**, *20*, 7151. [CrossRef] [PubMed]
7. Hoogendoorn, S.; Knoop, V. Traffic flow theory and modelling. In *The Transport System and Transport Policy: An Introduction*; van Wee, B., Annema, J.A., Banister, D., Eds.; Edward Elgar Publishing Limited: Cheltenham, UK, 2012; pp. 125–159.
8. Coifman, B.; Wu, M.; Redmill, K.; Thornton, D. Collecting ambient vehicle trajectories from an instrumented probe vehicle: High quality data for microscopic traffic flow studies. *Transp. Res. Part C Emerg. Technol.* **2016**, *72*, 254–271. [CrossRef]
9. Li, L.; Jiang, R.; He, Z.; Chen, X.; Zhou, Z. Trajectory data-based traffic flow studies: A revisit. *Emerg. Technol.* **2020**, *114*, 225–240. [CrossRef]
10. Dingus, T.A.; Klauer, S.G.; Neale, V.L.; Petersen, A.; Lee, S.E.; Sudweeks, J.; Perez, M.A.; Hankey, J.; Ramsey, D.; Gupta, S.; et al. *The 100-Car Naturalistic Driving Study, Phase II—Results of the 100-Car Field Experiment*; Technical Report No. DOT HS 810 593; Virginia Tech Transportation Institute: Blacksburg, Virginia, 2006.
11. Anagnostopoulos, A.; Kehagia, F. Evaluating Fastest Path Procedures on Roundabouts by Extracting Vehicle Trajectories from Unmanned Aerial Vehicles. In *Advances in Intelligent Systems and Computing: Advances in Mobility-as-a-Service System. CSUM 2020. Advances in Intelligent Systems and Computing*; Nathanail, E.G., Adamos, G., Karakikes, I., Eds.; Springer: Cham, Switzerland, 2020; Volume 1278, pp. 1001–1011. [CrossRef]
12. Hidas, P.; Wagner, P. Review of Data Collection Methods for Microscopic Traffic Simulation. In Proceedings of the World Conference on Transport Research, Istanbul, Turkey, 8 June 2004.
13. Punzo, V.; Simonelli, F. Analysis and Comparison of Microscopic Traffic Flow Models with Real Traffic Microscopic Data. *Transp. Res. Rec. J. Transp. Res. Board* **2005**, *1934*, 53–63. [CrossRef]

14. Giuseppe, G.; Alessandro, V.; Fedel, F.S.; Carmine, D.F.; Vittorio, A.; Daniele, R.; Vincenzo, G. Using Smartphones as a Toll to Capture Road Traffic Attributes. *Appl. Mech. Mater.* **2013**, *432*, 513–519. [CrossRef]
15. Kim, E.J.; Park, H.C.; Ham, S.W.; Kho, S.Y.; Kim, D.K. Extracting Vehicle Trajectories Using Unmanned Aerial Vehicles in Congested Traffic Conditions. *J. Adv. Transp.* **2019**, *2019*. [CrossRef]
16. Punzo, V.; Borzacchiello, M.T.; Ciuffo, B. On the assessment of vehicle trajectory data accuracy and application to the Next Generation SIMulation (NGSIM) program data. *Transp. Res. Part C Emerg. Technol.* **2011**, *19*, 1243–1262. [CrossRef]
17. Iqbal, M.S.; Choundhury, F.C.; Wang, P.; Gonzalez, C.M. Development of origin-destination matrices using mobile phone call data. *Transp. Res. Part C Emerg. Technol.* **2014**, *40*, 63–74. [CrossRef]
18. Zhu, M.; Wang, X.; Tarko, A.; Fang, S. Modeling car-following behavior on urban expressways in Shanghai: A naturalistic driving study. *Transp. Res. Part C Emerg. Technol.* **2018**, *93*, 425–445. [CrossRef]
19. Shrestha, D.; Lovell, J.D.; Tripodis, Y. Hardware and software for collecting microscopic trajectory data on naturalistic driving behavior. *J. Intell. Transp. Syst.* **2017**, *21*, 202–213. [CrossRef]
20. Salvo, G.; Caruso, L.; Scordo, A.; Guido, G.; Vitale, A. Traffic data acquirement by unmanned aerial vehicle. *Eur. J. Remote Sens.* **2017**, *50*, 343–351. [CrossRef]
21. Bicici, S.; Zeybek, M. An approach for the automated extraction of road surface distress from a UAV-derived point cloud. *Autom. Constr.* **2021**, *122*, 103475. [CrossRef]
22. Outay, F.; Mengash, H.A.; Adnan, M. Applications of unmanned aerial vehicle (UAV) in road safety, traffic and highway infrastructure management: Recent advances and challenges. *Transp. Res. Part A Policy Pract.* **2020**, *141*, 116–129. [CrossRef]
23. Cardenal, J.; Fernández, T.; Pérez-García, J.L.; Gómez-López, J.M. Measurement of Road Surface Deformation Using Images Captured from UAVs. *Remote Sens.* **2019**, *11*, 1507. [CrossRef]
24. Almeshal, A.M.; Alenezi, M.R.; Alshatti, A.K. Accuracy Assessment of Small Unmanned Aerial Vehicle for Traffic Accident Photogrammetry in the Extreme Operating Conditions of Kuwait. *Information* **2020**, *11*, 442. [CrossRef]
25. Trubia, S.; Curto, S.; Severino, A.; Arena, F.; Puleo, L. The use of UAVs for civil engineering infrastructures. *AIP Conf. Proc.* **2021**, *2343*, 110012.
26. Khan, M.; Ectors, W.T.; Bellemans, D.; Jassens, D.; Wets, G. UAV-Based Traffic Analysis: A Universal Guiding Framework Based on Literature Survey. *Transp. Res. Proc.* **2017**, *22*, 541–550. [CrossRef]
27. Guido, G.; Gallelli, V.; Rogano, D.; Vitale, A. Evaluating the accuracy of the vehicle tracking data obtained from Unmanned Aerial Vehicles. *Int. J. Transp. Sci. Tech.* **2016**, *5*, 136–151. [CrossRef]
28. Kanistras, K.; Martins, G.; Rutherford, M.J.; Valavanis, K.P. Survey of Unmanned Aerial Vehicles (UAVs) for Traffic Monitoring. In *Handbook of Unmanned Aerial Vehicles*; Valavanis, K., Vachtsevanos, G., Eds.; Springer: Dordrecht, The Netherlands, 2014; pp. 2643–2666. [CrossRef]
29. Chen, P.; Zeng, W.; Yu, G.; Wang, Y. Surrogate Safety Analysis of Pedestrian-Vehicle Conflict at Intersections Using Unmanned Aerial Vehicle Videos. *J. Adv. Transp.* **2017**, *2017*. [CrossRef]
30. Barmpounakis, N.E.; Vlahogianni, E.; Golias, C.J.; Babinec, A. How accurate are small drones for measuring microscopic traffic parameters? *Int. J. Transp. Res.* **2019**, *11*, 332–340. [CrossRef]
31. Barmpounakis, N.E.; Vlahogianni, E.; Golias, J.C. Extracting Kinematic Characteristics from Unmanned Aerial Vehicles. In Proceedings of the Transportation Research Board 95th Annual Meeting, Washington, DC, USA, 10–14 January 2016.
32. Badassa, B.B.; Sun, B.; Qiao, L. Sustainable Transport Infrastructure and Economic Returns: A Bibliometric and Visualization Analysis. *Sustainability* **2020**, *12*, 2033. [CrossRef]
33. Guo, Y.-M.; Huang, Z.-L.; Guo, J.; Li, H.; Guo, X.-R.; Nkeli, M.J. Bibliometric Analysis on Smart Cities Research. *Sustainability* **2019**, *11*, 3606. [CrossRef]
34. Scopus. Available online: https://www.scopus.com/ (accessed on 17 March 2021).
35. VOSviewer. Available online: https://www.vosviewer.com/ (accessed on 17 March 2021).
36. Meng, L.; Wang Xiao, H.; Shi, K. Traffic Conflict Identification Technology of Vehicle Intersection Based on Vehicle Video Trajectory Extraction. *Procedia Comput. Sci.* **2017**, *109*, 963–968. [CrossRef]
37. Khan, M.A.; Ectors, W.; Bellemans, T.; Janssens, D.; Wets, G. Unmanned Aerial Vehicle-Based Traffic Analysis: A Case Study for Shockwave Identification and Flow Parameters Estimation at Signalized Intersections. *Remote Sens.* **2018**, *10*, 458. [CrossRef]
38. Salvo, G.; Caruso, L.; Scordo, A. Urban traffic analysis through an UAV. *Procedia Soc. Behav. Sci.* **2014**, *111*, 1083–1091. [CrossRef]
39. Krajewski, R.; Bock, J.; Kloeker, L.; Eckstein, L. The highD Dataset: A Drone Dataset of Naturalistic Vehicle Trajectories on German Highways for Validation of Highly Automated Driving Systems. In Proceedings of the 21st International Conference on Intelligent Transportation Systems (ITSC), Maui, HI, USA, 4–7 November 2018.
40. Deshaker. Available online: http://www.guthspot.se/video/deshaker.htm (accessed on 17 March 2021).
41. Adobe Lightroom. Available online: https://lightroom.adobe.com (accessed on 17 March 2021).
42. QGIS Geographic Information System. Available online: http://qgis.org (accessed on 17 March 2021).
43. Anagnostopoulos, A.; Kehagia, F. Turbo-roundabouts as an alternative to roundabouts in terms of traffic safety, capacity and pollutant emissions. In Proceedings of the 7th Pan-Hellenic Road Safety Conference, Larissa, Greece, 11–12 October 2018.
44. Damaskou, E.; Kehagia, F.; Pitsiava-Latinopoulou, M.; Anagnostopoulos, A. Factors Influencing Quality of Service in Road Safety at Urban Roundabouts, Based on Driver's Perception. In Proceedings of the 48th European Transport Conference, Milan, Italy, 9–11 September 2020.

*infrastructures*

*Article*

# Work-Related Accident Prevention in Norwegian Road and Maritime Transport: Examining the Influence of Different Sector Rules

**Tor-Olav Nævestad *, Beate Elvebakk and Karen Ranestad**

Institute of Transport Economics, Gaustadalléen 21, NO-0349 Oslo, Norway; beateelv@oslomet.no (B.E.); Karen.Ranestad@banenor.no (K.R.)
* Correspondence: ton@toi.no; Tel.: +47-2257-3800; Fax: +47-2260-9200

**Abstract:** About 36% of fatal road accidents in Norway involve at least one driver who is "at work". It has been argued that the implementation of rules clearly defining the responsibility of road transport companies to prevent work related accidents, by implementing safety management systems (SMS), could lead to increased safety. In the present study we tested the validity of this suggestion, by examining the influence of different sector rules on work-related accident prevention in Norwegian road and maritime transport. In contrast to the road sector, the maritime sector has had rules requiring SMS for over 20 years, clearly defining the shipping companies responsibility for prevention of work-related accidents. The aims of the study were to: (1) examine how the different sector rules influence perceptions of whether the responsibility to prevent work-related accidents is clearly defined in each sector; and (2) compare respondents' perceptions of the quality of their sectors' efforts to prevent work-related accidents, and factors influencing this. The study was based on a small-scale survey (N = 112) and qualitative interviews with sector experts (N = 17) from companies, authorities, and NGOs in the road and the maritime sectors. Results indicate that respondents in the maritime sector perceive the responsibility to prevent work-related accidents as far more clearly defined, and they rate their sector's efforts to prevent accidents as higher than respondents in road. Multivariate analyses indicate that this is related to the scope of safety regulations in the sectors studied, controlled for several important framework conditions. Based on the results, we conclude that the implementation of SMS rules focused on transport companies' responsibility to prevent work-related accidents could improve safety in the road sector. However, due to barriers to SMS implementation in the road sector, we suggest starting with a simplified version of SMS.

**Keywords:** safety management; regulation; transport; road; maritime

**Citation:** Nævestad, T.-O.; Elvebakk, B.; Ranestad, K. Work-Related Accident Prevention in Norwegian Road and Maritime Transport: Examining the Influence of Different Sector Rules. *Infrastructures* **2021**, *6*, 72. https://doi.org/10.3390/infrastructures6050072

Academic Editors: Krzysztof Goniewicz, Robert Czerski and Marek Kustra

Received: 13 March 2021
Accepted: 6 May 2021
Published: 11 May 2021



## 1. Introduction

### 1.1. Background

A study from Norway indicates that 36% of fatal road accidents involved at least one driver who was "at work" at the time of the accident [1]. An average of 1.490 people is injured (lightly or seriously) in these accidents and the majority (81%) of these people are other road users [2]. This means that measures to improve transport safety in companies with working drivers will not only reduce the number of injuries among drivers at work, but particularly among other road users.

Although there are relatively few systematic studies in this area, research indicates that implementation of safety management systems (SMS) can lead to increased road safety. A comprehensive literature review indicates that the implementation of SMS is related to positive safety outcomes [3]. SMS is legally required as a tool for implementing safety culture in several high-risk industries, e.g., the nuclear sector [4], aviation [5,6], and oil and gas (e.g., [7]).

SMS denote the formal aspects of safety in organizations ("how things should be done"). The informal aspects of safety management generally refer to safety culture ("how things are actually done"), which can be defined as shared and safety relevant ways of thinking or acting that are (re)created through the joint negotiation of people in social settings [8]. The development of a positive safety culture is a formal aim and justification of SMS in the maritime sector [9], in aviation [5] in rail [10], and also in the voluntary ISO:39001 standard in the road sector. Thus, it is believed that the development of formal procedures ("how things should be done") will influence informal practices ("how things actually are done") [11]. Studies also indicate positive effects of SMS on safety culture in aviation [12], in the maritime sector [13] and in rail [14,15].

SMS typically comprise formal routines and measures enabling the organization to work systematically with safety, e.g., by establishing formal safety policies and goals, establishing key roles and responsibilities, systematically collecting information about incidents and hazards, developing countermeasures, monitoring the effects of these, and adjusting measures if necessary (cf. [3]). Moreover, SMS clearly define companies' responsibility to prevent work-related accidents, through the implementation of such formal measures [16].

Studies of SMS implementation from the road sector report of reductions in accidents and incidents, improved safety culture and improved road safety behaviours [17–20]. In addition, previous studies show that hauliers transporting dangerous goods (road tanker) by road have a 75% lower risk of accidents than other goods transport companies [21]. These companies also work more systematically with SMS and safety culture than other hauliers [22].

Despite the promising safety outcomes of SMS in road and other sectors, Norwegian research from the road sector indicates that neither transport companies nor authorities focus sufficiently well on the importance of SMS and the organizational responsibility for safety [23]. Similar tendencies have been found in research from other countries, indicating that work-related road safety traditionally has been managed using single driver-focused measures, and not SMS and safety culture (e.g., [22,24]).

The tendency to focus on the driver instead of the organization in efforts to prevent accidents has been related to the legal rules governing work-related accident prevention in the road sector. Interviewees in a previous Norwegian study reported that authorities largely focus on the Road Traffic Act, which places the main responsibility for safety on the driver, in their enforcement of the safety of drivers at work [23]. This means that drivers at work in practice are treated as private drivers, although the employers of the former have a legal responsibility for their safety through the Working Environment Act. The interviewees also stated that very few employers recognize this responsibility, e.g., by implementing SMS. Based on this, sector experts in the study of Nævestad and Phillips [23] suggested that the road sector should learn from other sectors, which focuses on the organizational responsibility to prevent work related accidents, e.g., by implementing SMS. The same suggestion is discussed in an ITF roundtable session about SMS in transport [22].

In the present study we test the validity of this suggestion, by examining the influence of different sector rules on work-related accident prevention in Norwegian road and maritime transport. More specifically, we examine whether the maritime sector performs better on the prevention of work-related accidents because of the different rules regulating safety in the two sectors. We have chosen to compare road with the maritime sector, as the maritime sector has had rules requiring SMS for over 20 years, clearly focusing on the organizational responsibility to prevent accidents. In contrast, formal SMSs for companies in the road sector are voluntary so far (e.g., ISO:39001).

### 1.2. Aims

The aims of the study are to: (1) examine how the different sector rules influence perceptions of whether the responsibility to prevent work-related accidents is clearly defined in road and the maritime sector; and (2) compare respondents' perceptions of the quality of their sectors' efforts to prevent work-related accidents, and factors influencing this.

## 2. Theoretical Approach and Previous Research

### 2.1. The Rules Governing Safety and SMS in the Road and Maritime Sector

SMS was legally required in the maritime sector in 1998 through the International Safety Management (ISM) code of the International Maritime Organization (IMO), which requires SMS in all commercial ships over 500 GT. The ISM code was introduced after several severe maritime accidents were found to be caused by human error and insufficient SMS. One of the main purposes of the ISM-code is to firmly define the shipping company and the ship master's responsibility for the management of safety and the environment, through the implementation of ISM compliant SMS [25]. According to the ISM code, an SMS should include, for instance: (1) a safety and environmental protection policy; (2) procedures to ensure the safe operation of ships; and (3) defined lines of communication between shore and shipboard personnel [9,26]. The ISM code is implemented as a provision to the Norwegian Ship Safety and Security Act [27]. Actors in the sector have considered this act to clarify responsibilities, through increasing the focus on shipping companies' responsibility for accident prevention [28].

International research indicates low SMS implementation among companies in the road sector, as this is not legally required [22]. Some of the large companies have, however, adopted advanced SMS practices, particularly companies transporting dangerous goods including oil and chemical products [22]. The closest one comes to overarching legislation for SMS in the road sector is the EU Framework Directive on Safety and Health at Work (Directive 89/391/EEC) and corresponding national legislation that sets out the need for employers of drivers at work to manage accident risks associated with road users, trips, and vehicles [16]. The corresponding national legislation in Norway is the Working Environment Act (WEA). However, although employers of drivers at work in Norway have a legal responsibility for their safety through the WEA, very few employers recognize this responsibility, e.g., by implementing SMS [23]. The most important legislation regulating road safety in Norway is the Road Traffic Act (RTA), which applies to all road users, and which places the main responsibility for safety on the driver. Nævestad and Phillips [23] report that authorities tend to enforce the RTA more often than WEA when dealing with drivers at work. This indicates a less clear responsibility for work-related accident prevention in the road sector, and a more driver-centered approach, which also is found in international approaches [24]. The most well-known SMS approach in the road sector is the ISO:39001 traffic safety standard. This is, however, voluntary. The standard is often described as a management system for traffic safety and a tool for building safety culture. An explicit goal of this standard is to create a positive safety culture by implementing SMS. Only eight companies had, however, implemented this standard in Norway in 2018.

### 2.2. Safety Outcomes of SMS

Although there are few studies comparing safety culture and safety outcomes across transport sectors, previous research indicates more focus on safety management systems, more advanced safety cultures and better safety outcomes in aviation, rail, and the maritime sector, compared with the road sector (cf. [22,29,30]. This can be explained by the fact that companies in the road sector do not have the same legal requirements for safety management systems as in aviation (IATA 2019), the maritime sector [13], and railways [10]. In these sectors, requirements are set for systems aiming to facilitate key aspects of safety culture; e.g., a safety culture including reporting, justice, and learning. These requirements are often cited to explain why companies in aviation [31,32], the maritime sector [13], and rail transport [14] perform better than the road sector on safety. Several studies find relationships between implementation of SMS, or SMS elements, and positive safety culture and safety outcomes in aviation [31,32], in rail [15], in the maritime sector [13] and in the road sector [17].

Finally, it should also be noted that identifying the safety outcomes of SMS is a challenging methodological issue. There are few robust evaluations of this (i.e., with pre-post measurements, control, and test groups). Additionally, studies have not yet managed to study the separate effects of the different elements in SMS. There are also several different definitions of SMS. It should also be noted that relationships are complex, and that it may be difficult to discern between elements of safety culture interventions and elements in SMS interventions. In his systematic review of the effects of safety management systems in the transport sector, Thomas [3] concludes that, despite little research in the field, there seems to be a relationship between SMS and objective safety outcomes (behavior and accidents). Although there is no agreement on which components of safety management systems contribute most to safety, Thomas [3] concludes that the following two factors are the most important: management commitment to safety and safety communication. Additionally, there are few studies comparing safety management across sectors as we do in the present study. Making such comparisons may be difficult, as other framework conditions (in addition to SMS rules) are also important in explaining different safety levels between sectors (cf. [29]). Such framework conditions may be, e.g., competition, business structure (number and size of companies), economy, and customer focus on safety. We return to this issue.

### 2.3. Mechanisms through Which SMS May Influence Safety Outcomes

SMS may lead to positive safety outcomes through at least two mechanisms. The first is that SMS provides a systematic way of managing organizational safety, and that it clearly places responsibility for this process in the company. The philosophy that the ISM code is based on is total quality management, highlighting continuous improvement through management commitment and personnel empowerment (Lappalainen 2008 in [29]). The process of continuous improvement follows Deming's circle ('plan–do–check–act') [29]. Implementing an SMS involves analyzing the safety status and setting goals (plan), implementing measures to fulfil the goals (do), developing indicators to measure goal attainment (check), and adjusting the measures if necessary (act).

The second mechanism through which SMS may produce positive safety outcomes is through the development of a positive safety culture. As noted, this is the explicit motivation for most SMS legislation, hypothesizing that the development of formal procedures ("how things should be done"), will influence informal practices ("how things actually are done") [11]. Implementing an SMS largely concerns implementing certain routines and ways of doing things in the organization, e.g., carrying out risk assessments, documenting the process, developing procedures, and training new employees etc. [13,16,17]. The implementation of such activities can lead to improved safety culture, especially if it is followed by increased focus on safety among managers and employees in the organization.

### 2.4. Potential Barriers to SMS Implementaion

Contrary to the hypothesized relationship between SMS and safety culture that is described above, several studies report discrepancies between formal and informal aspects of safety in organizations [26,33,34]. Thus, it seems that a positive safety culture does not necessarily follow from SMS implementation. This can be explained by, e.g., SMS that are poorly adapted to the companies in question, by referring to the nature of the working activities, to the competence of the personnel, etc. [26,34]. These factors can also be related to the size and maturity of companies, etc. The report from the ITF [22] roundtable on SMS in transport mentions several such potential barriers to successful SMS implementation in the road sector, for example: (1) there is no international regulatory or standard setting body in road transport of the kind responsible for aviation (ICAO) or maritime transport (IMO); (2) there is a large share of non-professional road users; (3) there are many small companies; (4) high proportion of owner-drivers; and (5) low organizational maturity, indicated, e.g., by low degree of reporting of incidents and little systematic focus and follow up of indicators measuring performance [22]. These factors may challenge the possibilities to implement SMS and continuous improvement (PDCA) in companies in the road sector.

### 2.5. Hypotheses

As the SMS rules in the maritime sector firmly places the responsibility for safety on the shipping company and the shipmaster, we hypothesize that respondents in the maritime sector have a stronger perception that the responsibility for accident prevention is clearly defined in their sector regulations (Hypothesis 1). Moreover, based on this we also expect respondents in the maritime sector to rate their efforts to prevent work related accidents as higher than respondents in the road sector (Hypothesis 2). Finally, we expect that respondents in the maritime sector rate SMS as more important for the safety level in their sector than respondents in the road sector (Hypothesis 3).

## 3. Methods

We have used two methods to fulfil the study aims. The first method is semi structured qualitative interviews with 17 sector experts. We conducted these to get rich information, based on the interviewees' experiences and viewpoints, and also as a background to the development of the quantitative survey. The qualitative interviews resulted in textual data that we used to complement the numerical data from the survey. The use of quantitative survey data is the second method, and this is based on 112 respondents. We use this to make statistical comparisons between the answers of respondents from the two sectors.

### 3.1. Interviews

We have conducted qualitative interviews with 17 sector experts to gain knowledge on the aims of the study. Interviewees were selected from transport companies, the Labour Inspection Authority, the Public Roads Administration, including personnel from the Accident Analysis Groups, the Norwegian Maritime Directorate, the Accident Investigation Board, the Norwegian Coastal Administration, and other relevant actors. The interviews were conducted in 2016 and 2017. The interviews were conducted face-to-face and by telephone. The interviews generally lasted for between one and one and a half hours. We used a semi structured interview guide, and the themes and questions in the guide focused on the aims of the study.

The interview guide focused on the following themes:

(1) Background information about the interviewees' work;
(2) Registration and overview of work-related accidents in the sector of the interviewee;
(3) Registration and overview of work-related risk factors in the sector of the interviewee;
(4) Views on responsibilities related to the occurrence and prevention of work-related accidents;
(5) Current, past (and potential future) measures aiming to prevent work-related accidents;
(6) Views on efforts to prevent work-related accidents in companies.

The purpose of the interviews was to give us more insight into the interviewees' understanding of their organizations' knowledge and information sources about work-related accidents, views on risk factors and thoughts on roles and responsibilities. We collected this information to be able to conduct rich comparisons between the studied sectors. Interviewees were encouraged to "think out loud" and they were assured that the purpose of the interview was to provide us with nuanced viewpoints and thoughts that we cannot collect by means of survey methods. Although the themes in the interviews were fairly similar to those in the survey, the qualitative interviews involved open ended questions which allowed the interviewees to elaborate freely when answering.

### 3.2. Survey

#### 3.2.1. Recruitment of Respondents and Sample Characteristics

A small-scale web-based survey was distributed to representatives from government agencies, NGOs, and personnel in transport companies in the two sectors. Relevant representatives from government agencies were identified with assistance from the project's reference group. The survey was sent to relevant persons in the Transport Accident Investigation Board Norway, the Ministry of Transport and Communications, the Norwegian Public Road Authority, the Norwegian Maritime Authority, the Norwegian Labour Inspection Authority, and the Norwegian Public Roads Administration's Accident Analysis Groups. The survey was also sent to transport companies in the studied sectors, and they were asked to distribute the survey among elected safety officials and trade union representatives. Thus, the survey includes what we may term sector experts, with good knowledge resulting from efforts to prevent work-related accidents within the sectors. Table 1 shows the distribution of sector experts in the different sectors, by type of organization.

**Table 1.** Distribution of sector experts in the studied sectors, by type of organization.

| Sector | Directorate | Inspectorate | Investigation Board | Transport Company | Other | Total |
|---|---|---|---|---|---|---|
| Road | 14% | 20% | 6% | 55% | 6% | 66 |
| Maritime | 30% | 9% | 0% | 54% | 7% | 46 |
| Total | 21% | 15% | 4% | 54% | 6% | 112 |

There were 112 individual respondents: 59% (N = 66) from the road sector and 41% (N = 46) from the maritime sector. The respondents from transport companies in both sectors were largely recruited from two unions: one union from the road sector including drivers and one union from the maritime sector which largely includes ship navigators. Thus, although both groups of union members are transport operators, the operators from the maritime sector rank higher in the organizational hierarchy than those in the road sector. While the method of distribution makes it impossible to calculate the response rate, it is obvious that it has been very low. This, in addition to the limited number of responses, means that results must be treated with considerable caution.

#### 3.2.2. Survey Themes

The survey contains seven different themes:

(1) Background questions, e.g., sector, type of organization, position;
(2) Views on risk factors related to work-related accidents;
(3) Questions on why the number of work-related accidents has been reduced in recent years, whether respondents have a good overview of the occurrence of work-related accidents and causes, sources of information, and whether companies report all accidents;
(4) Questions on the responsibility for the prevention of work-related accidents and whether responsibility is clearly defined in current legislations;
(5) Rating of respondents' organizations efforts to prevent work-related accidents, views on the safety rules in the sectors, and questions about the significance of framework conditions for safety.

#### 3.2.3. Quantitative Analysis

Regression analysis. We have performed two regression analyzes. The first was conducted to assess the conditions explaining variation in the respondents' answer to the question: "Is responsibility for accident prevention sufficiently clearly defined in current regulations in the sector?" The second was to assess respondents' agreement with the statement: "How would you rate your organization's efforts to prevent work-related accidents?". We used logistic regression in the first analysis, as the dependent variable was made dichotomous (1: Yes, 2: No/do not know). We used linear regression in the second analysis, since the dependent variables are continuous. The regression analyzes show the effects of the independent variables that we include on the two dependent variables, controlled for the other variables in the analysis.

## 4. Results

### *4.1. Is Responsibility for Accident Prevention Is Clearly Defined?*

The first aim of the study was to examine how the different sector rules influence perceptions of whether the responsibility to prevent work-related accidents is clearly defined in the maritime sector and in the road sector. As the SMS rules in the maritime sector firmly places the responsibility for safety on the shipping company and the shipmaster, we hypothesize that respondents in the maritime sector have a stronger perception that the responsibility for accident prevention is clearly defined in their sector regulations (Hypothesis 1).

In the survey, we asked whether responsibility for accident prevention was defined clearly enough in current regulations in the sector. The road sector stands out with a relatively low share of respondents stating that responsibility is defined clearly enough; 37% answered yes, compared with 78% in the maritime sector. The corresponding shares for no were 31% in road and 13% in the maritime sector. The road sector also had a larger percentage of respondents stating that they "do not know" (31%), compared with 9% in the maritime sector. Differences between the sectors were statistically significant at the 1% level.

Respondents from the road sector who gave reasons for their answers referred to the relationship between drivers and their employer organizations and/or their customers. They referred to stress or pressure as a result of short deadlines, and the fact that drivers are held responsible even though they are not the ones who define the route and the time frame. In this manner, they underlined that transport buyers also indirectly influence the safety of transport assignments. Moreover, they also pointed to drivers' legal responsibilities as a problem, as they may provide an opportunity for managers or customers to ignore their actual influence and liability. This indicates a discrepancy between the legal responsibilities of drivers and the practical responsibilities of, e.g., transport buyers in the road sector.

The majority of interviewees from the road sector thought employers should take more responsibility for their employees' behaviour and safety in traffic, as part of their HSE work. Specifically, they believed that work assignments should be based on risk assessments, including an analysis of the road and conditions, and employers should develop safety-promoting routines, procedures and guidelines. It was noted that many businesses fail to fulfil these requirements today. Road transport differs from most professional sectors in that individual drivers usually carry the entire responsibility for safety, and some of the interviewees stated that the companies have—or should take on— the overarching responsibility for the interplay between the various elements and actors involved in road traffic. Some of the interviewees from the road sector believed that relations of responsibility in this area should be more clearly defined, especially HSE-requirements or safety standards. Others found responsibilities to be well-defined in theory, but they said that the practical follow-up was inconsistent. The Working Environment Act gives employers a wide-ranging responsibility for their workers' safety, but interviewees noted that this is rarely enforced. The Road Traffic Act—which places all responsibility with the driver—is enforced through controls and in police investigations following accidents, but the responsibility of the firms is not enforced to the same degree. So while the law divides responsibility between different actors, this is not the case in practice.

Interviewees in the maritime sector underline that safety in the maritime sector is circumscribed by the International Maritime Organisation (IMO). This is a specialized agency of the United Nations whose primary purpose is to develop and maintain a comprehensive regulatory framework for shipping. The Norwegian Maritime Authority (NMA) is the government agency responsible for life, health, and working conditions for Norwegian-registered ships and ships at Norwegian ports and is also in charge of active safety work, such as inspections regulated by international law. The Norwegian Coastal Administration is responsible for maritime infrastructure and maritime safety services, while the Labour Inspection Agency is responsible for working conditions in ports. Safety in the maritime sector in Norway is regulated through the Ship Safety and Security Act, which came into existence in 2007. According to this act:

> "The company has an overall duty to see to that the construction and operation of the ship is in accordance with the rules laid down in or pursuant to this Act, including that the master and other persons working on board comply with the legislation". (§6)

Section 58 in this act relates to the establishment of SMS (as required by the ISM code).

### *4.2. Respondents' Assessment of the Quality of Their Sectors' Efforts*

#### 4.2.1. Ratings of the Sector's Efforts to Prevent Work-Related Accidents

The second aim of the study was to examine respondents' perceptions of the quality of their sectors' efforts to prevent work-related accidents, and factors influencing this. As responsibilities for the prevention of work-related accidents are more clearly in the maritime sector, we expected respondents in the maritime sector to rate their efforts to prevent work related accidents as higher than respondents in the road sector (Hypothesis 2). This is compared in Figure 1, where we show results for the question: "How would you rate your own organizations' work with work-related accidents on a scale from 1 (= very deficient) to 7 (= very good).

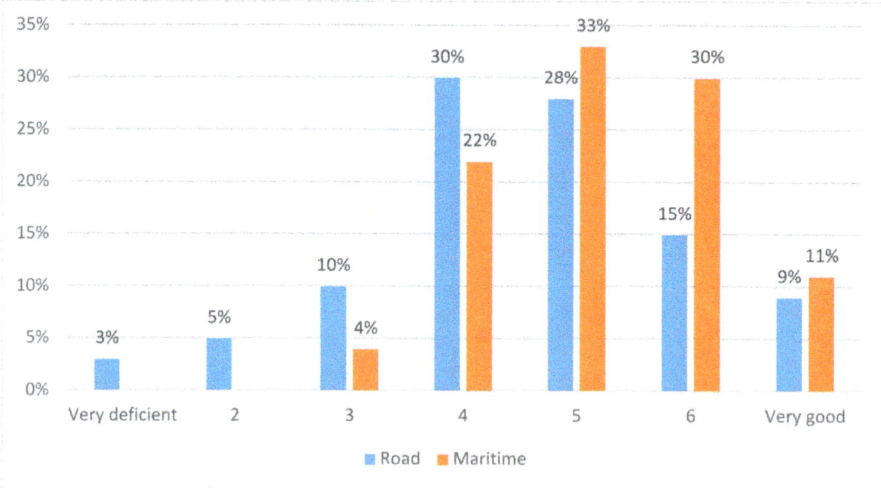


**Figure 1.** How would you rate your own organizations' work with work-related accidents on a scale from 1 (= very deficient) to 7 (= very good) by sector. Shares from Road (N = 66) and the maritime sector (N = 46).

Figure 1 indicates that respondents from the road sector rate their own efforts to prevent work-related accidents as lower than respondents from the maritime sector. If we assume that scores ranging from 5–6 means "good", we see that 74% of the respondents in the maritime sector rate their own organization's work with work-related accidents as good, compared to 52% in the road sector. Correspondingly, 18% rate their organization's efforts as deficient in the road sector, compared to 4% in the maritime sector. The sector experts that we interviewed often referred to the rules governing safety in their sector and the enforcement of these rules when discussing their sectors' and organizations' efforts to prevent work-related accidents. Interviewees in the road sector referred, e.g., to the lacking enforcement of the Working Environment Act, while interviewees in the maritime sector referred to the SMS requirements of the ISM-code.

#### 4.2.2. Respondents' Rating of the Safety Level and Framework Conditions

Respondents were also asked to rate the safety level in their own sector compared to that of international commercial aviation on several key aspects. Respondents were asked: "Imagine a scale from 1 to 10 indicating the level of safety, where 10 corresponds to the level of safety in international commercial aviation", "How would you rate the level of safety in your sector?" We also asked three additional questions, worded in the same manner, focusing on authorities' focus on safety, customer focus on safety and scope of safety regulations. The results are indicated in Figure 2.

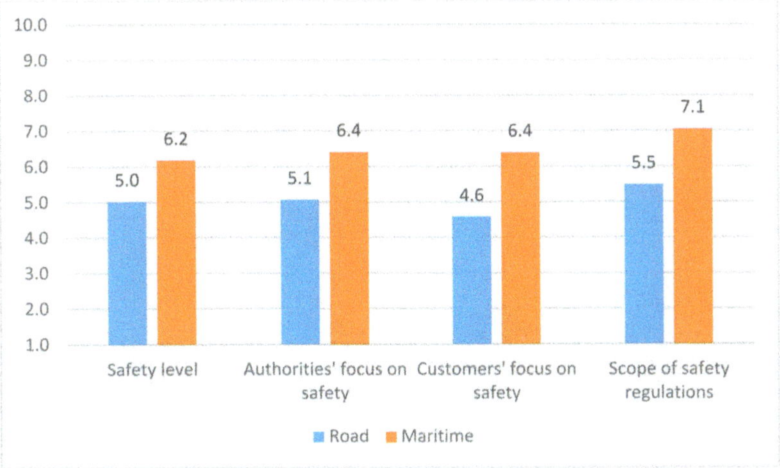


**Figure 2.** Results for four questions based on the formulation: "Imagine a scale from 1 to 10 indicating the level of safety, where 10 corresponds to the level of safety in international commercial aviation", "How would you rate your sector?" Similar questions were asked for: authorities' focus on safety, customer focus on safety and scope of safety regulations. Respondents from road (N = 66) and Maritime (N = 46).

Results indicate a general pattern; respondents from the maritime sector rate the safety level in their sector as higher than respondents in the road sector. All differences were statistically significant at the 1% level. The comparisons were "anchored" in an absolute reference point (i.e., the commonly known standard of international commercial aviation), as previous research has indicated that comparisons across contexts may be difficult, as respondents' assessments are relative, based on the different reference points and expectations in their respective sectors [35].

#### 4.2.3. Respondents' Ratings of Factors Influencing the Safety Level in Their Sector

We expect that respondents in the maritime sector rate SMS as more important for the safety level in their sector than respondents in the road sector (Hypothesis 3). In a previous study, we found a strong decline in the number of people injured in work-related accidents in both the road- and the maritime sector [2]. Based on this, we asked respondents about the following: "The number of work-related accidents in your sector has fallen sharply in recent years. What do you think are the reasons for this decline?" Seven answer alternatives were provided (cf. Figure 3).

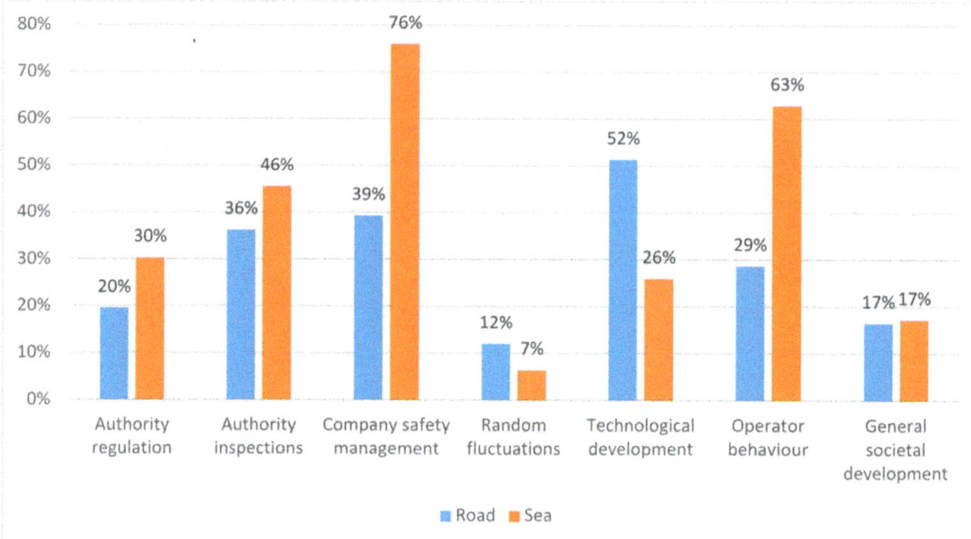


**Figure 3.** Results for respondents answer to the question: "The number of work-related accidents in your sector has fallen sharply in recent years. What do you think are the reasons for this decline?" Seven answer alternatives were provided. Respondents from road (N = 66) and Maritime (N = 46).

Figure 3 indicates that the most important answer provided by respondents from the road sector is technological development; half of the respondents from road answered this, which is twice as much as in the maritime sector. The most prevalent answer provided by respondents from the maritime sector is companies' safety management. This is in accordance with Hypothesis 3, and we can probably attribute this result to the focus on SMS in the maritime sector. The share answering "company safety management" in the maritime sector (76%) is nearly twice as high as that in the road sector (39%). This result is not surprising, given the fact that SMS is not mandatory in the road sector.

In the interviews, we also asked the sector experts to point to the most important measures against work-related transport accidents that have been introduced in recent years. Interviewees in the maritime sector pointed to the SMS requirements of the ISM code:

> "It is the ISM safety management systems that have been introduced. We think they work, based on the decline in work accident rates, but the background is a bit unclear. But I believe that the [SMS] requirements have led to a certain enlightenment in the shipping companies about how to implement measures, an increased focus."

Another interviewee stated, in line with this, that the focus on the human factors and safety management has increased because of the SMS-requirements of the ISM code.

### 4.3. *Multivariate Analyses*

#### 4.3.1. Which Factors Influence Respondents' Perception That Responsibility for the Prevention of Work-Related Accidents Is Clearly Defined in Their Sector?

In Table 2, we examine factors influencing respondents' perception whether responsibility for the prevention of work-related accidents is clearly defined in their sector

**Table 2.** Logistic regression. Dependent variable: "Is the responsibility for the prevention of work-related accidents sufficiently clearly defined in your sector? (0 = Yes, 1 = No/don't know). B values.

| Variable | Mod. 1 | Mod. 2 | Mod. 3 |
|---|---|---|---|
| Type of org. (Company = 0, Other = 1) | −1.147 *** | −1.419 *** | −1.616 *** |
| Sector (Maritime = 0, Road = 1,) | | 2.044 *** | 1.791 *** |
| Scope of safety regulations | | | −0.267 ** |
| Adjusted R2 | 0.100 | 0.319 | 0.376 |

* $p < 0.1$ ** $p < 0.05$ *** $p < 0.01$.

The first main result is that we see a positive and significant relationship between the road sector and disagreement with the statement that the responsibility for accident prevention is clearly defined. This is as expected, based on the bivariate results, however, in this analysis we also control for type of organization and the scope of safety regulations in the sector.

The second main result is that type of organization contributes negatively and significantly. This means that respondents from companies tend to assess that responsibilities for accident prevention is more clearly defined than respondents from other types of organizations, e.g., authorities. This could have been due to SMS rules applying to companies in the maritime sector, but we control for sector.

Third, results indicate a negative relationship between the scope of safety regulations and the dependent variable. This indicates that respondents who are subjected to comprehensive safety regulations (i.e., in the maritime sector) are more likely to perceive that the responsibility for prevention of work-related accidents are clearly defined.

The Nagelkerke R value is 0.376, which means that the model explains 38 % of the variation in the dependent variable.

#### 4.3.2. Which Factors Influence Respondents' Ratings of Their Organizations' Efforts to Prevent Work-Related Accidents?

In Table 3, we examine factors influencing respondents' ratings of their organizations' efforts to prevent work-related accidents.

**Table 3.** Linear regression. Dependent variable: "How would you rate your organization's efforts to prevent work-related accidents?" (Min = 1, Max = 7) Standardized beta coefficients.

| Variable | Mod. 1 | Mod. 2 | Mod. 3 | Mod. 4 | Mod. 5 | Mod. 6 | Mod. 7 |
|---|---|---|---|---|---|---|---|
| Type of org. (Oth. = 1, Company = 2) | 0.170 * | 0.171 * | 0.076 | 0.163 | 0.141 | 0.145 | 0.138 |
| Sector (Road = 1, Maritime = 2) | | 0.239 ** | 0.189 ** | 0.106 | 0.040 | 0.036 | 0.050 |
| Companies report all incidents | | | 0.246 ** | 0.187 * | 0.143 | 0.141 | 0.126 |
| Responsibility is clearly defined (Yes = 1, No/don't know = 2) | | | | −0.232 ** | −0.166 | −0.171 | −0.152 |
| Scope of safety regulations | | | | | 0.307 *** | 0.300 *** | 0.289 *** |
| Heavy competition between comp. | | | | | | −0.026 | −0.029 |
| Safety more important than price | | | | | | | 0.083 |
| Adjusted R2 | 0.020 | 0.069 | 0.111 | 0.142 | 0.215 | 0.208 | 0.207 |

* $p < 0.1$ ** $p < 0.05$ *** $p < 0.01$.

The analyses in Table 3 indicates three main results. First, the most important result is that the variable "Scope of safety regulations" is the variable which has the strongest contribution to respondents' rating of their efforts to prevent work-related accidents. The positive beta coefficient indicates that respondents (in the maritime sector) who have the most comprehensive safety regulations, rate their efforts as better (than the road sector), also when we control for companies' reporting of accidents (which we have included as an indicator of sector safety culture) and framework conditions like competition between companies in the sector, and customers' focus on transport safety over price. The two latter framework conditions are measured by the following statements: "Heavy competition between companies is detrimental to safety in my sector" and "Safety is more important than price to customers". As illustrated in Figure 2, the maritime sector scores significantly higher than the road sector on the "Scope of safety regulations" variable. As noted, the full wording of the Scope of safety regulation variable is: "Imagine a scale from 1 to 10 indicating the scope of safety regulations, where 10 corresponds to the amount of safety regulations in international commercial aviation. How would you rate your sector?"

The second main result is that there is a close relationship between the scope of safety regulations variable and the variable "Responsibility for prevention of accidents is clearly defined". This variable contributed significantly and negatively in Model 4, indicating that lack of clearly defined responsibility for work-related accident prevention is related to lower ratings of your own organization's efforts to prevent such accidents. The clearly defined responsibility variable ceases, however, to contribute significantly in Model 5, when "scope of safety regulations" is included, indicating the close correlation between the two.

The third main result is that these variables are also closely related to sector. The sector variable contributes significantly in Models 2 and 3, indicating higher ratings of efforts to prevent work-related accidents in the maritime sector. The sector variable ceases, however, contribute significantly in Model 4, when the clearly defined responsibility variable is included, indicating the close relationship between the two, i.e., that this is more clearly defined in the maritime sector.

The fourth main result is that companies' reporting of incidents (i.e., sector safety culture), also is related to the scope of sector regulations, as the variable reporting of incidents ceases to contribute significantly when the variable scope of sector regulations is included in Model 5. The positive contribution indicates that reporting of incidents is related to higher ratings of efforts to prevent work-related accidents (and presumably a positive safety culture in the sector).

Finally, we see that neither customer focus on safety, nor heavy competition between companies influence respondents' rating of their efforts to present work-related accidents.

The Adjusted R value is 0.207, which means that the model explains 21% of the variation in the dependent variable.

## 5. Concluding Discussion

### *5.1. Is the Responsibility to Prevent Work-Related Accidents Clearly Defined?*

In contrast to the road sector, the maritime sector has had rules requiring SMS, clearly defining shipping companies' responsibilities for prevention of work-related accidents, for over 20 years. In the present study we tested the influence of different sector rules on work-related accident prevention in Norwegian road and maritime transport. The first aim of the study was to examine how the different sector rules influence perceptions of whether the responsibility to prevent work-related accidents is clearly defined in the maritime sector and in the road sector. As the SMS rules in the maritime sector firmly place the responsibility for safety on the shipping company and the shipmaster [25], we hypothesized that respondents in the maritime sector have a stronger perception that the responsibility for accident prevention is clearly defined in their sector regulations than respondents in the road sector (Hypothesis 1).

Survey results supported Hypothesis 1; the road sector had a relatively low share of respondents agreeing that the responsibility for accident prevention was defined clearly enough in current regulations in the sector. The shares agreeing were 37% in the road sector, compared with 78% in the maritime sector. Respondents from the road sector who gave reasons for their answers underlined that transport buyers also influence the safety of transport assignments. Moreover, in the road sector, interviewees stated that drivers at work usually carry the entire responsibility, as the Road Traffic Act, which places all responsibility with the driver, is enforced through controls and in police investigations. Interviewees pointed out that the Working Environment Act, which focuses on the responsibility of the employer and work-related risk factors is rarely enforced in practice in the road sector. The practical focus on the driver in the road sector is line with previous research from Norway [23] and research from other countries (e.g., [22,36]). Work-related road safety has traditionally been managed using single driver-focused measures, and not SMS and safety culture (e.g., [24]). In contrast, one of the main purposes of the ISM-code is to firmly define the shipping company and the ship master's responsibility for the management of safety and the environment [25,26].

To sum up, results from the qualitative data indicate that respondents from the road sector found responsibility for work-related accident prevention unclear as: (1) the safety of drivers at work is regulated through at least two different rules; (2) only one of these is enforced in practice; and (3) in addition, other parties (e.g., transport buyers) also have a strong influence work-related road safety, but their influence is not recognised legally.

### *5.2. The Quality of Efforts to Prevent Work-Related Accidents*

The second aim of the study was to compare respondents' perceptions of the quality of their sectors' efforts to prevent work-related accidents, and factors influencing this. Quantitative results indicate that respondents from the maritime sector rate their own organizations' efforts to prevent work-related accidents, and the safety level in their sector, as higher than respondents from the road sector. Moreover, respondents from the maritime sector also rate their sector authorities' focus on safety as higher, and the customer focus on safety in their sector as higher than respondents in the road sector. Respondents from the maritime sector also rate the scope of safety regulations as more comprehensive than respondents in road.

We conducted multivariate analyses to examine the factors influencing respondents' rating of their own organizations' efforts to prevent work-related accidents. The multivariate analyses generally indicate that respondents in the maritime sector rate their organizations' efforts to prevent work-related accidents as higher, as responsibility for accident prevention is more clearly defined, which in turn is related to the scope of the safety regulations. These results are in line with previous research, which indicates more focus on safety management systems, more advanced safety cultures and better safety outcomes in transport sectors with legal SMS requirements compared to the road sector (cf. [22,29,30]). Moreover, studies find relationships between SMS, or SMS elements and positive safety culture and safety outcomes in aviation [12,32], in rail [15], in the maritime sector [13], and in the road sector [17]. These results indicate the importance of sector rules requiring SMS for the prevention of work-related accidents. In accordance with this, the sector experts that we interviewed often referred to the rules governing safety in their sector and the enforcement of these rules when discussing their sectors' efforts to prevent work-related accidents.

It is difficult to compare transport sectors, as several framework conditions are likely to differ, in addition to the rules. In Figure 2, we saw, for instance, that customer focus on safety and authority focus on safety was rated higher among respondents in the maritime sector than in the road sector. In the multivariate analyses, we therefore controlled for such sector characteristics that could potentially represent confounding variables, e.g., competition between companies and customers' focus on safety versus price. In conclusion, we found that these variables do not influence respondents' rating of their efforts to present work-related accidents.

Additionally, we should ideally compare the risk of work-related accidents in each sector to compare the quality of efforts to prevent work-related accidents. It is however difficult to make such comparisons, as the measures of exposure differ in the sectors (e.g., kilometre in the road sector and days/hours at work in the maritime sector). This is an important issue for future research. Another interesting issue for future research is the influence of sector rules on safety culture in the sectors. Our multivariate analyses (Table 3) indicate relationships between sector rules, companies' reporting of incidents, which can be used as an indicator of sector safety culture (cf. [37]), and respondents' rating of their organization's efforts to prevent work-related accidents. This is in line with previous research indicating that SMS rules may facilitate key aspects of safety culture; e.g., reporting, justice, and learning culture [12,13,15].

### *5.3. The Perceived Importance of SMS for Safety in the Maritime Sector*

The specific characteristic of the safety regulations that we focus on in the present study is the defined responsibility of companies for safety management through SMS rules, which are legally required in the maritime sector [13]. Based on this, our third hypothesis was that we expected that respondents in the maritime sector rate SMS as more important for the safety level in their sector than respondents in the road sector. We tested this hypothesis by asking respondents in the two sectors about the most important reasons for the decline in the number of work-related accidents in their sector, which has occurred in recent years [2]. The most important answer provided by respondents from the maritime sector was "companies' safety management" (76% in the maritime sector vs. 39% in the road sector). This is in accordance with Hypothesis 3, and we can probably attribute this result to the focus on SMS in the maritime sector. This result is not surprising, given the fact that SMS is mandatory in the maritime sector, but not in the road sector. In contrast, the most important answer provided by respondents from the road sector was technological development. The SMS requirements of the ISM code was also mentioned by interviewees in the maritime sector when asked to identify the most important measures against work-related accidents that has been introduced in recent years.

### *5.4. Methodological Weaknesses and Issues for Future Research*

The main methodological weakness of the present study is the relatively small samples sizes of respondents from the road and maritime sectors that the quantitative survey is based on. The quantitative data is based on only 112 questionnaires in total. This is a small sample, which should be labelled a pilot study, especially since the groups of people working in transport companies were only 35 people in road transport and 25 people in maritime transport. The people in the transport companies are very important in a study like the current, because they directly encounter the issue of work-related accidents. Thus, we recommend that future studies further examining the themes that we discuss here include larger samples of people working in transport companies. This is required to establish robust conclusions. We have, however, not seen studies comparing sectors like we do in the present study, and it therefore provides an important contribution, although it is based on a small sample.

The small samples are due to the fact that recruitment of sector expert respondents was difficult, as we targeted very specialized personnel in the public authorities, NGOs, etc., and that there are relatively few of these specialized personnel in Norway. We made several efforts, e.g., by sending several reminders, to recruit relevant study participants.

The small samples may make comparisons across sectors difficult, in the sense that it may increase the risk of type II errors (false negative observations). This means that if we do not see significant differences between the studied sectors, it could potentially indicate that the groups are too small, rather than that the observed difference is unimportant.

Another potential challenge related to the small sample is the issue of representativity. With the low number of respondents, it is reasonable to ask whether they actually are representative for their own sector. Unfortunately, it is impossible to calculate response rates, due to the method of survey distribution. When discussing the relatively small quantitative sample, it is important to note that we complement the quantitative data with rich qualitative interview data. Comparisons of quantitative data across sectors may be difficult, due to different reference points and baselines among the respondents. The qualitative data allows us to "control" for this in some sense, as we are able to get rich descriptions of these reference points and baselines, and comprehensive and complex accounts of the situation in each sector.

Since the quantitative and qualitative data was collected in 2016/17, it is important to discuss its current relevancy for policy and research. All in all, the main results of the present study can still be considered valid, as the rules regarding SMS and responsibility in road and the maritime sector have not changed since the data was collected. It is of course possible that some of the specific details provided in the qualitative interviews may have changed, but the legal contexts in the two sectors are still the same [27,38,39], indicating that the main results regarding the comparisons of the sectors still provide important lessons for policy makers and researchers. Additionally, international research also indicates that the main conclusions regarding the comparisons of the sectors are valid for the situation in other countries (cf. [22,24,30,40], indicating the importance of our study.

### 5.5. Policy Implications

We may draw three main policy implications based on our study. The first is that our results indicate that the responsibility for the prevention of work-related accidents in the road sector is unclear in practice, and that this responsibility should be clarified. Both the Road Traffic Act and the Working Environment Act apply to drivers at work, but it seems that only the former is enforced in practice. The consequence is that drivers at work are treated as other private drivers, and that the potential of organizational safety management largely remains relatively unexploited in the road sector. As noted, about 36% of fatal road accidents involved at least one driver who was "at work" [1], and measures focusing on SMS and safety culture may lead to reductions in accident risk with up to 60% [40]. In a previous study, we estimated that between 7 and 56 deaths and severe injuries could have been avoided annually in Norway in the period 2007–2016, if more haulier companies had worked systematically with SMS and safety culture [41]. The potential is even greater if we focus on all drivers at work. It seems that this conclusion also applies to the international context (cf. [24]).

The second main policy implication of our study is that the responsibility should be clarified by also introducing SMS requirements in the road sector. The present study indicates that SMS rules are related to more clearly defined responsibilities for the prevention of work-related safety, a higher rating of the prevention of work-related accidents, and a higher perceived safety level in the maritime sector. Additionally, several studies also indicate that implementation of SMS is related to positive safety outcomes in the road sector [18–20] and in other sectors [3].

We have, however, seen that there are several differences between the road sector and the transport sectors with SMS requirements, which may represent barriers to SMS implementation in the road sector, including: (1) no international regulatory or standard setting body in road transport of the kind responsible for aviation (ICAO) or maritime transport (IMO); (2) a large share of non-professional road users; (3) many small companies; (4) high proportion of owner-drivers; and (5) low organizational maturity, indicated, e.g., by low degree of reporting of incidents and little systematic focus and follow up of indicators measuring performance [22]. The factors related to small companies and maturity have also been found to be relevant in some subsectors in the maritime sector, where studies indicate poorly adapted SMS and violations of procedures [29,34]. These studies indicate that SMS implementation may fail, and that it does not necessarily leads to improved safety culture.

The barriers to SMS implementation in the road sector that were discussed in the ITF [22] roundtable on SMS in transport point to an important paradox: on the one hand, SMS is supposed to contribute to positive safety culture, but if companies have a poor safety culture, they may not be mature enough for successful SMS implementation (and thus improved safety culture). Insufficient organizational maturity, e.g., due to many small companies is listed as a barrier to SMS implementation in the road sector by the ITF [22]. One of the possible solutions to this dilemma, which is suggested in the ITF report, is to implement less comprehensive and simplified SMS in the road sector. This seems to be a fruitful approach, given the barriers to implementation. Nævestad et al. [42] provides such an alternative, which is called the Safety Ladder for safety management. Based on a systematic literature review, taking Norwegian research as its point of departure, Nævestad et al. [42] concludes that four measures seem to be most realistic for small goods-transport businesses, and that these measures seem to have the greatest safety potential. These four measures can be arranged on a ladder, where businesses start at the lowest and most basic level, before proceeding to the next step. The validation and implementation of such simplified SMS approaches is an important issue for future research and policy development.

The third main policy implication of our study is that the responsibility of other parties involved in road transport also should be clarified, e.g., transport buyers, as these also are perceived to have a considerable influence on road safety (cf. [22]).

## 6. Conclusions

The present study supports the assertion that the implementation of rules focusing on the responsibility of road transport companies to prevent work related accidents, by implementing safety management systems (SMS), could lead to increased safety in the road sector. The study indicates that the SMS rules in the maritime sector are related to more clearly defined responsibilities for the prevention of work-related safety. Our study indicates that this in turn is related to a higher rating of the prevention of work-related accidents and a higher perceived safety level in the maritime sector. Additionally, respondents in the maritime sector view SMS as the most important safety measure in the sector in recent years. However, due to barriers to SMS implementation in the road sector, we suggest starting with a simplified version of SMS.

**Author Contributions:** Conceptualization, T.-O.N. and B.E.; methodology, T.-O.N., B.E., K.R.; formal analysis, T.-O.N., B.E., K.R.; writing—original draft preparation, T.-O.N., B.E., K.R.; writing—review and editing, T.-O.N.; visualization, T.-O.N.; project administration, B.E., T.-O.N.; funding acquisition, T.-O.N., B.E. All authors have read and agreed to the published version of the manuscript.

**Funding:** The study was financed by the TRANSIKK program of the Research Council of Norway. Grant number 236643.

**Institutional Review Board Statement:** The study was conducted according to the guidelines of the Declaration of Helsinki, and approved by NSD, Norwegian Centre for Research Data.

**Informed Consent Statement:** Informed consent was obtained from all subjects involved in the study.

**Data Availability Statement:** The data presented in this study are available on request from the corresponding author.

**Acknowledgments:** The study was financed by the TRANSIKK program of the Research Council of Norway, as part of a larger research project "Work-related accidents in road, sea and air transport: Prevalence, causes and measures" (2014-2017). The information described based on the qualitative interviews is based on the situation in 2016-2017, and some of the details may have changed since then. Results from the project are also presented in Elvebakk et al [43].

**Conflicts of Interest:** The authors declare no conflict of interest.

## References


1. Nævestad, T.-O.; Phillips, R.O.; Elvebakk, B. Traffic accidents triggered by drivers at work–A survey and analysis of contributing factors. Transportation. *Res. Part. F Traffic Psychol. Behav.* **2015**, *34*, 94–107. [CrossRef]
2. Nævestad, T.O.; Phillips, R.; Elvebakk, B.; Bye, R.J.; Antonsen, S. *Work-Related Accidents in Norwegian Road, Sea and Air Transport: Prevalence and Risk Factors*; TØI Report 1428/2015; Transportøkonomisk Institutt: Oslo, Norway, 2015.
3. Thomas, M.J.W. *A Systematic Review of the Effectiveness of Safety Management Systems (No. AR-2011-148)*; Australian Transport Safety Bureau: Canberra, Australia, 2012.
4. Bernard, B. Safety culture oversight: An intangible concept for tangible issues within nuclear installations. *Saf. Sci.* **2018**, *4*, 45. [CrossRef]
5. ICAO. ICAO Annex 19, Safety Management. Available online: https://www.skybrary.aero/index.php/ICAO_Annex_19,_Safety_Management (accessed on 14 March 2021).
6. IATA. Creating a Positive Safety Culture. *Best Practices to Align with Annex 19's New Recommendations.* Available online: https://go.updates.iata.org/safetyculture?_ga=2.26439165.1941341082.1571071913-370565390.1570852392 (accessed on 14 March 2021).
7. Kringen, J. Culture and Control: Regulation of Risk in the Norwegian Petroleum Industry. Ph.D. Thesis, Center for Technology, Innovation and Culture, Faculty of Social Sciences, University of Oslo, Oslo, Norway, 2009.
8. Nævestad, T.-O. Culture, Crises and Campaigns: Examining the Role of Safety Culture in the Management of Hazards in a Highrisk Industry. Ph.D. Thesis, University of Oslo, Oslo, Norway, 2010.
9. IMO. *2018: ISM Code. International Safety Management Code with Guidelines for Its Implementation*; IMO: London, UK, 2018.
10. European Rail Agency. Available online: https://www.era.europa.eu/activities/safety-management-system_en (accessed on 14 March 2021).
11. Nævestad, T.-O.; Hesjevoll, I.S.; Ranestad, K.; Antonsen, S. Strategies regulatory authorities can use to influence safety culture in organizations: Lessons based on experiences from three sectors. *Saf. Sci.* **2019**, *118*, 409–423. [CrossRef]
12. Adjekum, D.K.; Tous, M.F. Assessing the relationship between organizational management factors and a resilient safety culture in a collegiate aviation program with Safety Management Systems (SMS). *Saf. Sci.* **2020**, *131*, 104909. [CrossRef]
13. Lappalainen, F.J.; Kuronen, J.; Tapaninen, U. Evaluation of the ISM Code in the Finnish shipping companies. *J. Marit. Res.* **2012**, *9*, 23–32.
14. Amtrak. *Safety and Security: Opportunities Exist to Improve the Safe-2-Safer Program, Audit Report OIG-A-2015-007*; Amtrak: Washington, DC, USA, 2015.
15. Zuschlag, M.; Ranney, J.M.; Coplen, M. Evaluation of a safety culture intervention for Union Pacific shows improved safety and safety culture. *Saf. Sci.* **2016**, *83*, 59–73. [CrossRef]
16. Phillips, R.O.; Nævestad, T.-O.; Jordbakke, G. *Increasing the Implementation of Traffic Safety Management Systems by Organisations, TØI Report 1664/2018*; TØI: Oslo, Norway, 2018.
17. Naveh, E.; Katz-Navon, T. A longitudinal study of an intervention to improve road safety climate: Climate as an organizational boundary spanner. *J. Appl. Psychol.* **2015**, *100*, 216–226. [CrossRef] [PubMed]
18. Murray, W.; Ison, S.; Gallemore, P.; Nijjar, H.S. Effective occupational road safety programs a case study of Wolseley. *Transp. Res. Rec. J. Transp. Res. Board* **2009**, *2096*, 55–64. [CrossRef]
19. Murray, W.; White, J.; Ison, S. Work-related road safety: A case study of Roche Australia. *Saf. Sci.* **2012**, *50*, 129–137. [CrossRef]
20. Wallington, D.; Murray, W.; Darby, P.; Raeside, R.; Ison, S. Work-related road safety: Case study of British telecommunications (BT). *Transp. Policy* **2014**, *32*, 194–202. [CrossRef]
21. Elvik, R.; Vaa, T.; Erke, A.; Sorensen, M. *The Handbook of Road Safety Measures*; Emerald Group: Oslo, Norway, 2009.
22. ITF. Safety Management Systems. Summary Report of rountable meeting held at OECD headquarters on 23–24 March 2017. In *ITF/TRC (2017)21*; ITF: London, UK, 2017.
23. Nævestad, T.-O.; Phillips, R.O. *Trafikkulykker ved Kjøring i Arbeid—En Kartlegging og Analyse av Medvirkende Faktorer, TØI Rapport 1269/2013*; Transportøkonomisk Institutt: Oslo, Norway, 2013.
24. Newnam, S.; Watson, B. Work-related driving safety in light vehicle fleets: A review of past research and the development of an intervention framework. *Saf. Sci.* **2011**, *49*, 369–381. [CrossRef]
25. NOU 1999: 30—Regjeringen. No. Available online: https://www.regjeringen.no/no/dokumenter/nou-1999-30/id142198/?ch=15 (accessed on 14 March 2021).
26. Størkersen, K.V.; Thorvaldsen, T. Traps and Tricks of Safety Management at Sea. *Saf. Sci.* **2021**, *134*, 105081. [CrossRef]
27. SSA. Norwegian Ship Safety Act. Available online: https://lovdata.no/dokument/NL/lov/2007-02-16-9 (accessed on 14 March 2021).
28. Elvebakk, B. *Between Control. and Collaboration: Transport. Safety Inspectorates in Norway, TØI Report 1404/2015*; Institute of Transport Economics: Oslo, Norway, 2015.
29. Bjørnskau, T.; Longva, F. *Sikkerhetskultur i Transport*; TØI Rapport 1012/2009; Transportøkonomisk Institutt: Oslo, Norway, 2009.
30. Nævestad, T.-O.; Phillips, R.O. *The Relevance of Safety Culture as a Regulatory Concept and Management Strategy in Professional Transport.: Comparing the Experiences of Regulators and Companies from Four Sectors*; TØI Rapport 1668/2018; Transportøkonomisk Institutt: Oslo, Norway, 2018.
31. Hudson, P. Applying the lessons of high risk industries to health care. *BMJ Qual. Saf.* **2003**, *12*, i7–i12. [CrossRef] [PubMed]

32. Patankar, M.S. Chapter 13—Maintenance Resource Management for Technical Operations. In *Crew Resource Management*, 3rd ed.; Kanki, B.G., Anca, J., Chidester, T.R., Eds.; Elsevier: Amsterdam, The Netherlands, 2019; pp. 357–405.
33. Antonsen, S. The relationship between culture and safety on offshore supply vessels. *Saf. Sci.* **2009**, *47*, 1118–1128. [CrossRef]
34. Bye, R.J.; Aalberg, A.L. Why do they violate the procedures?—An exploratory study within the maritime transportation industry. *Saf. Sci.* **2020**, *123*, 104538. [CrossRef]
35. Nævestad, T.-O.; Phillips, R.; Levlin, G.M.; Hovi, I.B. Internationalisation in Road Transport of Goods in Norway: Safety Outcomes, Risk Factors and Policy Implications. *Safety* **2017**, *3*, 22. [CrossRef]
36. Mooren, L.; Grzebieta, R.; Williamson, A.; Olivier, J.; Friswell, R. Safety management for heavy vehicle transport: A review of the literature. *Saf. Sci.* **2014**, *62*, 79–89. [CrossRef]
37. Reason, J. *Managing the Risk of Organisational Accidents*; Ashgate: Aldershot, UK, 1997.
38. RTA. Norwegian Road Traffic Act. Available online: https://lovdata.no/dokument/NL/lov/1965-06-18-4 (accessed on 14 February 2021).
39. WEA. Norwegian Working Environment Act. Available online: https://lovdata.no/dokument/NL/lov/2005-06-17-62 (accessed on 14 March 2021).
40. Gregersen, N.P.; Brehmer, B.; Morén, B. Road safety improvement in large companies. An experimental comparison of different measures Accident Analysis. *Prevention* **1996**, *28*, 297–306.
41. Nævestad, T.-O.; Phillips, R.O.; Hovi, I.B.; Elvik, G.N.J. Miniscenario: Sikkerhetsstigen. In *Innføre tiltak for Sikkerhetsstyring i Godstransportbedrifter. TØI Rapport 1620/2018*; Transportøkonomisk Institutt: Oslo, Norway, 2018.
42. Nævestad, T.O.; Phillips, R.O.; Elvebakk, B. The safety ladder: Developing an evidence-based safety management strategy for small road transport companies. *Transp. Rev.* **2018**, *38*, 372–393. [CrossRef]
43. Elvebakk, B.; Nævestad, T.-O.; Ranestad, K. *Work-Related Accidents in Norwegian Road, Sea and Air Transport. Roles and Responsibilities*; TØI Report 1567/2017; TØI: Oslo, Norway, 2017.

*infrastructures*

*Article*

# Performance Evaluation of Electric Trolley Bus Routes. A Series Two-Stage DEA Approach

**Ioannis E. Tsolas**

School of Applied Mathematics and Physics, National Technical University of Athens, 15780 Athens, Greece; itsolas@central.ntua.gr

**Abstract:** A common concern for bus operators is efficiency measurement in order to monitor transit performance. The purpose of this paper is to propose a series two-stage data envelopment analysis (DEA) approach integrated with bootstrapping in order to evaluate the performance of electric trolley bus routes of Athens and Piraeus, Greece. Production and sales efficiency were measured in the first and second stages, respectively. In the light of the results, the routes assessed have a comparable higher DEA-based efficiency in both stages when compared to the perfect possible performance, but production and sales efficiency are not associated. Nevertheless, arterial bus routes have a marginally better performance in the production process on average, whereas the feeder–local bus routes produce a slightly better sales performance. The proposed modeling approach is an addition to the current literature, and can be employed by managers and operators.

**Keywords:** data envelopment analysis; bootstrapping; bus routes

**Citation:** Tsolas, I.E. Performance Evaluation of Electric Trolley Bus Routes. A Series Two-Stage DEA Approach. *Infrastructures* **2021**, *6*, 44. https://doi.org/10.3390/infrastructures6030044

Academic Editor: Krzysztof Goniewicz

Received: 24 February 2021
Accepted: 12 March 2021
Published: 15 March 2021



## 1. Introduction

The need to measure and assess the efficiency of the transit system has led to the development of several performance metrics [1–4]. Two primary indicator-based assessment methods are key performance indicator (KPI) analysis and composite score analysis. KPI analysis sets indicator targets or thresholds to achieve a composite score, whereas composite score analysis normalizes and weights indicators. In KPI analysis and composite score analysis, however, the thresholds and weights are often subjectively determined [5]. In addition, individual performance measures do not yield consistent results on transit performance [6–8] and this implies the need for a composite indicator or a smaller set of more detailed indicators to describe the transit system.

Competitive methods are used to evaluate the performance of transit systems in terms of efficiency, such as parametric stochastic frontier analysis (SFA) [9,10] and non-parametric data envelopment analysis (DEA) [11]. SFA involves the selection of an econometrically calculated functional form for output or cost frontier function using two error term components, namely statistical noise and inefficiency. For these terms, the normal and half-normal assumptions for noise and inefficiency are typically made respectively.

DEA, published by Charnes et al. [11] in the literature, is a mathematical programming technique that is a non-parametric frontier-based approach. It is used to derive the efficiency of a group of decision-making units (DMUs), e.g., bus routes, by defining a best practicing frontier from the data set. DEA-based efficiency is measured relative to that frontier and the efficiency ratings take values between zero and unity (i.e., perfect efficiency for units located on the frontier); units located off the frontier are considered inefficient. DEA has been applied to ports, railways, airlines, urban transit, and airports. For recent reviews the reader is referred to Lozano and Gutiérrez [12].

In general terms, efficiency can be defined as output-oriented by achieving the maximum possible output with a given amount of input, or as input-oriented by producing a given level of output at the lowest cost possible. A distinction should be made between supply-related measures and demand-related measures (i.e., operator-oriented outputs and user-oriented outputs, respectively) in the calculation of public transport efficiency; the former is typically vehicle-kilometers, seat-kilometers, or vehicle-hours, whereas the latter consists of passenger-kilometers, passenger-trips, or revenues. Practical issues such as data accessibility or method choice often determine the choice of the output variable(s) in practice [13].

In the modeling approach, the transport service rendered by the operator and ultimately used by the customer must be considered sequentially by simultaneously reflecting the operator's and user's outputs. One way to address this problem is to use a series of two-stage DEA model to devise both production and sales (consumption) operations, because they can provide more detailed information on a DMU's performance than the conventional single black box DEA model. This modeling approach makes it possible to investigate the inner workings of the entire process in more detail, ultimately leading to a deeper understanding of it [14].

The current study focuses on DEA because it is more versatile than SFA and can also be used to analyze the production and sales process of the transit system. There are few studies that analyze the DEA-based efficiency of the urban transit system with an emphasis on the production and sales process. In this context, the current research aims to improve on the DEA single-stage black box [15] and to evaluate the performance of a group of electric bus routes in Greece using the series two-stage DEA.

The purpose of this paper is to provide a series two-stage DEA framework to assess the efficiency of public trolley bus transit. The case study concerns an electric (trolley) bus network of twenty routes that mainly serve the Athens and Piraeus city centers. The network today is operated by Road Transport S.A. (Odikes Sygkoinonies S.A. (OSY S.A.)) which is a subsidiary of Athens Area Urban Transport Organization S.A. (OASA S.A). Relevant studies for the performance assessment of trolley bus transit that serve Athens and Piraeus are the single-stage DEA and SFA works by Kagiantalidis [16] and Michaelides et al. [17], respectively.

This study contributes in many respects to the current literature. Firstly, it fills the gap created for bus routes by the single DEA black-box model, using a series two-stage DEA model to measure both production and sales performance. For a group of Greek bus routes, it decides to what degree, given the inputs, the operator should increase the services produced and whether the efficiency of the routes could be enhanced in the sales process by reducing the chosen inputs given the output. In addition, it follows a bootstrapping approach, unlike most previous related DEA studies that have lacked estimates of the uncertainties concerning individual efficiencies.

The remainder of this paper is structured as follows. Section 2 provides a review of the use of DEA in transit system efficiency measurement. In Section 3, the problem to be solved for the case of bus route efficiency assessment is stated. Section 4 deals with methods and the dataset for the analysis. In Section 5, the results are presented and discussed. The final section concludes.

## 2. Literature Review

There are numerous publications on DEA-based transit system efficiency measurement that are divided into single, two-stage, and serial two-stage works. In the works reviewed below, bus routes are defined as DMUs. The typical single-stage DEA studies evaluate transit networks without throwing light on their function within a black-box background in which they are viewed as a whole (i.e., black box) system [15].

There are several DEA applications in transit systems to establish a single measure of the system's effectiveness [18–21]; some of the first studies are those of Chu et al. [18], Odeck and Alkadi [19], Nolan et al. [20], and Viton [21]. The reader is directed to Mahmoudi et al. [22] for a recent review. Model construction is based on the series two-stage DEA in another research strand. A series two-stage DEA structure distinguishes sub-processes and aims at measuring their efficiency [15], unlike the single DEA black-box model. In this strand lies the work of Yu [23], Yu and Fan [24], Sheth et al. [25], Lao and Liu [26], and Hahn et al. [14,27].

The efficiency of a multi-mode bus transit system is measured by DEA by identifying as sub-processes: (i) highway bus and urban bus service [23] and (ii) highway bus, urban bus service, and consumption process [24]. Sheth et al. [25] uses network DEA combined with goal programming to analyze the efficiency of the bus route from two separate perspectives: the point of view of the providers and customers. Two DEA models are used by Lao and Liu [26] to analyze the operational performance and spatial effectiveness of bus lines. Hahn et al. [14,27] employ a network DEA model to assess the performance of arterial bus routes and bus companies, respectively, in the city of Seoul.

Li et al. [28] implemented a bootstrap super-data-envelopment analysis model for route-level transit operational efficiency assessment with respect to DEA-bootstrap modeling, and Hahn et al. [27] used a double bootstrap (DEA-bootstrap and truncated bootstrap regression) to test the performance of arterial bus routes. Other approaches, such as SFA [29] and multi-objective programming [30], can also be combined with DEA. It should be noted that the multi-stage DEA approach, such as the three-stage DEA approach, has also appeared in the related literature [5].

The following gaps have been identified based on the above review of literature: there are few studies in the context of transit efficiency that use the series two-stage DEA, and DEA is subject to uncertainty, which can lead to skewed estimates and misleading conclusions. The current study fills the gaps described above by combining DEA with bootstrapping and using a two-stage DEA model.

## 3. Problem Statement

The current study aims to address the performance assessment of electric bus routes by means of a series two-stage DEA. Data analysis and benchmarks are the basis for an examination of the performance of electric bus transit. Benchmarks (i.e., best-in-class routes) for production and sales processes can be identified by means of DEA and, moreover, their use as reference points is important for the preparation of appropriate performance improvement measures. Corrective steps to enhance efficiency should focus not only on improving production, but also on meeting demand through the sales process. Thus, benchmarks for the production and sales phase should be developed for bus routes.

To produce the efficiency metric representing the relationship between inputs and outputs, classic single-stage DEA modeling only uses input and output information, i.e., the maximum output provided to fixed inputs or the minimum input given to a fixed output [31]. In the case of electric bus transit, each route is seen as a system with two sub-processes: the production and sales process. Instead of evaluating the performance of each route as a whole, without understanding its internal structure (i.e., production and sales process), the system is divided into these two sub-processes and assessed separately for each of them. Thus, two DEA efficiency metrics are involved in the success of each bus route: efficiency of production and efficiency of sales. A DEA with a two-stage structure is proposed in the current study: In the first stage (production sub-process) the number of vehicle-km and trips are considered as outputs that are produced using production factors. In the second stage (sales sub-process) the outputs of the first stage are considered to be the inputs, and the number of tickets is the considered output.

## 4. Methods—Data Set

### 4.1. Series Two-Stage DEA Structure

The current study uses the series two-stage DEA model to derive bus route efficiency scores in both the production and consumption (as measured by sales) phases, taking into account the availability of data. Bus routes are considered to be entities engaging in similar activities that generate comparable results and offer similar services per length of the route. However, deficits have increased the need for government subsidies, resulting in inefficiencies [32]. Due to unavailability of data, subsidized and non-subsidized routes are not differentiated in the current study.

The independent approach [33] is used to assess the bus routes (i.e., each stage is treated separately and their common feature is that the outputs of the first stage are inputs for the second stage), and the efficiency of each stage is calculated separately. Figure 1 demonstrates the two-stage layout of the DEA sequence used to assess sampled bus routes. The selected variables are discussed in detail in Section 4.3.

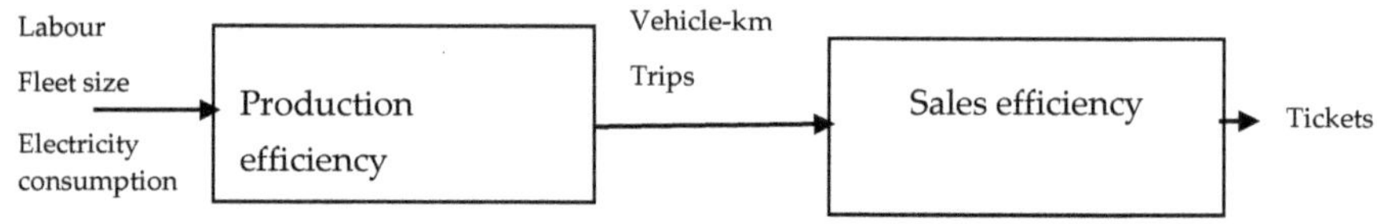


**Figure 1.** Series two-stage data envelopment analysis (DEA) approach.

### 4.2. Model Building

The main idea of DEA is measuring the relative efficiency of a homogeneous set of decision-making units (DMUs). Indeed, DEA believes that the performance of a DMU should be evaluated in the presence of competitors (other DMUs). CCR (Charles, Cooper and Rhodes) [7], BCC (Banker, Charles and Cooper) [34], and SBM (Slacks-Based Measure) [35] are the most popular models used in the literature [22].

The category of bus routes evaluated in the current research comprises routes of various fleet sizes, and the BCC model was therefore chosen to take account of the impact of economies of scale. Input minimizing models calculate the input decrease that could be achieved with the current output level in relation to the model orientation, whereas output maximization models indicate the maximum possible output increase for the given input number.

In stage 1 (production process), the optimization of performance is aimed at maximum output in terms of vehicle-km and trips per route given the inputs and, thus, the output-oriented version of the BCC model was used. There is no direct control over demand by bus route operators in stage 2 (sales process) and thus input orientation (i.e., BCC input-oriented model) was chosen. In the case study application, it was sought to determine to what degree the efficiency of bus routes could be improved during the production process by increasing the produced outputs given the input factors and, moreover, to determine whether the operator could be successful by reducing the number of vehicle-km and trips per route, given the demand as expressed by the number of tickets.

Assuming that there is a group of $n$ bus routes, $j = 1, \ldots, n$ using inputs $X$ Î $\hat{A}^{m}{}_{+}$ to generate outputs $Y$ Î $\hat{A}^{k}{}_{+}$, the following BCC (envelopment form) or variable returns to scale (VRS) output-oriented Model (1) and input-oriented Model (2) [36] were selected to assess the production and sales efficiency of bus routes, respectively:

$$
\begin{aligned}
& Max\phi \\
& \text{subject to} \\
& \sum_{j=1}^{n} \lambda_j x_{ij} \leq x_{ij_0} \\
& \sum_{j=1}^{n} \lambda_j y_{rj} \geq \phi y_{rj_0} \\
& \sum_{j=1}^{n} \lambda_j = 1 \\
& \lambda_j, s_r^{+}, s_i^{-} \geq 0, j = 1,2,\cdots,n, i = 1,2,\ldots m, r = 1,2,\ldots,k
\end{aligned}
\quad (1)
$$

$$
\begin{aligned}
&Min\theta \\
&\text{subject to} \\
&\sum_{j=1}^{n} \lambda_j x_{ij} \leq \theta x_{ij0} \\
&\sum_{j=1}^{n} \lambda_j y_{rj} \geq y_{rj0} \\
&\sum_{j=1}^{n} \lambda_j = 1 \\
&\lambda_j, s_r^+, s_i^- \geq 0, j = 1, 2, \cdots, n, i = 1, 2, \ldots m, l = 1, \ldots, p, r = 1, 2, \ldots, k
\end{aligned}
\quad (2)
$$

where $x_{ij}$ *is* the $i$th input used by the $j$th bus route; $y_{rj}$ is the $r$th output produced by the $j$th route; $1/\phi$ and $\theta$ denote the efficiency score of route "$_0$" derived from Models (1) and (2), respectively; "$_0$" denotes the route under assessment; and $\lambda_j$ is the intensity factor indicating the contribution of route $j$ in the derivation of efficiency of route "$_0$".

The production efficiency of route "$_0$" is defined by $q = 1/\phi^*$, where $\phi^*$ is the optimal solution of Model (1). The efficiency of route "$_0$" deals with the route that has inputs $x_{ij0}$ and outputs $y_{rj0}$, respectively. The model looks for a group of routes that are generated by weighting each route $j$ by a coefficient $\lambda_j$ so that they do not use more inputs than the evaluated route and maximize outputs compared to the evaluated route. For each route, the solving process is repeated. Routes for which, respectively, $q = 1$ and $q < 1$ are considered efficient and inefficient, respectively.

For the route "$_0$", the optimal solution $\theta^*$ of Model (2) yields a sales efficiency score. The model searches for a group of routes generated by weighting each route $j$ by a coefficient $\lambda_j$ so that they do not produce more outputs than route "$_0$" and reduce inputs compared to route "$_0$". Routes for which, respectively, $\theta^* = 1$ and $\theta^* < 1$, are considered efficient and inefficient.

Without taking into account the ambiguity surrounding estimates of DEA ratings, it is presumed that any deviation from the frontier is due to inefficiency in traditional DEA applications. Uncertainty is present in DEA through sampling variability or the uncertainty arising from the estimation of the frontier and may lead to biased DEA (point) estimates and thus to misleading conclusions. The bootstrap, developed by Efron [37] and Efron and Tibshirani [38], was advocated as a way of analyzing the sensitivity to the sampling variance of calculated efficiency scores [39–41] and evaluating the robustness of DEA point estimates through confidence interval construction [39,42,43].

The proposed modeling approach can be expanded to include undesirable outputs, such as air pollution in the case of non-electric buses or accidents [14,44], which are components of the transportation cost [45]. Moreover, bootstrapped truncated regression can also be used to identify the drivers of performance. The bootstrapped bias-corrected DEA efficiency ratings should be regressed on explanatory variables using bootstrapped truncated regression [46].

### *4.3. Data Set*

A group of twenty electric bus routes was examined for the purpose of the present paper. They are considered homogeneous because they use the same production technology and can therefore be compared with the DEA in terms of their performance.

In the evaluation of the trolley bus transit system in Greece in this paper, the unit of analysis or the DMU is the provision of the transportation services along a trolley bus route. The basic principle behind the DEA performance appraisal is that the DMU being measured uses limited resources (inputs) (in this case fleet size, man-hours, electricity) and generates output, i.e., goods (vehicle-km, trips) and services (tickets) for society; see [47] for a similar discussion.

Fleet size, man-hours, and electricity are considered as route inputs and the number of vehicle-km and trips as the route output variables during a particular year in the production sub-process. Labor is measured by the number of man-hours per year working on each route. The capital is measured by the size of the fleet, which is the available number of vehicles working on a route annually. Electricity is determined by the overall consumption of electricity. The sales sub-process deals with the optimization of ticket sales on each route and, as a result, the number of ticket validations is set as an output variable, whereas the (intermediate) outputs of the first sub-process (vehicle-km, trips) are considered as inputs. Other factors that reflect attractiveness, such as the number of stops, punctuality, and spatial design of bus routes, may also affect the consumption phase (sales) but these factors were not considered due to unavailability of data.

The selection of input and output variables in the DEA evaluations is justified by two isotonicity tests [48] for the production and sales process. To investigate whether input increases lead to higher outputs, these tests were carried out by measuring all inter-correlations among all variables. Tests were passed for the two processes and the selection of variables was therefore justified. The twenty routes selected comply with the Cooper et al. thumb rule criteria [36].

With the exception of the average number of trips per length of route, which was calculated in this paper, data on variables in the production and sales process were collected from a previous study [16]. Table 1 displays the descriptive statistics of the bus route variables used. An Internet-based map [49] provides a geospatial representation of the existing multimodal transport network, including the electric (trolley) bus network that serves the city centers of Athens and Piraeus. A previously developed map of a similar nature is also mentioned in the literature [50].

**Table 1.** Electric bus routes: Descriptive statistics.

| Descriptive Statistics | Man-Hours | Fleet Size (Number of Vehicles) | Electricity Consumed (kWh) | Vehicle-km | Trips per Legth Route | Tickets |
|---|---|---|---|---|---|---|
| Mean | 21,226 | 336 | 1,489,200 | 548,822 | 109 | 1,647,906 |
| Standard deviation | 8595 | 130 | 676,716 | 244,111 | 40 | 924,663 |
| Median | 20,511 | 359 | 1,523,294 | 511,144 | 91 | 1,652,333 |
| Min | 7749 | 119 | 385,181 | 157,024 | 73 | 470,973 |
| Max | 38,559 | 594 | 2,472,323 | 955,629 | 189 | 3,839,893 |

## 5. Results

### 5.1. Production and Sales Efficiency

The DEA point estimates, the bias-corrected estimates, and the estimated 95 percent confidence bounds are shown in Table 2. The results were created using 2000 bootstrap replications.

Taking into account the results provided by the BCC output-oriented Model (1), 10 (50 percent) of the 20 routes were found to be relatively productive efficient; mean production efficiency: 0.94. The median production efficiency was around 0.99. The efficiency score of 0.94 means that by generating more outputs by around 6 percent (= (1/0.94) − 1) while retaining the same input level, performance can be improved. The BCC input-oriented Model (2) results indicate that 10 (50 percent) of the 20 routes were found to be relatively efficient; mean sales efficiency: 0.94. In addition, by reducing the current input level by 6% (= 1 − 0.94) while retaining the same output level, performance in the sales process can be increased.

**Table 2.** Bus route efficiency measures for production and sales process and descriptive statistics.

| **Sub-Process Efficiency/Bus Routes (BR)** | **Production Efficiency** | | | | **Sales Efficiency** | | | |
|---|---|---|---|---|---|---|---|---|
| DEA estimates | BCC-O point estimates | BCC-O bias-corrected | BCC-O L | BCC-O U | BCC-I point estimates | BCC-I bias-corrected | BCC-I L | BCC-I U |
| BR1 | 0.96 | 0.95 | 0.89 | 0.96 | 0.96 | 0.94 | 0.90 | 0.96 |
| BR2 | 0.77 | 0.76 | 0.74 | 0.77 | 1.00 | 0.96 | 0.91 | 1.00 |
| BR3 | 1.00 | 0.96 | 0.89 | 1.00 | 1.00 | 0.94 | 0.78 | 1.00 |
| BR4 | 0.82 | 0.81 | 0.79 | 0.82 | 1.00 | 0.98 | 0.93 | 1.00 |
| BR5 | 1.00 | 0.95 | 0.88 | 1.00 | 1.00 | 0.97 | 0.91 | 1.00 |
| BR6 | 0.92 | 0.91 | 0.87 | 0.92 | 0.91 | 0.90 | 0.87 | 0.91 |
| BR7 | 1.00 | 0.94 | 0.81 | 1.00 | 1.00 | 0.95 | 0.82 | 1.00 |
| BR8 | 1.00 | 0.96 | 0.86 | 1.00 | 1.00 | 0.98 | 0.88 | 1.00 |
| BR9 | 0.88 | 0.86 | 0.84 | 0.87 | 1.00 | 0.97 | 0.91 | 1.00 |
| BR10 | 0.84 | 0.83 | 0.81 | 0.84 | 0.97 | 0.95 | 0.89 | 0.97 |
| BR11 | 0.93 | 0.91 | 0.88 | 0.92 | 0.84 | 0.83 | 0.81 | 0.84 |
| BR12 | 1.00 | 0.97 | 0.90 | 1.00 | 1.00 | 0.98 | 0.92 | 1.00 |
| BR13 | 0.95 | 0.94 | 0.91 | 0.95 | 1.00 | 0.97 | 0.93 | 1.00 |
| BR14 | 0.81 | 0.80 | 0.76 | 0.81 | 0.97 | 0.96 | 0.93 | 0.97 |
| BR15 | 1.00 | 0.97 | 0.91 | 1.00 | 0.93 | 0.91 | 0.88 | 0.92 |
| BR16 | 1.00 | 0.96 | 0.89 | 1.00 | 0.75 | 0.73 | 0.70 | 0.75 |
| BR17 | 0.97 | 0.95 | 0.90 | 0.97 | 0.78 | 0.77 | 0.73 | 0.78 |
| BR18 | 1.00 | 0.97 | 0.92 | 1.00 | 0.72 | 0.71 | 0.68 | 0.72 |
| BR19 | 1.00 | 0.97 | 0.93 | 1.00 | 1.00 | 0.96 | 0.87 | 1.00 |
| BR20 | 1.00 | 0.97 | 0.93 | 1.00 | 0.936 | 0.92 | 0.89 | 0.94 |
| Mean | 0.94 | 0.92 | 0.87 | 0.94 | 0.94 | 0.91 | 0.86 | 0.94 |
| Standard deviation | 0.08 | 0.07 | 0.06 | 0.08 | 0.09 | 0.08 | 0.08 | 0.09 |
| Median | 0.99 | 0.95 | 0.88 | 0.98 | 0.98 | 0.95 | 0.89 | 0.98 |
| Min | 0.77 | 0.76 | 0.74 | 0.77 | 0.72 | 0.71 | 0.68 | 0.72 |
| Max | 1.00 | 0.97 | 0.93 | 1.00 | 1.00 | 0.98 | 0.93 | 1.00 |

BCC-O: BCC output-oriented model; BCC-I: BCC input-oriented model; L: Lower bound; U: Upper bound.

The output-oriented bootstrap results of the bias-corrected BCC boost the discriminating power of the output-oriented BCC model because the BCC estimates seem to be skewed upwards. Because all routes are inefficient, according to bootstrap estimates, there is scope for improvement in production efficiency by generating more outputs by about 9 percent (= $(1/0.92) - 1$). The median of the bias-corrected efficiency is around 0.95. The bias-corrected BCC input-oriented bootstrap results also enhance the BCC input-oriented model's discriminating power, because the BCC estimates tend to be skewed upwards. There is space for improvement in sales efficiency by minimizing inputs by about 9 percent, according to bootstrap estimates. The median of the bias-corrected efficiency is approximately 95 percent.

There is no connection between production and sales efficiency, i.e., a bus route that performs well in the production process does not appear to also perform well in the sales process.

### *5.2. Arterial vs. Feeder–Local Bus Routes*

Two types of bus routes were classified: arterial and feeder–local. Suburban areas and downtown Athens are connected by arterial buses. In downtown Athens and Piraeus, feeder buses connect major subway stations or bus terminals, and local buses operate on circular routes in downtown Athens and Piraeus, especially for access to major shopping and business areas.

In view of the results of the current analysis (Table 3), the average performance of arterial bus routes in the production process is marginally better (point estimate: 96 percent; bootstrapping biased corrected: 93 percent), relative to feeder–local bus routes (point estimate: 93 percent; bootstrapping biased corrected: 90 percent). On average, the feeder–local bus routes achieve a marginally better sales performance (point estimate: 0.96; bootstrapping biased corrected: 0.93), compared to arterial bus routes (point estimate: 91 percent; bootstrapping biased corrected: 89 percent).

**Table 3.** Descriptive statistics of arterial vs. feeder–local bus route efficiency measures for production and sales process.

| **Bus Route Type** | **Arterial Bus Routes** | | | | **Feeder–Local Bus Routes** | | | |
|---|---|---|---|---|---|---|---|---|
| **Sub-Process Efficiency** | **Production Efficiency** | | **Sales Efficiency** | | **Production Efficiency** | | **Sales Efficiency** | |
| DEA estimates | BCC-O point estimates | BCC-O bias-corrected | BCC-I point estimates | BCC-I bias-corrected | BCC-O point estima-tes | BCC-O bias-corrected | BCC-I point estimates | BCC-I bias-corrected |
| Mean | 0.96 | 0.93 | 0.91 | 0.89 | 0.93 | 0.90 | 0.96 | 0.93 |
| Standard deviation | 0.05 | 0.04 | 0.10 | 0.09 | 0.10 | 0.08 | 0.08 | 0.07 |
| Median | 0.97 | 0.95 | 0.95 | 0.93 | 1.00 | 0.95 | 1.00 | 0.96 |
| Min | 0.84 | 0.83 | 0.72 | 0.71 | 0.77 | 0.76 | 0.75 | 0.73 |
| Max | 1.00 | 0.97 | 1.00 | 0.98 | 1.00 | 0.97 | 1.00 | 0.98 |

BCC-O: BCC output-oriented model; BCC-I: BCC input-oriented model.

It should be noted that arterial buses, because they have the highest speed in the suburban area, achieve an average higher speed and thus perform better in the production process. The feeder–local buses carry high passenger loads and more easily meet the increased demand for short trips, especially in downtown Athens, compared to the arterial buses that should concentrate on meeting the long-trip demand. As a result, feeder–local buses show greater results in sales efficiency because all electric bus routes have an equal fare. The length of a bus route may influence its relative efficiency, but the bootstrapped truncated regression [46] does not support this.

## 6. Conclusions and Implications

Several enhancements to transit performance assessment were suggested by the current study. The first enhancement lies in the implementation of a series two-stage DEA approach to evaluate the efficiency of electric bus routes in the sub-processes of production and sales. The series two-stage DEA model was used in order to overcome the limitation of single DEA model that cannot accommodate an internal structure and interrelationships between the variables of the sub-processes. The second development is that, by combining DEA with bootstrapping, the current study provides new empirical evidence on the performance of electric bus routes. In addition, bootstrapping in the current research serves as a tool to fully rank the assessed routes, thus overcoming the limitations of conventional DEA models.

The current research is a first step towards deriving DEA-based production and sales efficiency scores for a sample of electric bus routes. The assessed routes display a comparable efficiency in both processes, i.e., production and consumption, but production and sales efficiency are not associated. In the light of the results, the arterial buses perform better in the production process, whereas the feeder–local buses show greater performance in sales efficiency. From these findings, some policy implications can be obtained. In particular, more focus should be given to sales efficiency for arterial bus routes, while production efficiency should be concerned for the feeder–local bus routes.

The modeling approach used in this research may be useful to managers and operators because it can help them to identify best-in-class and lagging bus routes in both production and sales sub-process. Policy makers could employ it to monitor both production and sales performance, select the best-in-class routes that can use the as benchmarks, and develop necessary interventions to improve the performance.

The results derived are sample specific, so future researches can use the proposed framework to appraise other bus routes, in order to quantify performance and investigate whether their findings are similar with those of the current study. As more data become available, the number of bus stops and waiting time can be used as explanatory variables to further examine the drivers of performance. Moreover, although the current analysis involved only static DEA models, future research can be based on dynamic analysis. If a long-time series of data is made available, DEA can provide a dynamic evaluation of transit performance.

**Funding:** This research received no external funding.

**Conflicts of Interest:** The author declares no conflict of interest.

## References

1. Tomazinis, A.R. *Productivity, Efficiency, and Quality in Urban Transportation Systems;* Heath and Company: Lexington, MA, USA, 1975.
2. Tomazinis, A.R. *A Study of Efficiency Indicators of Urban Public Transportation Systems;* Final Report DOT-TST-77-47; USDOT: Washington, DC, USA, 1977.
3. Fielding, G.L.; Glauthier, R.E.; Lave, C.A. Performance indicators for transit management. *Transportation* **1978**, *7*, 365–379. [CrossRef]
4. Fielding, G.L.; Glauthier, R.E.; Lave, C.A. *Distribution and Allocation of Transit Subsidies in California. Transit Management Program;* School of Sciences and Institute of Transportation Studies, University of California: Irvine, CA, USA, 1976.
5. Deng, Y.; Yan, Y. Evaluating route and frequency design of bus lines based on data envelopment analysis with network epsilon-based measures. *J. Adv. Transp.* **2019**, 12. [CrossRef]
6. Karlaftis, M.G.; McCarthy, P.S. Subsidy and public transit performance: A factor analytic approach. *Transportation* **1997**, *24*, 253–270. [CrossRef]
7. Benjamin, J.; Obeng, K. The effect of policy and background variables on total factor productivity for public transit. *Transp. Res.* **1990**, *24B*, 1–14. [CrossRef]
8. Stokes, B.R. The need for and use of performance indicators in transit. *Transit J.* **1979**, *1*, 3–10.
9. Aigner, D.J.; Lovell, C.A.K.; Schmidt, P.J. Formulation and estimation of stochastic frontier production function models. *J. Econom.* **1977**, *6*, 21–37. [CrossRef]
10. Meeusen, W.; van den Broeck, J. Efficiency estimation from Cobb-Douglas production functions with composed error. *Int. Econ. Rev.* **1977**, *18*, 435–444. [CrossRef]
11. Charnes, A.; Cooper, W.W.; Rhodes, E. Measuring the efficiency of decision making units. *Eur. J. Oper. Res.* **1978**, *2*, 429–444. [CrossRef]
12. Lozano, S.; Gutiérrez, E. A slacks-based network DEA efficiency analysis of European airlines. *Transp. Plan. Technol.* **2014**, *37*, 623–637. [CrossRef]
13. Holmgren, J. The effects of using different output measures in efficiency analysis of public transport operations. *Res. Transp. Bus. Manag.* **2018**, *28*, 12–22. [CrossRef]
14. Hahn, J.-S.; Kim, D.-K.; Kim, H.-C.; Lee, C. Efficiency analysis on bus companies in Seoul city using a network DEA model. *KSCE J. Civ. Eng.* **2013**, *17*, 1480–1488. [CrossRef]
15. Kao, C. Network data envelopment analysis: A review. *Eur. J. Oper. Res.* **2014**, *239*, 1–16. [CrossRef]
16. Kagiantalidis, N. Measurement of Technical Efficiency. Case Study: The Routes of ILPAP S.A. Diploma Thesis, National Technical University of Athens, Athens, Greece, 2004.
17. Michaelides, P.G.; Belegri-Roboli, A.; Marinos, T. Evaluating the Technical Efficiency of Trolley Buses in Athens, Greece. *J. Public Transp.* **2010**, *13*, 93–109. [CrossRef]
18. Chu, X.; Fielding, G.J.; Lamar, B.W. Measuring transit performance using data envelopment analysis. *Transp. Res.* **1992**, *26A*, 223–230. [CrossRef]
19. Odeck, J.; Alkadi, A. Evaluating efficiency in the Norwegian bus industry using data envelopment analysis. *Transportation* **2001**, *28*, 211–232. [CrossRef]
20. Nolan, J.F.; Ritchie, P.C.; Rowcroft, J.E. Identifying and measuring public policy goals: ISTEA and the US bus transit industry. *J. Econ. Behav. Organ.* **2002**, *48*, 291–304. [CrossRef]
21. Viton, P.A. Changes in multi-mode bus transit efficiency, 1998–1992. *Transportation* **1998**, *25*, 1–21. [CrossRef]
22. Mahmoudi, R.; Emrouznejad, A.; Shetab-Boushehri, S.N.; Hejazi, S.R. The origins, development and future directions of Data Envelopment Analysis approach. *Transp. Syst. Socio-Econ. Plan. Sci.* **2020**, *69*, 100762.
23. Yu, M.M. Measuring the efficiency and return to scale status of multi-mode bus transit—Evidence from Taiwan's bus system. *Appl. Econ. Lett.* **2008**, *15*, 647–653. [CrossRef]
24. Yu, M.M.; Fan, C.K. Measuring the performance of multimode bus transit. A mixed structure network DEA model. *Transp. Res. Part E* **2009**, *45*, 501–515. [CrossRef]
25. Sheth, C.; Triantis, K.; Teodorović, D. Performance evaluation of bus routes: A provider and passenger perspective. *Transp. Res. Part E* **2007**, *43*, 453–478. [CrossRef]
26. Lao, Y.; Liu, L. Performance evaluation of bus lines with Data Envelopment Analysis and Geographic Information Systems. *Comput. Environ. Urban Syst.* **2009**, *33*, 247–255. [CrossRef]
27. Hahn, J.S.; Kim, H.R.; Kho, S.Y. Analysis of the efficiency of Seoul arterial bus routes and its determinant factors. *KSCE J. Civ. Eng.* **2011**, *15*, 1115–1123. [CrossRef]

28. Li, X.; Yu, J.; Shaw, J.; Wang, Y. Route-level transit operational-efficiency assessment with a bootstrap super-data-envelopment analysis model. *J. Urban Plan. Dev.* **2017**, *143*, 04017007. [CrossRef]
29. Zhang, K.; Xu, Y.; Sun, D. A mixed frontier model for urban bus performance evaluation. *Proc. Inst. Civ. Eng. Transp.* **2018**, *171*, 65–74. [CrossRef]
30. Wei, R.; Liu, X.; Mu, Y.; Wang, L.; Golub, A.; Farber, S. Evaluating public transit services for operational efficiency and access equity. *J. Transp. Geogr.* **2017**, *65*, 70–79. [CrossRef]
31. Farrell, M.J. The measurement of productive efficiency. *J. R. Stat. Soc. Ser. A* **1957**, *120*, 253–290. [CrossRef]
32. Boame, K.A.; Obeng, K. Sources of productivity change: A Malmquist total factor productivity approach. *Transp. Rev.* **2005**, *25*, 103–116. [CrossRef]
33. Koronakos, G. A taxonomy and review of the network data envelopment analysis literature. In *Machine Learning Paradigms. Learning and Analytics in Intelligent Systems*; Tsihrintzis, G., Virvou, M., Sakkopoulos, E., Jain, L., Eds.; Springer: Cham, Switzerland, 2019; Volume 1, pp. 255–311. [CrossRef]
34. Banker, R.D.; Charnes, A.; Cooper, W.W. Models for estimating technical and scale efficiencies in Data Envelopment Analysis. *Manag. Sci.* **1984**, *30*, 1078–1092. [CrossRef]
35. Tone, K. A slacks-based measure of efficiency in data envelopment analysis. *Eur. J. Oper. Res.* **2001**, *130*, 498–509. [CrossRef]
36. Cooper, W.W.; Seiford, L.M.; Tone, T. *Data Envelopment Analysis: A Comprehensive Text with Models, Applications, References and DEA-Solver Software*; Springer Science + Business Media, Inc.: New York, NY, USA, 2007.
37. Efron, B. *The Jackknife, the Bootstrap, and Other Resampling Plans*; Society for Industrial and Applied Mathematics Philadelphia: Philadelphia, PA, USA, 1982.
38. Efron, B.; Tibshirani, R.J. *An Introduction to the Bootstrap*; Chapman & Hall: New York, NY, USA, 1993.
39. Simar, L.; Wilson, P.W. Sensitivity analysis of efficiency scores: How to bootstrap in nonparametric frontier models. *Manag. Sci.* **1998**, *44*, 49–61. [CrossRef]
40. Ferrier, G.D.; Hirschberg, J.G. Bootstrapping confidence intervals for linear programming efficiency scores: With an illustration using Italian banking data. *J. Product. Anal.* **1997**, *8*, 19–33. [CrossRef]
41. Löthgren, M.; Tambour, M. Bootstrapping DEA-based efficiency measures and Malmquist productivity indices. A study of Swedish eye-care service provision. *Appl. Econ.* **1999**, *31*, 417–425.
42. Simar, L.; Wilson, P.W. Statistical inference in nonparametric frontier models: The state of the art. *J. Product. Anal.* **2000**, *13*, 49–78. [CrossRef]
43. Simar, L.; Wilson, P.W. A general methodology for bootstrapping in nonparametric frontier models. *J. Appl. Stat.* **2000**, *27*, 779–802. [CrossRef]
44. Hahn, J.-S.; Kho, S.-Y.; Choi, K.; Kim, D.-K. Sustainability evaluation of rapid routes for buses with a network DEA model. *Int. J. Sustain. Transp.* **2017**, *11*, 659–669. [CrossRef]
45. Polyzos, S.; Tsiotas, D. The contribution of transport infrastructures to the economic and regional development: A review of the conceptual framework. *Theor. Empir. Res. Urban Manag.* **2020**, *15*, 5–23.
46. Simar, L.; Wilson, P.W. Estimation and inference in two-stage, semi-parametric models of productive processes. *J. Econom.* **2007**, *136*, 31–64. [CrossRef]
47. Graham, D.J. Productivity and Efficiency in Urban Railways: Parametric and Non-Parametric Estimates. *Transp. Res. Part E: Logist. Transp. Rev.* **2008**, *44*, 84–99. [CrossRef]
48. Mostafa, M.M. Modeling the competitive market efficiency of Egyptian companies: A probabilistic neural network analysis. *Expert Syst. Appl.* **2009**, *36*, 8839–8848. [CrossRef]
49. Athens Live Bus Map. Available online: https://oasa.live/ (accessed on 9 March 2021).
50. Stathopoulos, A.; Tsekeris, T. The Athens dynamic traffic map for multimodal travel information services. *J. Maps* **2008**, *4*, 119–133. [CrossRef]

infrastructures

*Article*

# Evaluation of Microsimulation Models for Roadway Segments with Different Functional Classifications in Northern Iran

**Amir Masoud Rahimi [1], Maxim A. Dulebenets [2,*] and Arash Mazaheri [1]**

[1] Department of Civil Engineering, University of Zanjan, University Blvd., P.O. Box 313, Zanjan 45371-38791, Iran; amrahimi@znu.ac.ir (A.M.R.); arashmaz@gmail.com (A.M.)
[2] Department of Civil & Environmental Engineering, Florida A&M University-Florida State University, 2525 Pottsdamer Street, Building A, Suite A124, Tallahassee, FL 32310-6046, USA
* Correspondence: mdulebenets@eng.famu.fsu.edu; Tel.: +1-(850)-410-6621

**Abstract:** Industrialization, urban development, and population growth in the last decades caused a significant increase in congestion of transportation networks across the world. Increasing congestion of transportation networks and limitations of the traditional methods in analyzing and evaluating the congestion mitigation strategies led many transportation professionals to the use of traffic simulation techniques. Nowadays, traffic simulation is heavily used in a variety of applications, including the design of transportation facilities, traffic flow management, and intelligent transportation systems. The literature review, conducted as a part of this study, shows that many different traffic simulation packages with various features have been developed to date. The present study specifically focuses on a comprehensive comparative analysis of the advanced interactive microscopic simulator for urban and non-urban networks (AIMSUN) and SimTraffic microsimulation models, which have been widely used in the literature and practice. The evaluation of microsimulation models is performed for the four roadway sections with different functional classifications, which are located in the northern part of Iran. The SimTraffic and AIMSUN microsimulation models are compared in terms of the major transportation network performance indicators. The results from the conducted analysis indicate that AIMSUN returned smaller errors for the vehicle flow, travel speed, and total travel distance. On the other hand, SimTraffic provided more accurate values of the travel time. Both microsimulation models were able to effectively identify traffic bottlenecks. Findings from this study will be useful for the researchers and practitioners, who heavily rely on microsimulation models in transportation planning.

**Keywords:** transportation engineering; transportation planning; traffic simulation; microsimulation; SimTraffic; AIMSUN

**Citation:** Rahimi, A.M.; Dulebenets, M.A.; Mazaheri, A. Evaluation of Microsimulation Models for Roadway Segments with Different Functional Classifications in Northern Iran. *Infrastructures* **2021**, *6*, 46. https://doi.org/10.3390/infrastructures6030046

Academic Editor: Krzysztof Goniewicz

Received: 28 January 2021
Accepted: 10 March 2021
Published: 15 March 2021

**Publisher's Note:** MDPI stays neutral with regard to jurisdictional claims in published maps and institutional affiliations.



## 1. Introduction

Roadway density and traffic congestion substantially increased over the last years across the world, especially near large metropolitan areas, primarily due to rapid industrialization, fast population growth, urban development, and increasing demand for passenger and freight transport [1–4]. The congestion mitigation alternatives (e.g., adding another lane to a given roadway segment, adjust cycles of traffic signals, build an interchange, implement some of the access management approaches, and others) must be implemented in order to alleviate the increasing congestion issues and serve communities. Transportation planners must evaluate various congestion mitigation alternatives, and the most promising alternative should be recommended for implementation. Nowadays, transportation planners often tend to use traffic simulation software packages for comparison of various congestion mitigation alternatives. The increasing application of traffic simulation software packages is supported by numerous advancements in computer and software sciences.

A simulation analysis of traffic flow is based on specific indices and parameters that must be set within a given software package. The major traffic flow parameters within simulation models must be established based on the data collected as a result of field studies and surveys. Then, the transportation network performance indicators (e.g., travel time, travel speed, travel delay), produced by the traffic simulation model, can be compared to the actual values collected from the field. Based on a comparative analysis against the field data, the required modifications should be applied within the traffic simulation model to ensure that it will replicate realistic travel conditions, which are observed for a given transportation network, with an acceptable degree of error. Once parameters of the given traffic simulation model are calibrated, the model can be executed to estimate the values of transportation network performance indicators for different congestion mitigation alternatives. Upon completion of the simulation analysis, transportation planners will be able to determine the most promising congestion mitigation alternative (i.e., the alternative, which will yield the most favorable impact on the travel conditions). One of the major advantages of using traffic simulation consists in the fact that the traffic simulation models allow visualizing the study area, identification of the roadway sections that experience bottlenecks and require future improvements, and efficient scenario analysis (e.g., evaluation of different congestion mitigation alternatives) [5].

Traffic simulation models can be categorized into three types [5–9]: (1) macroscopic, (2) microscopic, and (3) mesoscopic. Some of the principles used within macroscopic simulation models are adopted from fluid dynamics. Simulation of the traffic flow is performed for a given roadway section of the transportation network without considering interactions among the roadway users. Macroscopic simulation models primarily rely on such parameters as traffic volume, average speed, and density. Transportation planners use macroscopic simulation models for the analysis of the level of service and demand, as well as evaluation of regional plans and comprehensive transport programs.

As for microscopic simulation models, they rely on the car-following theory and the concepts of lane-changing, gap-acceptance and route choice in order to simulate the traffic behavior of each vehicle in a given transportation network. The car-following parameters determine the acceleration of vehicles, their interaction with other roadway users. Lane-changing allows the vehicles to shift from one lane to another based on the driver's objectives and surrounding vehicles. The gap-acceptance parameters determine the synthetic links of vehicles to the traffic flow on the route. The route choice parameters determine the selection of specific routes of a given transportation network for each driver. Microscopic simulation produces more detailed outputs as compared to macroscopic simulation and, therefore, is generally applied for a comprehensive evaluation of a given transportation network. However, microscopic simulation models require more input parameters as opposed to macroscopic simulation models. Moreover, it is quite difficult to determine the accurate values of the microsimulation model parameters due to challenges associated with modeling the driver behavior along the roadways [5,6].

On the other hand, mesoscopic simulation models combine features of macroscopic and microscopic simulation models [8,9]. Mesoscopic simulation models allow a detailed emulation of the vehicle platoon dispersion (e.g., a platoon of vehicles is moving along a roadway segment, and the dispersion occurs due to the differences in vehicle speeds). Furthermore, mesoscopic simulation models allow emulation of the vehicle platoon behavior (e.g., a platoon of vehicles is moving along a roadway segment with similar speeds and a short headway). A detailed platoon modeling allows accurate computation of travel times of vehicles. The total number of vehicles in a platoon, vehicle speeds in a platoon, and distribution of speeds in a platoon are some of the major characteristics required for modeling vehicle platoons in mesoscopic simulation models.

The selection of the appropriate traffic simulation package is critical for roadway improvement projects. In particular, the appropriate traffic simulation model will allow accurate estimation of the major transportation network performance indicators before and after implementation of various roadway improvement projects (therefore, the efficiency of potential roadway improvement projects could be accurately assessed). Generally, microscopic simulation models (e.g., AIMSUN, VISSIM, CORSIM, CUBE, SimTraffic, and

PARAMICS) are used for the analysis of the major roadway segments, which have large traffic volumes and experience significant delays. Considering increasing congestion issues near large metropolitan areas of Iran [6], this study focuses on the application of microsimulation for the analysis of the transportation network located in the northern part of Iran. The AIMSUN and SimTraffic microsimulation models, which have been widely used for the analysis of the transportation networks in Iran [5,10,11], are compared in terms of the accuracy in estimating the major transportation network performance indicators, including travel time, travel speed, vehicle flow, fuel consumption, and total travel distance. The values of performance indicators, suggested by both microsimulation models, are compared to the actual field data. Findings from this research will be valuable for transportation planners and will assist with the selection of the appropriate microsimulation model for the analysis of the transportation networks in Iran.

The remaining sections of the manuscript are organized in the following order. The next section presents a review of the relevant literature with a focus on the implementation of various microsimulation models for the analysis of transportation networks. The third section presents some background information for the AIMSUN and SimTraffic microsimulation models. Furthermore, the third section describes the major transportation network performance indicators, which will be considered in this study and estimated using AIMSUN and SimTraffic. The fourth section discusses the adopted research methodology along with data collection and provides a detailed analysis of the collected data. The fifth section presents the description of numerical experiments, which were conducted to evaluate the AIMSUN and SimTraffic microsimulation models, while the last section summarizes the findings of this research and outlines potential future research extensions.

## 2. Literature Review

As mentioned in the introduction section of the manuscript, different traffic simulation models have been widely used for the evaluation of transportation networks. There are many advantages of using traffic simulation; however, there exist some drawbacks associated with traffic simulation as well. The highway capacity manual of the Transportation Research Board [12] provides a detailed discussion of the traffic simulation advantages and disadvantages. The advantages of using traffic simulation include the following [12]: (1) simulated methods are appropriate where analytical studies cannot be administered; (2) simulation models allow comprehensive understanding of the transportation network parameters and their relative interactions; (3) simulation models provide the outputs that can be used for the statistical analysis of the spatial and temporal data; (4) simulation models can be used to evaluate and compare the status of network options; (5) simulation models can be used to analyze modifications in the network efficiency; and (6) simulation models consider the distinctive demands of the network parameters.

The disadvantages of using traffic simulation include the following [12]: (1) simulation models are sophisticated and could provide simpler administrative procedures; (2) simulation models should be analyzed, calibrated, and validated; (3) any shortcoming in the implementation of the latter procedures can make the results unreliable and inefficient; and (4) some users apply simulation models without being aware of its limitations and modalities. This section of the manuscript focuses on a review of the relevant previously conducted studies, which applied traffic simulation models for the analysis of transportation networks, assessed their accuracy in estimating various transportation network performance indicators, and discussed the advantages and disadvantages of using traffic simulation. A more comprehensive review of the state-of-the-art on various traffic simulation models can be found in Pell et al. [7], Azlan and Rohani [8], and Gora et al. [9].

### 2.1. Detailed Review of the Collected Studies

Many previous research efforts have aimed to compare different microsimulation models. For example, Bloomberg and Dale [13] focused on the comparison of the VISSIM and CORSIM microsimulation models in terms of the network coding structure, car-following logic, gap acceptance model, and other attributes. The analysis results indicated that the differences among the considered microsimulation models were minimal, and the selection of the appropriate microsimulation model was primarily affected by the user needs and project requirements. Furthermore, it was found that CORSIM generally provided greater travel time as compared to VISSIM. Shaw and Nam [14] performed a comparative analysis of the VISSIM, PARAMICS, and CORSIM microsimulation models for the Southeast Wisconsin freeway system. The microsimulation models were compared based on the following aspects: (1) model capabilities; (2) ease of use; and (3) freeway system operational assessment application requirements. As a result of a detailed analysis, PARAMICS was found to be the most appropriate microsimulation model.

Tian et al. [15] studied the differences between the VISSIM, SimTraffic, and CORSIM microsimulation models. Based on the conducted numerical experiments, CORSIM produced the lowest variations in vehicle delays and throughput flow rates, while SimTraffic returned the highest variations. Moreover, it was noticed that higher variations were generally recorded for the scenarios where the capacity conditions were reached. Jones et al. [16] performed a comprehensive comparative analysis of the AIMSUN, SimTraffic, and CORSIM microsimulation models based on different criteria (i.e., software requirements, ease of network coding, data requirements, appropriateness of the default parameter values, etc.). SimTraffic was reported to have the most user-friendly interface, while CORSIM was more efficient for modeling complex transportation networks. Furthermore, the study recommended that the microsimulation model selection should be based on the user needs and project requirements/expectations. In some cases, the synthesis of microsimulation models might be encouraged.

Fang and Elefteriadou [17] assessed the performance of the CORSIM, VISSIM, and AIMSUN microsimulation models for two interchanges in Arizona. The following factors were identified to be the most critical ones in the selection of the appropriate microsimulation model: (1) capability of representation of certain geometric characteristics; (2) capability of emulating certain signal control plans; (3) calibration process and comparison against the field conditions; and (4) extraction of certain performance indicators. Xiao et al. [18] proposed a comprehensive approach for the identification of the appropriate microsimulation model using quantitative and qualitative criteria. The quantitative evaluation criteria included calibration testing, while the qualitative evaluation criteria consisted of functional capabilities, service quality, input/output features, and ease of use. A case study was conducted for the AIMSUN and VISSIM microsimulation models. It was found that preferences to use a specific microsimulation model were primarily determined by the type of user. Shariat and Babaie [19] compared the car-following models adopted within the VISSIM and AIMSUN microsimulation models. Although the Gipps car-following model (used in AIMSUN) was simpler and generally emulated the traffic flow faster, the Whiteman–Ritter car-following model (used in VISSIM) was found to be more logical and typically yielded more accurate results.

Shariat [5] focused on the calibration of the AIMSUN, VISSIM, and SimTraffic microsimulation models for the Tehran metropolitan area. It was found that AIMSUN was superior to VISSIM and SimTraffic in terms of knowledge management, user-friendliness, software cost, and current application by various organizations in Iran. Pourreza et al. [20] evaluated the performance of CORSIM, AIMSUN, INTEGRATION, PARAMICS, and VISSIM for the analysis of transportation networks. The following aspects were considered: (1) expected application of the model; (2) model capabilities; (3) previous software implementation; (4) software support; (5) software costs; and (6) user-friendliness, graphics, and interface. CORSIM was found to be the most advantageous microsimulation model based on the considered performance indicators. Da Rocha et al. [21] conducted a study aiming to assess the accuracy of traffic microsimulation models in estimating fuel consumption and emissions. The researchers examined the Gipps and Newell car-following models. It was found that the Gipps car-following model demonstrated higher accuracy in terms of the simulated vehicle trajectories. The analysis results showed that the selection of the non-optimal parameters substantially increased the variance of the model outputs.

Ibrahim and Far [22] undertook a simulation-based analysis to determine potential benefits from the implementation of pattern recognition in intelligent transportation systems. The AIMSUN microsimulation model was developed using real-life operational data. The numerical experiments demonstrated that AIMSUN was able to reduce the travel time by ~5–30%, while the congestion duration was decreased by ~8–41%. Praticò et al. [23] performed a study aiming to assess the accuracy in estimating vehicle travel speed on roundabouts. The VISSIM microsimulation model was used to emulate the traffic flow. The computational experiments showed that the proposed microsimulation model could provide accurate travel speed estimates if the microsimulation model parameters were carefully calibrated. Shaaban and Kim [24] focused on modeling two-lane and three-lane roundabouts in the VISSIM and SimTraffic environments. The microsimulation models were compared in terms of the estimated traffic delay values. It was found that, for the high-traffic flow scenarios, VISSIM provided higher delay values as compared to SimTraffic. However, no significant differences between the delay values were observed for the low-traffic flow scenarios.

Essa and Sayed [25] performed a comparative analysis of the PARAMICS and VISSIM microsimulation models. The numerical experiments showed that the default model parameters gave poor correlation with the field-measured data. Furthermore, it was found that both microsimulation models could not estimate traffic conflicts accurately without proper calibration. However, a good correlation between the field-measured conflicts and the simulated conflicts was achieved after calibration for both PARAMICS and VISSIM models. Astarita et al. [26] aimed to assess intersection safety by means of different traffic simulation models. The following types of intersections were considered: (1) a roundabout; (2) an intersection regulated with a traffic light; and (3) an unregulated intersection. AIMSUN, VISSIM, and different versions of Tritone were used for simulating the intersection traffic flows. The experiments showed some variations in the simulation outputs. However, the roundabout intersection generally had the largest number of conflicts. Kan et al. [27] studied freeway corridors that had dedicated lanes and periodically experienced congestion. Two driving behavior models were proposed and implemented in AIMSUN and MOTUS. The experiments demonstrated the high accuracy of the developed models and provided some insights into driver behavior on freeways.

Shaaban et al. [28] aimed to evaluate potential impacts from converting roundabouts into traffic signals at one of the urban arterial corridors in Qatar. A microscopic simulation approach based on VISSIM and MOVES (module for estimating emissions) was developed in the study. It was found that the replacement of roundabouts with traffic signals could reduce emissions by 37%−43%. Granà et al. [29] used AIMSUN to determine passenger car equivalent units for two-lane and turbo roundabouts. The results showed that the operational performance of roundabouts could be significantly affected by the percentage of heavy vehicles. Kim et al. [30] proposed a systematic guideline that could be used for calibrating reliable microscale estimates of vehicle emissions. The VISSIM environment was used to simulate the traffic flow. The proposed methodology demonstrated its effectiveness based on the available traffic data.

Song et al. [31] investigated the accuracy of TransModeler and VISSIM for the estimation of nontraffic performance indicators, including emissions, fuel consumption, and safety. The experiments showed that, even after calibration, both microsimulation models had significant errors when comparing to the actual values. Van Beinum et al. [32] examined the VISSIM and MOTUS traffic simulation models in their ability to emulate merging situations in high-traffic scenarios. It was found that the considered simulation packages were not able to accurately emulate turbulent traffic flows in terms of the headway distribution and lane-changing locations. However, the emulated gap acceptance distributions seemed to be appropriate.

A number of studies conducted a detailed review of different traffic simulation models. For example, Pell et al. [7] conducted a detailed analysis of 17 simulation packages, mostly focusing on the adaptability of simulation models to heterogeneous traffic and roadways networks. It was found that many software packages still have a significant number of drawbacks in modeling capabilities. Azlan and Rohani [8] provided a comprehensive overview of microscopic, mesoscopic, and macroscopic traffic simulation models. The models were overviewed in terms of their main purpose and the key parameters used. The study highlighted that the selection of the appropriate traffic simulation software is directly interrelated with the project needs. Gora et al. [9] studied the existing literature on the applications of microscopic traffic simulation for modeling connected and autonomous vehicles. A large variety of different traffic modeling approaches were discussed, including car-following models (e.g., Gipps model, Wiedemann model, Nagel–Schreckenberg model, intelligent driver model), lane-changing models, and software packages (e.g., VISSIM, SUMO).

### 2.2. Literature Summary and Contribution

A summary of the conducted literature review is presented in Table 1, including the following data: (a) author(s); (b) year; (c) software used; and (d) key findings and important notes. A review of the literature indicates that different microsimulation models have been widely used by researchers in the past. The selection of the appropriate microsimulation software package is generally dependent on a number of factors, which may include, but are not limited to [5,14,16,17,20]: (1) software capabilities; (2) ease of use; (3) user interface/graphics; (4) software cost; (5) hardware/software requirements; (6) capability of emulating certain operations features; (7) previous software implementation; (8) accuracy in estimating various transportation network performance indicators (e.g., travel speed, travel time, vehicle delay, vehicle flow, and others); (8) user needs; (9) objectives of the project; and others. This study extends the work conducted by Shariat [5] and Shariat and Babaie [19] and focuses on the selection of the appropriate microsimulation software package for modeling the traffic movements in the northern part of Iran. The AIMSUN and SimTraffic microsimulation models are evaluated for the roadway sections with different functional classifications in terms of various performance indicators, including travel time, travel speed, vehicle flow, fuel consumption, and total travel distance.

**Table 1.** Literature review summary.

| Author(s) | Year | Software Used | Key Findings and Important Notes |
|---|---|---|---|
| **Bloomberg and Dale** [13] | 2000 | CORSIM; VISSIM | The differences among the considered microsimulation models were minimal, and the selection of the appropriate microsimulation model was primarily affected by the user needs. |
| Shaw and Nam [14] | 2002 | CORSIM; PARAMICS; VISSIM | PARAMICS was found to be the most appropriate model for the Southeast Wisconsin freeway system based on the model capabilities, ease of use, and application requirements. |
| Tian et al. [15] | 2002 | CORSIM; SimTraffic; VISSIM | CORSIM produced the lowest variations in both vehicle delays and throughput flow rates, while SimTraffic returned the highest variations. |
| Jones et al. [16] | 2004 | AIMSUN; CORSIM; SimTraffic | SimTraffic was reported to have the most user-friendly graphical interface, while CORSIM was found to be more efficient for modeling complex transportation networks. |

**Table 1.** *Cont.*

| Author(s) | Year | Software Used | Key Findings and Important Notes |
|---|---|---|---|
| Fang and Elefteriadou [17] | 2005 | AIMSUN; CORSIM; VISSIM | Identified the most critical factors that should be considered in the selection of the appropriate microsimulation model. Familiarity with the facility was found to be one of the main factors that could improve the modeling accuracy. |
| Xiao et al. [18] | 2005 | AIMSUN; VISSIM | The models were evaluated based on the functional capabilities, service quality, and ease of use. Preferences to use a specific model were primarily determined by the type of user. |
| Shariat and Babaie [19] | 2006 | AIMSUN; VISSIM | The Whiteman–Ritter car-following model (used in VISSIM) was found to be more logical and typically yielded more accurate results. |
| Shariat [5] | 2011 | AIMSUN; SimTraffic; VISSIM | AIMSUN was superior to VISSIM and SimTraffic in terms of knowledge management, user-friendliness, software cost, and popularity among organizations. |
| Pourreza et al. [20] | 2011 | AIMSUN; CORSIM; INTEGRATION; PARAMICS; VISSIM | CORSIM was found to be the most advantageous microsimulation model based on the considered performance indicators (i.e., model capabilities, previous software implementation, software support, software costs, user-friendliness, graphics, and interface). |
| Da Rocha et al. [21] | 2015 | N/A | The Gipps and Newell car-following models were studied. The Gipps car-following model demonstrated higher accuracy in terms of the simulated vehicle trajectories. The selection of the non-optimal parameters substantially increased the variance of the model outputs. |
| Ibrahim and Far [22] | 2015 | AIMSUN | The numerical experiments demonstrated that the AIMSUN microsimulation model was able to reduce the travel time by ~5–30%, while the congestion duration was decreased by ~8–41%. |
| Praticò et al. [23] | 2015 | VISSIM | Aimed to estimate vehicle travel speeds on roundabouts. The accurate travel speed estimates could be provided when the model parameters were carefully calibrated. |
| Shaaban and Kim [24] | 2015 | SimTraffic; VISSIM | For the high traffic flow scenarios, VISSIM provided higher delay values as compared to SimTraffic. |
| Essa and Sayed [25] | 2016 | PARAMICS; VISSIM | Default model parameters gave poor correlation with the field-measured data. Both microsimulation models could not estimate conflicts accurately without proper calibration. |
| Astarita et al. [26] | 2019 | AIMSUN; Tritone; VISSIM | The experiments showed some variations in the simulation outputs. However, the roundabout intersection generally had the largest number of conflicts. |
| Kan et al. [27] | 2019 | AIMSUN; MOTUS | Studied freeway corridors that had dedicated lanes and experienced congestion. The experiments provided some insights into driver behavior on freeways. |

**Table 1.** *Cont.*

| Author(s) | Year | Software Used | Key Findings and Important Notes |
|---|---|---|---|
| Shaaban et al. [28] | 2019 | VISSIM | It was found that the replacement of roundabouts with traffic signals could reduce emissions by 37%–43% at one of the urban arterial corridors in Qatar. |
| Granà et al. [29] | 2020 | AIMSUN | The results showed that the operational performance of roundabouts could be significantly affected by the percentage of heavy vehicles. |
| Kim et al. [30] | 2020 | VISSIM | The study proposed a systematic guideline that could be used for calibrating reliable microscale estimates of vehicle emissions. |
| Song et al. [31] | 2020 | TransModeler; VISSIM | The experiments showed that, even after calibration, both microsimulation models had significant errors in some performance indicators when comparing to the actual values. |
| Van Beinum et al. [32] | 2020 | MOTUS; VISSIM | The considered models were not able to accurately emulate turbulent traffic flows in terms of the headway distribution and lane-changing locations. |
| Pell et al. [7] | 2017 | Survey study | Conducted a detailed analysis of 17 simulation packages. It was found that many software packages have a significant number of drawbacks in modeling capabilities. |
| Azlan and Rohani [8] | 2018 | Survey study | Provided a comprehensive overview of microscopic, mesoscopic, and macroscopic traffic simulation models. The study highlighted that the project needs mostly affect the final selection of the appropriate traffic simulation model. |
| Gora et al. [9] | 2020 | Survey study | Studied the existing literature on the applications of microscopic traffic simulation for modeling connected and autonomous vehicles. It was highlighted that new algorithms should be developed to better capture the travel behavior of vehicles. |

AIMSUN and SimTraffic have been widely used for the analysis of the transportation networks in Iran [5,10,11], and such a tendency can be explained by several reasons. First, both AIMSUN and SimTraffic are user-friendly in simulating traffic flow as compared to other microsimulation software packages (e.g., VISSIM). Second, AIMSUN and SimTraffic are quite popular microsimulation software packages and have been adopted by many consulting companies in Iran. Third, the cost of AIMSUN and SimTraffic is more affordable as compared to other microsimulation software packages (e.g., VISSIM). Fourth, the calibration process for AIMSUN and SimTraffic is less complicated when comparing to other microsimulation software packages. Last, but not least, AIMSUN and SimTraffic were found to be efficient in terms of replicating typical traffic conditions in Iran [5]. Findings from the present study are expected to provide more insights regarding the performance of AIMSUN and SimTraffic in terms of the modeling accuracy of the traffic movements in the northern part of Iran. These insights will be valuable for transportation planners and will assist with the selection of the appropriate microsimulation model for the analysis of the transportation networks in Iran.

## 3. Basic Background Information for AIMSUN and SimTraffic

This section of the manuscript focuses on the description of the background information for the AIMSUN and SimTraffic microsimulation models. Furthermore, this section of the manuscript provides a detailed description of how the key transportation network performance indicators are calculated within the AIMSUN and SimTraffic microsimulation models.

### 3.1. AIMSUN

The advanced interactive microscopic simulator for urban and non-urban networks (AIMSUN2), the AIMSUN's prototype, was developed by the members of the former Simulation and Operations Research Laboratory (LIOS), located at the Polytechnic University of Catalonia [33] in 1989. In 1997, the Transport Simulation Systems (TSS) company was founded. Technical developments continued at the Polytechnic University of Catalonia, while TSS was commercializing the AIMSUN microsimulation software package. AIMSUN includes two components that enable a dynamic simulation, including the microscopic simulator and the mesoscopic simulator. AIMSUN can be applied for modeling roadways of different classifications, including urban networks, highways, freeways, arterials, ring roads, and their combinations. Its comprehensive graphic environment allows modeling different levels of travel demand. Furthermore, AIMSUN allows efficient correspondence with monitoring and signal mechanisms. The AIMSUN microsimulation software package can be used to administer maintenance mechanisms of the transportation corridors, facilitate transport security, and evaluate intelligent transport systems, toll mechanisms, and pricing procedures.

The AIMSUN microscopic simulator is a combined discrete/continuous simulator, where for certain elements of the system (e.g., detectors, vehicles), states alter continuously over the given simulated time, which is separated into fairly short, fixed-time intervals that are called simulation steps or cycles. AIMSUN contains some other important elements (e.g., entrance points, traffic signals), for which states alter discretely at specific points over the given simulation time. AIMSUN has many modeling capabilities, including detailed modeling of the traffic network, different types of drivers and vehicles, a wide range of the network geometric layouts, traffic incidents, conflicting maneuvers, and others. Along with traffic lights and traffic detectors, AIMSUN allows emulating variable message signs (VMS) and ramp metering devices. In order to design a simulation scenario, AIMSUN requires certain input data, which can be categorized into four classes: (1) network description; (2) traffic control plans; (3) traffic demand data; and (4) public transport plans. Some of the input parameters are primarily related to the simulation scenario features (e.g., warm-up time, simulation time), while some parameters characterize the nature of the traffic flow and transportation network and must be calibrated (e.g., reaction times, lane-changing zones). The AIMSUN microsimulation software package allows producing a graphical representation of the transportation network in both 2D and 3D formats, statistical data output (journey times, flow, delays, speed, stops), and the data, which were gathered by the simulated detectors (occupancy, counts, speed).

AIMSUN relies on the car-following, lane-changing, and gap-acceptance models. The car-following model determines changes in the velocity of a given vehicle, depending on its position and the positions of the surrounding vehicles. AIMSUN relies on the Gipps car-following model, which is based on the physical probability of lane-changing patterns, location of permanent traffic barriers, express routes, the future driver turns, and the existence of heavy vehicles. The lane-changing model triggers the vehicle movement from one lane to another. Generally, lane changes occur due to alterations in the traffic flow, connecting the origin and the destination, and driver routes. The vehicle lane changes are classified into discretionary and urgent lane changes. The gap-acceptance model allows defining whether the available gap will be accepted by a given driver to maneuver.

### 3.2. *SimTraffic*

SimTraffic is a microsimulation module, which is available within the Synchro Studio software. The Synchro Studio was developed by Trafficware, Inc., which was acquired by Naztec in 2005 [34]. Along with SimTraffic, the Synchro Studio has another module (Synchro), which is primarily used for optimizing the timing schemes at signalized intersections and for traffic signal coordination. The Synchro Studio is widely used for different traffic projects and studies on public transport. Synchro optimizes the cycle length, offsets, split times, and phase sequences, aiming to minimize the driver stops and delay. SimTraffic utilizes the information regarding the optimized signal timing provided by Synchro in order to execute microsimulation and emulate the traffic flows. Although the Synchro Studio is heavily used for improving the efficiency of traffic signals, the availability of the SimTraffic module extends its application for the analysis of congested transportation networks. SimTraffic allows modeling individual vehicles traveling along the predefined transportation network. Different types of vehicles can be modeled using SimTraffic, including trucks, passenger cars, and busses.

Unlike a number of other microsimulation software packages, SimTraffic displays animation while the simulation is being executed. The input data, assigned within Synchro (e.g., traffic flows, intersection cycle length, network geometric characteristics), are transferred automatically in the SimTraffic module. The driver and vehicle parameters, including yellow reaction time, green reaction time, gap-acceptance factor, vehicle acceleration, vehicle length, vehicle width, and occupancy, are adopted based on the values that are recommended by the Federal Highway Administration (FHWA). The trip generation and the route assignment are determined based on the traffic flows, which are assigned to each roadway segment. The traffic flows can be adjusted using growth factors, peak hour factor (PHF), or percentile adjustments. SimTraffic assumes that each vehicle will travel at its cruise speed if there are no impediments (i.e., in case there are no obstacles on a given roadway segment, each vehicle will travel at its cruise speed). The cruise speed is estimated based on the assigned link speed and the speed factor, which is dependent on the driver type. The speed factors may range from 0.85 to 1.15 based on the driver type. Similar to the AIMSUN microsimulation software package, SimTraffic allows changing the driver characteristics within the simulation environment.

### 3.3. *Network Traffic Generation*

In AIMSUN, the user is able to select one of the following headway models for generating the network traffic [35]: (1) exponential; (2) uniform; (3) normal; (4) constant; (5) "ASAP"; and (6) external. The exponential headway model is the default, where vehicles are assumed to enter the network, following an exponentially distributed vehicle arrival pattern. As for the uniform headway model, the mean time headway values are sampled from the uniform distribution. The normal headway model generates the vehicles, entering the network based on the truncated normal distribution. The constant headway model assumes the time interval between two consecutive vehicles to be constant ($t = 1/\lambda$, where $t$—the headway (sec), and $\lambda$—the mean input flow (vehicles/sec)). The "ASAP" headway model allows the vehicle to enter the network "as soon as possible" (i.e., once the space becomes available). The ASAP model allows increasing utilization of the available transportation network space. The external headway model generates the entering network traffic using an external user-defined program.

In SimTraffic, the flows are generated at the network entry points based on the volume counts at the downstream intersection [36]. Trips can also be added to the midblock traffic if the midblock traffic is specified or a volume source is required to balance the traffic. If both balancing and midblock sources exist, the midblock traffic will be computed as the maximum of these two sources. The vehicle arrivals generally follow the Poisson distribution. The link flows are computed independently for heavy vehicles and passenger cars. The heavy vehicle volume is estimated as a product of the adjusted vehicle volume and the percentage of heavy vehicles, while the passenger car volume will be equal to the remaining vehicle volume. The user is able to assign two types of heavy vehicles, including: (a) trucks and (b) busses. The entering passenger cars can be assigned as standard passenger cars or carpool passenger cars.

### 3.4. Car-Following Models

AIMSUN relies on the car-following model, which is based on the Gipps experimental model [35]. The AIMSUN car-following model can be considered as an ad hoc model, where the model parameters are not set to be global and can be adjusted depending on the values of local parameters (e.g., type of driver, the geometry of the roadway section, the influence of vehicles on the adjacent lanes, etc.). The model is based on the two major components, including the following: (a) acceleration; and (b) deceleration. Acceleration represents an intention of a given vehicle to achieve a certain speed. On the other hand, deceleration occurs as a result of the following vehicle driving at a speed that is lower than the desired speed. Based on the AIMSUN car-following model, the maximum speed $V_a(n, t+T)$ to which vehicle $n$ is able to accelerate at the time $(t+T)$ can be calculated as follows [35]:

$$V_a(n,t+T) = V(n,t) + 2.5 \cdot a(n) \cdot T \cdot \left[1 - \frac{V(n,t)}{V^*(n)}\right] \cdot \sqrt{0.025 + \frac{V(n,t)}{V^*(n)}} \quad (1)$$

where:
$V(n,t)$—the speed of vehicle $n$ at time $t$ (m/sec);
$V^*(n)$—the desired speed of vehicle $n$ for a given roadway section (m/sec);
$a(n)$—the maximum acceleration of vehicle $n$ (m/sec$^2$);
$T$—the reaction time (sec).

The maximum speed $V_b(n,t+T)$ to which vehicle $n$ is able to accelerate at the time $(t+T)$, taking into account the vehicle characteristics and the limitations that are imposed by preceding vehicle $(n-1)$, can be computed using the following equation [35]:

$$V_b(n,t+T) = d(n) \cdot T + \sqrt{\begin{matrix} d(n)^2 \cdot T^2 - d(n) \cdot [2 \cdot \{x(n-1,t) - s(n-1) - x(n,t)\} \\ -V(n,t) \cdot T - \frac{V(n-1,t)^2}{\acute{d}(n-1)}] \end{matrix}} \quad (2)$$

where:
$d(n)$—the maximum deceleration desired by vehicle $n$ (m/sec$^2$);
$x(n,t)$—the position of vehicle $n$ at time $t$ (m);
$x(n-1,t)$—the position of the preceding vehicle $(n-1)$ at time $t$ (m);
$s(n-1)$—the effective length of the preceding vehicle $(n-1)$ (m);
$\acute{d}(n-1)$—the deceleration desired by the preceding vehicle $(n-1)$ (m/sec$^2$)

Based on Equations (1) and (2), the definitive speed of vehicle $n$ for a time interval $(t, t+T)$ can be calculated as follows [35]:

$$V(n,t+T) = min\{V_a(n,t+T), V_b(n,t+T)\} \quad (3)$$

SimTraffic relies on two car-following models: (a) fast following model and (b) slow following model. The fast following model is used for the cases when the leading vehicle speed is above 0.6 m/sec. On the other hand, the slow following model is applied for the slow-moving or stopped leading vehicle. The distance between vehicles or distance to the stopping point ($D$) can be calculated based on the following relationship [36]:

$$D = X^L - L^L - D^B - X^S \quad (4)$$

where:
$X^L$—the position of the lead vehicle or stopping point (m);

$L^L$—the length of the lead vehicle (m; 0 for stopping point);
$D^B$—the distance between (assumed to be 1.5 m);
$X^S$—the position of the subject vehicle (m).

In SimTraffic, the stopped vehicles will not start moving until the distance to the leading vehicle reaches 1.5 m. The latter creates a startup reaction time of approximately 1.0 sec per vehicle [36]. For example, the $10^{th}$ vehicle will not enter the network after approximately 10.0 sec the first vehicle entered the network. The following formula is used by SimTraffic to estimate the distance between vehicles, adjusted for the speed differential and reduced by the traveling vehicle's desired headway ($D^{Safe}$, m) [36]:

$$D^{Safe} = D + \frac{\min\left[\left(S^L\right)^2 - \left(S^S\right)^2; 0\right]}{2 \cdot a} - S^S \cdot H \tag{5}$$

where:

$S^L$—the speed of the leading vehicle (m/sec);
$S^S$—the speed of the subject vehicle (m/sec);
$a$—the vehicle deceleration (assumed to be 1.2 m/sec$^2$);
$H$—the desired headway (sec).

### 3.5. Travel Time Models

Travel time is one of the major performance indicators, which must be considered in the evaluation of transportation networks. The total vehicle travel time ($TT_{AIMSUN}$, sec) is calculated within AIMSUN based on the network entrance and exit times of all vehicles as follows [35]:

$$TT_{AIMSUN} = \sum_{i=1}^{N_{sys}} (TEX_i - TEN_i) \tag{6}$$

where:

$TEN_i$—the entrance time of vehicle $i$ in the network (sec);
$TEX_i$—the exit time of vehicle $i$ from the network (sec);
$N_{sys}$—the number of vehicles that cross the system during the considered time period (vehicles).

The total vehicle travel time ($TT_{SimTraffic}$, sec) on a given network segment is calculated within SimTraffic based on the total time spent by each vehicle on that segment and the total waiting time by each vehicle to enter that segment as follows [36]:

$$TT_{SimTraffic} = \sum_{i=1}^{N_{sys}} (t_i + w_i) \tag{7}$$

where:

$t_i$—the time spent by vehicle $i$ on a given network segment (sec);
$w_i$—the waiting time spent by vehicle $i$ to enter a given network segment (sec).

### 3.6. Average Speed Models

In AIMSUN, the average speed per vehicle ($S_{AIMSUN}$, m/sec) is computed based on the following relationship [35]:

$$S_{AIMSUN} = \frac{\sum_{i=1}^{N_{sys}} S_i}{N_{sys}} \tag{8}$$

where:

$S_i$—the average speed of vehicle $i$ (m/sec).

The average speed of vehicle $i$ is estimated as follows [35]:

$$S_i = \frac{D_i}{TEX_i - TEN_i} \quad (9)$$

where:

$D_i$—the total distance traveled by vehicle $i$ in the network (m).

In SimTraffic, the average speed per vehicle is computed by dividing the total distance by the total travel time [36]. The average speed is weighted by the vehicle flow and includes the stopped time and denied entry time.

### 3.7. Travel Distance Models

Both AIMSUN and SimTraffic estimate the total travel distance ($d^{tot}$, m) as a summation of the distances traveled by each vehicle in the network, based on the following formula:

$$d^{tot} = \sum_{i=1}^{N_{sys}} D_i \quad (10)$$

### 3.8. Fuel Consumption Estimation Models

AIMSUN estimates the fuel consumption of a vehicle based on the vehicle state (i.e., idling, cruising at a constant speed, deceleration, or acceleration). For the vehicles in a decelerating or idling state, the fuel consumption rate is assumed to be constant. The default fuel consumption rate is set to $F^{dec}_{AIMSUN} = 0.530$ mL/sec and $F^{idle}_{AIMSUN} = 0.330$ mL/sec for decelerating and idling states, respectively [35]. However, the aforementioned values can be modified by the user as needed. For the vehicles in an accelerating state, the fuel consumption rate ($F^{acc}_{AIMSUN}$, mL/sec) can be estimated as follows [35]:

$$F^{acc}_{AIMSUN} = c_1 + c_2 \cdot a \cdot V \quad (11)$$

where:

$c_1, c_2$—the model constants specified by the user;
$a$—the acceleration rate of a vehicle (m/sec$^2$);
$V$—the speed of a vehicle (m/sec).

For the vehicles traveling at a cruising speed, the fuel consumption rate ($F^{cru}_{AIMSUN}$, mL/sec) can be estimated as follows [35]:

$$F^{cru}_{AIMSUN} = k^a_1 \cdot \left[1 + \left(\frac{V}{2 \cdot V_m}\right)^3\right] + k^a_2 \cdot V \quad (12)$$

where:

$k^a_1, k^a_2$—the model constants empirically determined for the considered vehicles;
$V_m$—the speed of a vehicle at which the fuel consumption is minimal (m/sec);
$V$—the speed of a vehicle (m/sec).

SimTraffic, on the other hand, estimates the fuel consumption as follows [36]:

$$F_{SimTraffic} = k^s_1 \cdot TotT + k^s_2 \cdot TotD + k^s_3 \cdot Stops \quad (13)$$

where:

$F_{SimTraffic}$—the fuel consumption of a vehicle estimated in gallons (should be multiplied by 3.785 in order to convert to liters);
$k^s_1 = 0.075283 - 0.0015892 \cdot V + 0.000015066 \cdot V^2$;
$k^s_2 = 0.7329$;
$k^s_3 = 0.0000061411 \cdot V^2$;

*V*—the speed of a vehicle provided in mph (1 m/sec is 2.237 mph);
*TotT*—the travel distance provided in miles (1 mile has 1609.34 meters);
*TotD*—the total signal delay provided in hours;
*Stops*—the total number of vehicle stops per hour.

## 4. Research Methodology and Data Collection

In order to assess the performance of the considered microsimulation software packages, the field data were collected for the selected roadway sections located in the northern part of Iran. The available field data were refined, and the travel time-flow functions were calibrated using the SPSS statistical software for each one of the considered roadway sections. After processing the collected field data, the major transportation network performance indicators were estimated. Then, the considered roadway sections were modeled within the AIMSUN environment and the SimTraffic environment using the same geometric and physical characteristics. The network performance indicators, estimated using the microsimulation models, were compared to the ones, which were computed based on the collected field data. This section provides details on the field data collection and processing.

### *4.1. Roadway Sections Selected for the Field Survey*

The entire map of Rasht (one of the largest cities in the northern part of Iran and the capital city of Gilan province, located near the Caspian Sea, with a population of approximately 1.2 million, including students, workers, and other commuters [37]) was studied in order to select the roadway sections for further evaluation. A total of four roadway sections with different functional classifications were selected for a detailed analysis, including one major arterial roadway, two minor arterial roadways, and one collector-distributer (C–D) roadway. Note that the classification of roadway sections was adopted based on the Iran urban roadway design code [38]. In particular, the major arterial roadway is classified as a two-lane 2-way suburban roadway, generally passing through the small- and medium-sized cities. On the other hand, the minor arterial roadway is designed to facilitate mobility and accessibility of vehicles. The pedestrian traffic is controlled at intersections using the traffic control signals. The minor arterial roadways generally pass through the large-sized cities. Furthermore, the C-D roadways establish connections between the local and minor arterial streets. The C-D roadways typically have at least two lanes in each direction and an allowable travel speed of 40 km/h.

As stated earlier, a total of four roadway sections were selected for a detailed evaluation, including the following: (1) Beheshti Street; (2) Saadi Street; (3) Azadegan Street; and (4) Esteghamat Street. More information (i.e., classification and basic geometric characteristics) regarding the considered roadway sections is presented in Table 2. Furthermore, the satellite images of the selected roadway sections are presented in Figure 1. All the investigated roadway sections have 2 lanes in each direction. The lane width varies from 3.25 m (Azadegan Street) to 3.75 m (Saadi Street). Moreover, the surveyed section on the Beheshti Street was the longest (i.e., 1300 m), while the surveyed section on the Saadi Street was the shortest (i.e., 490 m). Note that none of the considered roadway sections had any junctions (i.e., the traffic flow along the considered roadway sections was not interrupted due to the presence of junctions).

**Table 2.** Geometric and physical characteristics of the selected roadway sections.

| Section Name | Section Type | Lanes in Each Direction | Lane Width (m) | Survey Length (m) |
|---|---|---|---|---|
| Beheshti | Major arterial | 2 | 3.50 | 1300 |
| Saadi | Minor arterial | 2 | 3.75 | 490 |
| Azadegan | Minor arterial | 2 | 3.25 | 546 |
| Esteghamat | C-D | 2 | 3.50 | 790 |

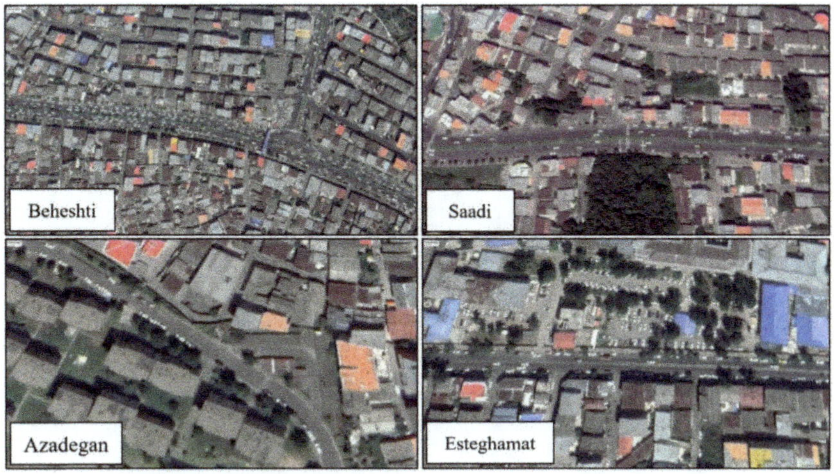


**Figure 1.** Satellite images of the selected roadway sections.

There exist different approaches for collecting the traffic data (e.g., counts, video recording). In this study, the field data were collected using the traffic counts. The total number of passing vehicles was recorded over 5-min time intervals for each one of the selected roadway sections. The data were collected from 8:00 am until 1:00 pm in five days during weekdays (from Saturday to Wednesday). Note that weekdays in Iran are from Saturday to Thursday. The Thursday data were not considered in the analysis, as the Thursday traffic flow patterns substantially differ from other weekdays for the considered study areas. Throughout the data collection, the weather was clear. Two vehicle plate registration stations were located at each one of the considered roadway sections (one station was located at the beginning of each roadway section, while the other station was located at the end of each roadway section). The following data were collected at the vehicle plate registration stations by the observers: (a) the vehicle entrance time; (b) the last three digits of the vehicle plate; and (c) vehicle type.

The data collected from the vehicle plate registration stations were stored on specific worksheets. Based on the vehicle entrance time at each vehicle plate registration station, the research team was able to determine the time when each vehicle entered and exited a given roadway section. The travel time along a given roadway section was estimated as a difference between the exit and entrance times for each vehicle. The last three digits of the vehicle plate were used as the vehicle's unique identifiers throughout this study. During the data collection, it was noticed that the travel time was relatively large for certain vehicles on some of the considered roadway sections. The latter can be explained by the fact that those vehicles could make stops along a given roadway section (e.g., to pick or drop-off passengers or cargo), which significantly increased the travel time. However, the number of vehicles with the abnormal travel time can be considered as insignificant as compared to the total number of vehicles, which were passing a given roadway section. In particular, over 17,000 records were collected for the considered roadway sections throughout this study, and less than 2% were eliminated from the analysis due to abnormal travel times.

Once the field data were collected, all registered vehicles were converted to the passenger car units (PCUs) using the standard PCU coefficients, which are presented in Table 3. Note that the adopted PCU coefficients have been widely used in the transportation planning of different networks in Iran [39–41]. Bikes and motorcycles are generally assumed to have the same PCU value (i.e., PCU = 0.3) since bikes are not very popular in Iran (i.e., installation of bike lanes is not desirable by the city authorities, as these bike lanes may occupy a substantial portion of urban streets). As for other types of vehicles, mid-size trucks and large-size trucks fall under the category "other types of vehicles". Mid-size trucks and large-size trucks may substantially impact the traffic flows during the day; however, their percentage was insignificant for the considered roadway sections.

**Table 3.** Adopted passenger car units (PCU) coefficients.

| Vehicle Types | Passenger Car | Taxi | Van | Pickup | Middle Bus | Urban Bus | Intercity Bus | Bike | Other Types of Vehicles |
|---|---|---|---|---|---|---|---|---|---|
| PCU coefficient | 1.0 | 1.5 | 1.0 | 2.0 | 2.5 | 5.0 | 3.0 | 0.3 | 3.0 |

### 4.2. Data Processing

Once the data collection was completed, the research team started the analysis of the worksheets, which contained the information gathered from the vehicle plate registration stations. The first step in processing the collected data was to identify the timestamps on the entry vehicle plate registration station and the exit vehicle plate registration station for each vehicle. The corresponding time stamps were retrieved using the vehicle plate information. The timestamp values were further used in estimating the total vehicle travel time for each one of the considered roadway sections. In the second step, the estimated travel time observations were analyzed, and the observations with abnormal travel time values were removed from the dataset (as discussed earlier, certain vehicles could make additional stops at a given roadway segment, which substantially increased the total travel time, as compared to the total travel time of the vehicles that did not make any stops). Elimination of the observations with abnormal travel time values was critical in order to ensure that the transportation network performance indicators would be calculated accurately. In the third step, the hourly vehicle flows were estimated for the time periods between 8:00 am and 1:00 pm. Note that the hourly vehicle flows were calculated using the PCU coefficients, which were applied to different types of vehicles. In the fourth step, the hourly travel time values were estimated for the time periods between 8:00 am and 1:00 pm in order to develop the functions, describing the relationship between the travel time and the hourly flow for each one of the considered roadway sections. The travel time and vehicle flow values were entered in the SPSS statistical software.

The SPSS statistical software was further used for the calibration of the travel time-flow functions for each roadway section. The Bureau of Public Roads (BPR) formula was adopted as a foundation throughout the analysis. The BPR formula can be expressed using the following relationship [42]:

$$t_i = t_i^0 \cdot \left[1 + 0.15 \cdot \left(\frac{v_i}{c_i}\right)^4\right] \; \forall i \in I \quad (14)$$

where:

$I$—the set of links in the transportation network;
$t_i$—the congested travel time on link $i$ (min);
$t_i^0$—the free-flow travel time on link $i$ (min);
$v_i$—the vehicle flow on link $i$ (vehicles/h);
$c_i$—the capacity of link $i$ (vehicle/h).

Based on the BPR formula, the congested travel time on a given link is defined based on the free-flow travel time on that link, the vehicle flow, and the link capacity. Increasing the flow of vehicles on a given link causes an increase in travel time. Once the link capacity is reached, the travel time will oscillate. The SPSS statistical software was used to estimate the free-flow travel time and capacity for each one of the considered roadway sections based on the collected data. The basic statistical information for the collected travel time data that were used for the development of BPR functions is presented in Table 4 (including the number of observations, minimum travel time, maximum travel time, average travel time, travel time standard deviation, and median travel time). Note that the collected number of observations used in developing the BPR function for each roadway section was found to be sufficient in order to obtain an acceptable degree of accuracy (i.e., the errors did not exceed $10^{-8}$ for the considered roadway sections).

**Table 4.** Statistical information for the collected travel time data.

| Statistic | Section Name | | | |
|---|---|---|---|---|
| | **Beheshti** | **Saadi** | **Azadegan** | **Esteghamat** |
| Number of observations | 1711 | 7773 | 5215 | 2348 |
| Minimum travel time (min/km) | 0.8002 | 0.9604 | 1.0003 | 1.3715 |
| Maximum travel time (min/km) | 2.4412 | 5.1720 | 4.2361 | 16.7479 |
| Average travel time (min/km) | 1.1901 | 1.9613 | 1.7693 | 5.0256 |
| Travel time standard deviation (min/km) | 0.5017 | 1.2875 | 0.9892 | 4.7005 |
| Median travel time (min/km) | 0.9502 | 1.3454 | 1.2961 | 2.7772 |

### 4.3. BPR Functions

Based on the results obtained from the SPSS statistical software, the following BPR functions were obtained for the Beheshti ($t^{beh}$), Saadi ($t^{saad}$), Azadegan ($t^{azad}$), and Esteghamat ($t^{est}$) roadway sections:

$$t^{beh} = 0.80 \cdot \left[1 + 0.15 \cdot \left(\frac{v}{260}\right)^4\right] \tag{15}$$

$$t^{saad} = 0.96 \cdot \left[1 + 0.15 \cdot \left(\frac{v}{215}\right)^4\right] \tag{16}$$

$$t^{azad} = 1.00 \cdot \left[1 + 0.15 \cdot \left(\frac{v}{232}\right)^4\right] \tag{17}$$

$$t^{est} = 1.37 \cdot \left[1 + 0.15 \cdot \left(\frac{v}{170}\right)^4\right] \tag{18}$$

The calibrated BPR functions are illustrated in Figure 2 for all the considered roadway sections. Since the length of the considered roadway sections is different, the absolute travel time values were converted into the relative travel time values (i.e., travel time per kilometer) in Table 4 and Figure 2, as this ratio would provide more insights into the travel conditions at the considered roadway sections. It can be observed that the travel time at the Esteghamat roadway section increases much faster with the increasing flow as compared to the other roadway sections.

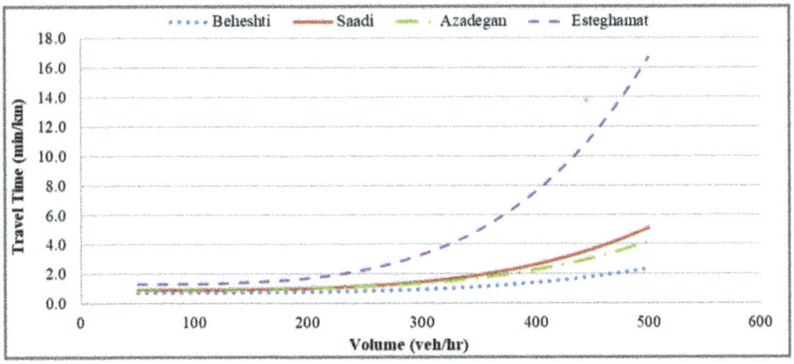


**Figure 2.** Calibrated Bureau of Public Roads (BPR) functions for the selected roadway sections.

### 4.4. Peak Hour Indicators

Based on the analysis of the collected data, the peak hour for the selected roadway sections was found to be 8 am—9 am. The average travel time for the peak hour was calculated based on the available travel time observations collected over the 8 am—9 am peak period. Furthermore, based on the roadway section length and the timestamps recorded at the vehicle plate registration stations, the average speed of vehicles was calculated for each direction of a given roadway section. Details regarding the peak hour indicators are presented in Table 5 for each one of the considered roadway sections, including the following: (1) section name; (2) section main direction; (3) vehicle flow in the main direction—$v^{main}$; (4) vehicle flow in the opposite direction—$v^{opp}$; (5) average travel time—$t^{ave}$; (6) average travel speed—$s^{ave}$; and (7) total distance traveled by all the vehicles—$d^{tot}$. Note that the main direction was determined based on the police reports and confirmed during the field survey that was conducted as a part of this study for each one of the considered roadway sections.

**Table 5.** The peak hour indicators for the selected roadway sections.

| Section Name | Direction | $v^{main}$ (veh) | $v^{opp}$ (veh) | $t^{ave}$ (min) | $s^{ave}$ (km/h) | $d^{tot}$ (km) |
|---|---|---|---|---|---|---|
| Beheshti | East to West | 2986 | 3764 | 1.8 | 43.32 | 8775.0 |
| Saadi | North to South | 2654 | 1789 | 1.9 | 15.42 | 2177.1 |
| Azadegan | East to West | 1677 | 1181 | 1.5 | 31.56 | 1560.5 |
| Esteghamat | East to West | 887 | 898 | 1.3 | 25.20 | 1410.2 |

The highest vehicle volume was recorded for the Beheshti roadway section, while the lowest vehicle flow was observed on the Esteghamat roadway section. The greatest travel time (≈1.9 min) was estimated for the Saadi roadway section, where the vehicles were traveling with an average travel speed of less than 20 km/h. On the other hand, the greatest average travel speed (≈43.32 km/h) was recorded for the Beheshti roadway section. In addition, based on the analysis of the collected data, the greatest vehicle travel distance was calculated for the Beheshti roadway section.

## 5. Numerical Experiments

Based on the existing physical and traffic characteristics, the selected roadway segments were simulated within the AIMSUN and SimTraffic environments. The major model parameters, such as vehicle specifications (e.g., length, width, maximum speed, acceleration, and others), driver behavior parameters (e.g., reaction time), lane-changing distance in ramp and weaving areas, and others, were calibrated for the travel conditions, observed in the northern part of Iran. The calibration of the major microsimulation model parameters (which are primarily used by the car-following models) was performed based on the field surveys, which were conducted by Shariat [5]. Specifically, Shariat [5] gathered the data for the representative roadway sections, passing through the Tehran metropolitan area. A number of professional Z series SONY cameras were installed along the roadway sections in order to collect the data. The speed and acceleration of passing vehicles were recorded with a time interval of less than 1.0 sec. Each one of the installed cameras could cover an area of up to 100 m in length. The videos created by each camera were overlapped. Then, the collected data were analyzed, and the required car-following model parameters were calculated. Although the study was conducted by Shariat [5] for the Tehran metropolitan area, the obtained results can be applied to this study due to similarities in the traffic flow patterns observed in the Tehran metropolitan area and the northern part of Iran (where the four roadway sections, selected for a detailed analysis in this study, are located).

Furthermore, some additional procedures were performed before adopting the calibration results from the previously conducted study. In particular, the validity of calibrated results (obtained for the Tehran metropolitan area) were verified using the field data that were collected for the considered roadway sections, located in the City of Rasht, based on the GEH formula, proposed by Geoffrey E. Havers [43]:

$$GEH = \sqrt{\frac{2 \cdot (v - \overline{v})^2}{v + \overline{v}}} \tag{19}$$

where:

$v$—the traffic volume obtained from the microsimulation model (vehicles);

$\overline{v}$—the actual traffic volume obtained from the field observations (vehicles).

As a result of the conducted analysis, it was found that the GEH values did not exceed 4.3 for the considered roadway sections, which shows a high accuracy level of the calibrated data for the car-following models that were adopted in this study. Additional field surveys were conducted in order to calibrate the physical and technical characteristics of a PCU in Iran [39–41]. More than 8800 vehicles of different types were analyzed in terms of the following parameters: (1) length; (2) width; (3) weight; (4) maximum speed (i.e., the maximum speed that a vehicle can achieve in a free flow traffic condition on a straight roadway section, assuming no speed limits and obstacles); and (5) maximum acceleration. The analysis results are summarized in Table 6. Based on the estimated PCU specifications and the report published by the Iran standard and quality inspection company [44], the PCU fuel consumption was set equal to 12.1 liters of fuel per 100 kilometers for the urban travel conditions. Using the data collected as a result of the field survey, the estimated driver reaction time comprised approximately 0.90 sec.

**Table 6.** Calibrated physical characteristics of a standard passenger car unit.

| Parameter | Length (mm) | Width (mm) | Weight (kg) | Maximum Speed (km/h) | Maximum Acceleration (m/sec$^2$) |
|---|---|---|---|---|---|
| Mean | 4141.8 | 1656.9 | 1044.6 | 164.5 | 1.93 |
| Minimum | 3838.0 | 1605.0 | 934.0 | 140.0 | 1.46 |
| Maximum | 4524.0 | 1755.0 | 1264.0 | 200.0 | 2.72 |
| Standard deviation | 280.7 | 47.0 | 104.1 | 21.5 | 0.41 |
| Coefficient of variation | 0.068 | 0.028 | 0.100 | 0.131 | 0.212 |

Certain microsimulation software packages (e.g., AIMSUN) require setting additional parameters for the lane-changing model. The latter set of parameters were estimated based on the available field observations and is presented in Table 7. In zone 1, the lane-changing decisions are primarily affected by the travel conditions on the lanes involved. The following factors are considered when assessing the improvement in driving conditions from changing lanes [35]: travel speed, desired speed, distance to the preceding vehicle, speed of the preceding vehicle, and others. The lane-changing model is typically implemented in zone 1 for overtaking maneuvers. As for zone 2, it is generally occupied by vehicles, which are not driving in the desirable lanes (i.e., the vehicles aim to move to alternative lanes in order to make turning maneuvers). Once the gap becomes acceptable, the vehicles within zone 2 will be moving closer to the desired lane. Note that the distances to zone 1 and zone 2 are given in seconds (Table 7) but can be converted to meters based on the vehicle travel speed. The on-ramp distance is used by the lane-changing model in the vicinity of ramps (e.g., certain vehicles will be switching lanes in order to get closer to the ramp).

**Table 7.** Calibrated lane-changing parameters.

| Lane-Changing Parameters | Mean Value (sec) |
|---|---|
| Distance to zone 1 | 13.74 |
| Distance to zone 2 | 4.40 |
| On-ramp distance | 7.10 |

The aforementioned calibrated parameters were assigned within both AIMSUN and SimTraffic microsimulation models in order to conduct the numerical experiments. The next sections of the manuscript elaborate on the evaluation of the considered microsimulation models for the selected roadway sections in terms of the major transportation network performance indicators.

### 5.1. Evaluation of the Microsimulation Models

Both AIMSUN and SimTraffic microsimulation models use statistical distributions in modeling the traffic flow, which causes differences in terms of the values of transportation network performance indicators from one replication to another. Therefore, multiple replications are required in order to obtain the average values of the performance indicators. A total of ten replications were used to calculate the average values of the performance indicators within the AIMSUN and SimTraffic microsimulation models in this study. Ten replications were found to be sufficient, as the coefficient of variation did not exceed 2.0% for the considered transportation network performance indicators (which will be presented in the following sections of the manuscript). Furthermore, the developed microsimulation models start each replication with an empty transportation network. In order to avoid significant variations in the performance indicators throughout the simulation run, a warm-up time of 15 min was assigned for both AIMSUN and SimTraffic. The peak hour volume was used in modeling the traffic flow for each one of the selected roadway sections. Based on the existing speed limits, the maximum allowable speed was set to 55 km/h for each roadway section.

### 5.2. Transportation Network Performance Indicators

The major transportation network performance indicators, estimated using the AIMSUN and SimTraffic microsimulation models, are presented in Tables 8 and 9. Tables 8 and 9 provide the following information: (1) section name; (2) input vehicle flow—$v$; (3) total travel time by all vehicles—$t^{tot}$; (4) average travel speed—$s^{ave}$; (5) average total travel time per vehicle—$t^{veh}$; (6) total fuel consumption by all the vehicles—$f^{tot}$; and (7) total distance traveled by all the vehicles—$d^{tot}$. The transportation network performance indicators, calculated using the AIMSUN and SimTraffic microsimulation models, were compared to the actual ones, which were calculated based on the collected field data. The actual input vehicle flow, average travel speed, average total travel time per vehicle, total fuel consumption by all the vehicles, and total distance traveled by all the vehicles, which were computed based on the collected field data, are presented in Table 10. Figure 3 presents the values of all the considered transportation network performance indicators obtained by different approaches (actual vs. AIMSUN vs. SimTraffic) for the selected roadway sections.

**Table 8.** AIMSUN performance indicators for the selected roadway sections.

| Section Name | $v$(veh) | $t^{tot}$(h) | $s^{ave}$(km/h) | $t^{veh}$(sec) | $f^{tot}$(liters) | $d^{tot}$(km) |
|---|---|---|---|---|---|---|
| Beheshti | 6745 | 183.7 | 48.02 | 98.03 | 321.6 | 8773.6 |
| Saadi | 4447 | 133.0 | 20.58 | 107.7 | 145.0 | 2729.2 |
| Azadegan | 2876 | 60.6 | 27.67 | 75.79 | 72.7 | 1603.3 |
| Esteghamat | 1789 | 40.5 | 32.62 | 81.55 | 53.2 | 1315.1 |

**Table 9.** SimTraffic performance indicators for the selected roadway sections.

| Section Name | $v$ (veh) | $t^{tot}$ (h) | $s^{ave}$ (km/h) | $t^{veh}$ (sec) | $f^{tot}$ (liters) | $d^{tot}$ (km) |
|---|---|---|---|---|---|---|
| Beheshti | 7129 | 220.0 | 43.00 | 111.09 | 836.9 | 9114.0 |
| Saadi | 4394 | 126.7 | 32.00 | 103.80 | 275.0 | 2701.5 |
| Azadegan | 2874 | 64.4 | 29.00 | 80.66 | 165.9 | 1763.0 |
| Esteghamat | 1791 | 47.8 | 32.00 | 96.08 | 131.7 | 1505.1 |

**Table 10.** Actual values of the performance indicators for the selected roadway sections.

| Section Name | $v$ (veh) | $s^{ave}$ (km/h) | $t^{veh}$ (sec) | $f^{tot}$ (liters) | $d^{tot}$ (km) |
|---|---|---|---|---|---|
| Beheshti | 6750 | 43.32 | 108.00 | 1061.8 | 8775.0 |
| Saadi | 4443 | 15.42 | 114.00 | 263.4 | 2177.1 |
| Azadegan | 2858 | 31.56 | 90.00 | 188.8 | 1560.5 |
| Esteghamat | 1785 | 25.20 | 78.00 | 170.6 | 1410.2 |

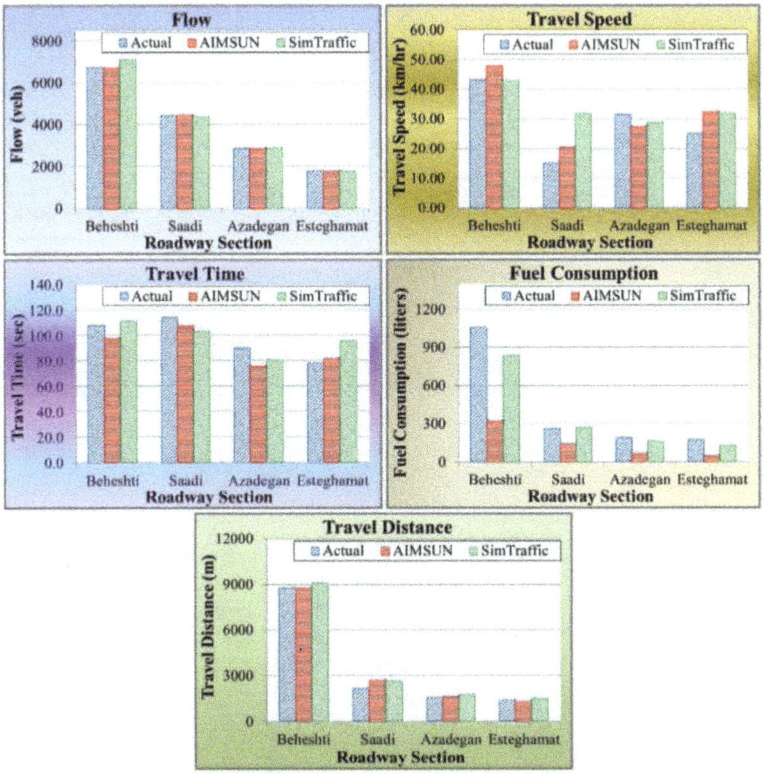


**Figure 3.** Transportation network performance indicators: actual vs. AIMSUN vs. SimTraffic.

The numerical experiments indicate that AIMSUN overestimated the vehicle flow on average by 0.13%, while SimTraffic overestimated the vehicle flow on average by 2.22% over the selected roadway sections. As for the average travel speed, both microsimulation models also overestimated the average travel speed as compared to the actual values, estimated based on the collected field data. Specifically, the average travel speed, suggested by the AIMSUN and SimTraffic microsimulation models, was greater on average by 11.59% and 17.75%, respectively, as compared to the actual average travel speed. It was found that AIMSUN underestimated the actual average total travel time per vehicle on average by 6.91%, while SimTraffic overestimated the average total travel time per vehicle on average by 0.42%.

As for the fuel consumption, both AIMSUN and SimTraffic microsimulation models underestimated the total fuel consumption by vehicles on average by 64.83% and 16.33%, respectively, as compared to the actual fuel consumption, calculated based on the Iran standard and quality inspection company guidelines (i.e., 12.1 liters of fuel per 100 kilometers). Such a significant difference in the fuel consumption, suggested by the microsimulation models, and the actual fuel consumption can be explained by the fact that both AIMSUN and SimTraffic deploy specific fuel consumption models, which are not just simply based on the total travel distance. Specifically, the AIMSUN fuel consumption model uses different equations for estimating the fuel consumption depending on the vehicle state (e.g., "idle" vs. "deceleration" vs. "traveling at the cruising speed" vs. "acceleration") and takes into consideration the vehicle speed, acceleration/deceleration rates, and different fuel consumption rates (which vary depending on the vehicle state) [35].

On the other hand, the SimTraffic fuel consumption model calculates the fuel consumption based on a nonlinear function, which includes the vehicle cruising speed, total travel distance, total delay caused by traffic signals, and total number of stops [36]. Therefore, based on the analysis results, it can be concluded that the current Iran standard and quality inspection company guidelines require some revisions in order to more accurately estimate fuel consumption. Other variables should be considered (e.g., vehicle state, vehicle speed, acceleration/deceleration rates, total delay caused by traffic signals, total number of stops)—not just the total travel distance. The numerical experiments also indicate that the total distance traveled by all the vehicles, suggested by the AIMSUN and SimTraffic microsimulation models, was greater on average by 3.58% and 8.34%, respectively, as compared to the actual total distance traveled by all the vehicles.

### 5.3. Discussion

The conducted numerical experiments provided some insights regarding the performance of the AIMSUN and SimTraffic microsimulation models for the selected roadway sections in the northern part of Iran. AIMSUN returned smaller errors for the vehicle flow, travel speed, and total travel distance, while SimTraffic provided more accurate values of the travel time. The errors of the microsimulation models in estimating various transportation network performance indicators can be justified by different issues that include, but are not limited to, the following: (1) capability of the adopted car-following models to replicate realistic traffic flow behavior; (2) capability of the adopted lane-changing models to replicate realistic lane-changing maneuvers; (3) network traffic generation accuracy; (4) errors that are associated with the calibration of BPR functions for the considered roadway sections; (5) errors that are associated with the calibration of physical and technical characteristics of a standard passenger car unit; and (6) errors that are associated with the field data collection and estimation of the actual values of the transportation network performance indicators. Addressing the aforementioned challenges is expected to improve the accuracy of both AIMSUN and SimTraffic microsimulation models.

The fuel consumption, suggested by both microsimulation models, was significantly different from the fuel consumption values, calculated based on the Iran standard and quality inspection company guidelines (where the fuel consumption is proportional to the total travel distance only). The latter finding can be justified by the fact that both AIMSUN and SimTraffic microsimulation models deploy more advanced fuel consumption models, which account not only for the travel distance but also for the other important factors (e.g., acceleration/deceleration rates, travel speed, vehicle state, number of stops, etc.). Despite the difference in terms of the computed fuel consumption values, both AIMSUN and SimTraffic microsimulation models were able to replicate the existing travel conditions on the considered roadway sections with a high degree of accuracy and identify bottlenecks for certain roadway sections. For example, both AIMSUN and SimTraffic were able to identify congestion on the Saadi roadway section, which is in line with the existing travel conditions (Figure 4). In particular, the AIMSUN and SimTraffic microsimulation models suggested the average travel speeds of 20.58 km/h and 32.00 km/h, respectively (Tables 8 and 9). Such values are significantly lower than the actual speed limit on the Saadi roadway section (55 km/h) and indicate moderate traffic congestion.

**Figure 4.** Congestion on the Saadi roadway section.

The entire section of the Saadi Street (i.e., 490-m roadway segment) experienced traffic congestion during peak hours primarily due to lack of capacity. The existing traffic demand in the area substantially exceeds the available capacity of the Saadi roadway section. Furthermore, throughout the field survey, it was noticed that many vehicles could make stops along the Saadi roadway section (e.g., to pick or drop-off passengers or cargo), which is another reason for the congestion and low travel speeds. Note that the travel speed estimation accuracy could be improved even further by enhancing the quality and quantity of the data that were used for the calibration of the AIMSUN and SimTraffic microsimulation models.

Despite the effectiveness of both microsimulation models in terms of the identification of bottlenecks, AIMSUN is recommended to be further used by transportation planners in northern Iran, as it outperformed SimTraffic in terms of the major transportation network performance indicators (i.e., vehicle flow, travel speed, and total travel distance).

## 6. Concluding Remarks and Future Research

The demand for passenger and freight transport has significantly increased over the last decades due to a number of reasons, including urban development, industrialization, and population growth. Some of the existing transportation networks are not able to serve the growing demand, which causes severe congestion. Different traffic simulation software packages have been widely used by transportation planners across the world, aiming to identify the appropriate congestion mitigation alternatives and eliminate recurring bottlenecks. Microsimulation models (e.g., VISSIM, CORSIM, PARAMICS, AIMSUN, and SimTraffic) have been commonly used for a detailed evaluation of transportation networks. A number of studies conducted in the past aimed to evaluate certain microsimulation packages. Most of those studies concluded that the selection of the appropriate microsimulation software package could be affected by the software capabilities, ease of use, user interface/graphics, accuracy in estimating various transportation network performance indicators, user needs, objectives of the project and other factors. Furthermore, the selection of the appropriate microsimulation model directly depends on the study area characteristics.

Taking into consideration the existing congestion issues in metropolitan areas of Iran, this study aimed to estimate the major transportation network performance indicators for the four roadway sections with different functional classifications located in the northern part of Iran. The AIMSUN and SimTraffic microsimulation models were developed for the selected roadway selections. The collected field data and the data from a previously conducted study for the Tehran metropolitan area were used for the calibration of microsimulation model parameters. The calibration of car-following models was performed using the previously conducted study for the Tehran metropolitan area, as it has similarities in the traffic flow patterns with the considered study areas. The AIMSUN and SimTraffic microsimulation models with calibrated parameters were used to estimate the major transportation network performance indicators, including travel time, travel speed, vehicle flow, fuel consumption, and total travel distance.

The numerical experiments indicated that AIMSUN returned smaller errors for the vehicle flow, travel speed, and total travel distance. On the other hand, SimTraffic provided more accurate values of the travel time. Significant variations were observed for the fuel consumption estimates, which could be explained by the fact that both microsimulation models had their own approaches for the calculation of fuel consumption. However, both AIMSUN and SimTraffic were able to accurately replicate the existing travel conditions and effectively identify congestion on the selected roadway sections. Despite the effectiveness of both microsimulation models in terms of the identification of bottlenecks, AIMSUN is recommended to be further used by transportation planners in northern Iran, as it outperformed SimTraffic in terms of the major transportation network performance indicators (i.e., vehicle flow, travel speed, and total travel distance). Moreover, findings from this study will be useful for the researchers and practitioners, who heavily rely on microsimulation models in transportation planning.

The scope of future research for this study may focus on the following extensions: (1) compare the AIMSUN and SimTraffic microsimulation models against other microsimulation models (e.g., VISSIM, CORSIM, and PARAMICS), which are widely used in transportation planning: (2) evaluate performance of the AIMSUN and SimTraffic microsimulation software packages for other congested roadway sections in Iran; (3) compare different congestion mitigation alternatives using the developed microsimulation models; (4) assess the effects from deployment of intelligent transportation systems for the considered roadway sections using the developed microsimulation models; (5) conduct an additional field survey and collect the data not only for the morning peak hour, but also for the evening peak hour (the developed microsimulation models could be evaluated using a larger data sample to improve the accuracy of results); (6) apply alternative methods for improving the transportation process (e.g., exact optimization, heuristic algorithms, and metaheuristic algorithms [45–47]); (7) compare vehicle trajectories proposed by AIMSUN and SimTraffic throughout the safety analysis (e.g., estimation of crash angles); and (8) collect additional field data to calibrate the parameters of car-following models for the considered roadway sections.

**Author Contributions:** The authors confirm contribution to the paper as follows: study conception and design: A.M.R., M.A.D., A.M.; data collection: A.M.R., A.M.; analysis and interpretation of results: A.M.R., M.A.D., A.M.; draft manuscript preparation: A.M.R., M.A.D., A.M. All authors have read and agreed to the published version of the manuscript.

**Funding:** This research received no external funding.

**Institutional Review Board Statement:** Not Applicable.

**Informed Consent Statement:** Not Applicable.

**Data Availability Statement:** The data that were used in this study can be requested by contacting the corresponding author.

**Conflicts of Interest:** The authors declare no conflict of interest.

## References


1. Markvica, K.; Hu, B.; Prandtstetter, M.; Ritzinger, U.; Zajicek, J.; Berkowitsch, C.; Hauger, G.; Pfoser, S.; Berger, T.; Eitler, S.; et al. On the development of a sustainable and fit-for-the-future transportation network. *Infrastructures* **2018**, *3*, 23.
2. Arena, F.; Pau, G.; Severino, A. An overview on the current status and future perspectives of smart cars. *Infrastructures* **2020**, *5*, 53.
3. Dulebenets, M.A. A comprehensive multi-objective optimization model for the vessel scheduling problem in liner shipping. *Int. J. Prod. Econ.* **2018**, *196*, 293–318.
4. De Carvalho, N.L.; Vieira, J.G.V.; da Fonseca, P.N.; Dulebenets, M.A. A multi-criteria structure for sustainable implementation of urban distribution centers in historical cities. *Sustainability* **2020**, *12*, 5538.
5. Shariat, A. *Calibration Of Traffic Engineering Software Based On Tehran's Traffic Condition*; A report prepared for the Tehran's municipality; Tehran, Iran, 2011.
6. Dulebenets, M.A.; Rahimi, A.M.; Mazaheri, A. Assessing the Effects of Indirect Left Turn on a Signalized Intersection Performance: A Case Study for the Tehran Metropolitan Area. *Open J. Appl. Sci.* **2017**, *7*, 617–634.
7. Pell, A.; Meingast, A.; Schauer, O. Trends in real-time traffic simulation. *Transp. Res. Procedia* **2017**, *25*, 1477–1484.
8. Azlan, N.N.N.; Rohani, M.M. Overview of application of traffic simulation model. In Proceedings of the MATEC Web of Conferences, Penang, Malaysia, 6–7 December 2017; EDP Sciences: Paris, France; Volume 150, p. 03006.
9. Gora, P.; Katrakazas, C.; Drabicki, A.; Islam, F.; Ostaszewski, P. Microscopic traffic simulation models for connected and automated vehicles (CAVs)—State-of-the-art. *Procedia Comput. Sci.* **2020**, *170*, 474–481.
10. Ahadi, M.R.; Salahi Moghadam, A.; Gholamin, P.; Nasrollahi, M. Modeling Vehicles Delay in WorkZone using Microscopic Simulation for Two-Lane Freeways. *J. Transp. Res.* **2017**, *14*, 1–8.
11. Rahimi, A.M.; Rahimi, F. Traffic Evaluation of SPUI and TUDI Interchanges Based on Traffic Conditions in Tehran with Aimsun and Synchro Software. *Iran. J. Sci. Technol.* **2019**, *44*, 1323–1334.
12. Transportation Research Board. *Highway Capacity Manual*, 5th ed.; National Academy of Sciences, Transportation Research Board; Washington, DC, USA, 2010.
13. Bloomberg, L.; Dale, J. Comparison of VISSIM and CORSIM simulation models on a congested network. *Transp. Res. Rec.* **2000**, *1727*, 52–60.
14. Shaw, J.W.; Nam, D.H. Microsimulation, freeway system operational assessment, and project selection in southeastern Wisconsin: Expanding the vision. In Proceedings of the 81st Annual Meeting of the Transportation Research Board, Washington, DC, USA, 13–17 January 2002.
15. Tian, Z.; Urbanik, T.; Engelbrecht, R.; Balke, K. Variations in capacity and delay estimates from microscopic traffic simulation models. *Transp. Res. Rec.* **2002**, *1802*, 23–31.
16. Jones, S.L.; Sullivan, A.J.; Cheekoti, N.; Anderson, M.D.; Malave, D. *Traffic Simulation Software Comparison Study*; A Report Prepared by the University Transportation Center of Alabama; Huntsville, AL, USA, 2004.
17. Fang, F.C.; Elefteriadou, L. Some guidelines for selecting microsimulation models for interchange traffic operational analysis. *J. Transp. Eng.* **2005**, *131*, 535–543.
18. Xiao, H.; Ambadipudi, R.; Hourdakis, J.; Michalopoulos, P. *Methodology for Selecting Microscopic Simulators: Comparative Evaluation of AIMSUN and VISSIM*; Report no. CTS 05-05; University of Minnesota: Minneapolis, MN, USA, 2005.
19. Shariat, A.; Babaie, M. An evaluation of car following models in microsimulations. In Proceedings of the 7th International Civil Engineering Congress, Tehran, Iran, 8–10 May 2006.
20. Pourreza, M.; Mirza Broujerdian, A.; Dindar, M. An evaluation of transport simulation models and choosing best microsimulation for traffic study. In Proceedings of the 9th International Conference on Traffic and Transportation Engineering, Tehran, Iran, 25 February 2011.
21. Da Rocha, T.V.; Leclercq, L.; Montanino, M.; Parzani, C.; Punzo, V.; Ciuffo, B.; Villegas, D. Does traffic-related calibration of car-following models provide accurate estimations of vehicle emissions? *Transp. Res. Part D Transp. Environ.* **2015**, *34*, 267–280.
22. Ibrahim, H.; Far, B.H. Simulation-based benefit analysis of pattern recognition application in intelligent transportation systems. In Proceedings of the IEEE 28th Canadian Conference on Electrical and Computer Engineering (CCECE), Halifax, NS, Canada, 3–6 May 2015.
23. Praticò, F.G.; Vaiana, R.; Gallelli, V. Micro-simulation effectiveness in predicting operating speed profiles in a roundabout. *Adv. Transp. Stud.* **2015**, *37*, 5–14.
24. Shaaban, K.; Kim, I. Comparison of SimTraffic and VISSIM microscopic traffic simulation tools in modeling roundabouts. *Procedia Comput. Sci.* **2015**, *52*, 43–50.
25. Essa, M.; Sayed, T. A comparison between PARAMICS and VISSIM in estimating automated field-measured traffic conflicts at signalized intersections. *J. Adv. Transp.* **2016**, *50*, 897–917.
26. Astarita, V.; Festa, D.C.; Giofrè, V.P.; Guido, G. Surrogate safety measures from traffic simulation models a comparison of different models for intersection safety evaluation. *Transp. Res. Procedia* **2019**, *37*, 219–226.
27. Kan, X.D.; Xiao, L.; Liu, H.; Wang, M.; Schakel, W.J.; Lu, X.Y.; van Arem, B.; Shladover, S.E.; Ferlis, R.A. Cross-comparison and calibration of two microscopic traffic simulation models for complex freeway corridors with dedicated lanes. *J. Adv. Transp.* **2019**, 1–15.
28. Shaaban, K.; Abou-Senna, H.; Elnashar, D.; Radwan, E. Assessing the impact of converting roundabouts to traffic signals on vehicle emissions along an urban arterial corridor in Qatar. *J. Air Waste Manag. Assoc.* **2019**, *69*, 178–191.

29. Granà, A.; Giuffrè, T.; Macioszek, E.; Acuto, F. Estimation of Passenger Car Equivalents for two-lane and turbo roundabouts using AIMSUN. *Front. Built Environ.* **2020**, *6*, 86.
30. Kim, J.; Kim, J.H.; Lee, G.; Shin, H.J.; Park, J.H. Microscopic traffic simulation calibration level for reliable estimation of vehicle emissions. *J. Adv. Transp.* **2020**, 1–13.
31. Song, Z.; Wang, H.; Sun, J.; Tian, Y. Experimental findings with VISSIM and TransModeler for evaluating environmental and safety impacts using micro-simulations. *Transp. Res. Rec.* **2020**, *2674*, 566–580.
32. Van Beinum, A.; Broekman, E.; Farah, H.; Schakel, W.; Wegman, F.; Hoogendoorn, S. Critical assessment of microscopic simulation models for simulating turbulence around motorway ramps. *J. Transp. Eng. Part A Syst.* **2020**, *146*, 04019066.
33. TSS-Transport Simulation Systems. Aimsun. Available online: https://www.aimsun.com (accessed on 15 January 2020).
34. Trafficware. Synchro Studio 8.0—Planning & Analysis Software. Available online: http://www.trafficware.com/synchro-studio.html (accessed on 15 January 2020).
35. AIMSUN. *Aimsun 8 Dynamic Simulators Users' Manual*; AIMSUN: Barcelona, Spain, 2014.
36. *Synchro Studio 8.0User Guide*; Trafficware: Sugar Land, TX, USA, 2017.
37. Mahyar, F. Analysis of the Bus Network of Rasht (Iran) and Description of Some Proposals to Improve the Service. Master's Thesis, Politecnico di Torino, Turin, Italy, 2019.
38. Islamic Republic of Iran. Vice Presidency for Strategic Planning and Supervision. In *Highway Geometric Design Code*; No. 415, Office of Deputy for Strategic Supervision, Department of Technical Affairs; Tehran, Iran, 2012.
39. Mazaheri, A. Determination of Appropriate Location of U-Turn at Urban Signalized Intersection. Master's Thesis, Islamic Azad University, Zanjan, Iran, 2014.
40. Mazaheri, A.; Rahimi, A.M. Determining a suitable position for U-turns near signal-controlled road junctions. *Proc. Inst. Civ. Eng. Transp.* **2017**, *170*, 1–9. [CrossRef]
41. Mazaheri, A.; Akbarzadeh, A.; Rahimi, A.M.; Akbarzadeh, M. Estimation of critical gap of U-turns at uncontrolled median openings considering Iran's driver behavior. *Transp. Lett.* **2020**, 1–13. [CrossRef]
42. Ortúzar, J.; Willumsen, L. *Modelling Transport*, 4th ed.; Wiley: Hoboken, NJ, USA, 2011.
43. Chitturi, M.V.; Shaw, J.W.; Campbell IV, J.R.; Noyce, D.A. Validation of origin–destination data from bluetooth reidentification and aerial observation. *Transp. Res. Rec.* **2014**, *2430*, 116–123.
44. Mahdinejad, M.; Jafari, H.; Nourani, M. *Iran's Vehicle Fuel Consumption Guide*; A Report Prepared by the Iranian Fuel Conservation Company; Tehran, Iran, 2016.
45. Pasha, J.; Dulebenets, M.A.; Kavoosi, M.; Abioye, O.F.; Theophilus, O.; Wang, H.; Kampmann, R.; Guo, W. Holistic tactical-level planning in liner shipping: An exact optimization approach. *J. Ship. Trade* **2020**, *5*, 1–35.
46. Dulebenets, M.A. A Delayed Start Parallel Evolutionary Algorithm for just-in-time truck scheduling at a cross-docking facility. *Int. J. Prod. Econ.* **2019**, *212*, 236–258.
47. Kavoosi, M.; Dulebenets, M.A.; Abioye, O.; Pasha, J.; Theophilus, O.; Wang, H.; Kampmann, R.; Mikijeljević, M. Berth scheduling at marine container terminals: A universal island-based metaheuristic approach. *Mar. Bus. Rev.* **2020**, *5*, 30–66.

*infrastructures*

*Article*

# On BRT Spread around the World: Analysis of Some Particular Cities

**Salvatore Trubia [1], Alessandro Severino [2,*], Salvatore Curto [1], Fabio Arena [1] and Giovanni Pau [1]**

1 Faculty of Engineering and Architecture, Kore University of Enna, 94100 Enna, Italy; salvatore.trubia@unikore.it (S.T.); ing.salvatorecurto@gmail.com (S.C.); fabio.arena@unikore.it (F.A.); giovanni.pau@unikore.it (G.P.)

2 Department of Civil Engineering and Architecture, University of Catania, 95123 Catania, Italy

* Correspondence: alessandro.severino@unict.it

Received: 31 August 2020; Accepted: 22 September 2020; Published: 20 October 2020

**Abstract:** The goal of civil engineering has always been the research and implementation of methods, technologies, and infrastructures to improve the community's quality of life. One of the branches of civil engineering that has the strongest effect on progress is transport. The quality of transport has a profound economic and social impact on our communities regarding trade (freight transport) and city livability (public transport systems). However, innovation is not the only way to improve the features above-mentioned, especially public transport, considering that it is usually beneficial to enhance and repurpose vehicles with appropriate adjustments to offer more efficient services. Other perspectives that influence public transport systems are the costs and times of design and construction, maintenance, operating costs, and environmental impact, especially concerning $CO_2$ emissions. Considering these issues, among the various types of existing public transport systems, those of the so-called Bus Rapid Transit (BRT) offer worthwhile results. The BRT system is a type of public road transport operated by bus on reserved lanes, and it is significantly profitable, especially from an economic point of view, in areas where there are existing bus routes. Nonetheless, for the construction of works minimization, it is closely linked to other features that improve its usefulness, depending on the vehicles' quality such as capacity, but above all, the propulsion or driving autonomy that would guarantee high efficiency. This paper introduces an analysis of some BRT systems operating worldwide, presenting the background, general technical features, and the correlation with autonomous vehicles.

**Keywords:** BRT; mass transit; autonomous vehicles; public transport; smart city

## 1. Introduction

The implementation of a public transport system in a city is not a usual event. This is why, before construction begins, every component and feature has to be designed to ensure its efficiency for long periods. For these reasons, both for existing mass transit systems and new ones, the perspective of maintenance and retraining appears fundamental. It is worth considering that with existing buses and a few infrastructure adjustments, like what Bus Rapid Transit (BRT) requires, an efficient service would be guaranteed, and offers a convenient solution for city administrations. The BRT public transport system was introduced in 1974 in Curitiba (Brazil). The reasons that led the administrators and technicians to make this choice were economic—reduced funds to construct a rail system—and social—because of the population increase in the city—requiring a public transport system with high capacity vehicles. After Curitiba, BRT spread worldwide, especially in Bogotà, with the implementation of "TransMilenio" in the 1990s. Such a system still represents a model for all public transport arrangements, and mostly it also showed how BRT is efficient for complex urban layouts. Before 1990, BRT operated only in eighteen cities, while, nowadays, it is active in 173 cities and serves 34,026,459 daily passengers [1] (Table 1).

**Table 1.** Global Bus Rapid Transit (BRT) data.

| Regions | Passengers per Day | Number of Cities | Length (km) |
|---|---|---|---|
| Africa | 491,578 (1.44%) | 5 (2.89%) | 131 (2.52%) |
| Asia | 9,471,593 (27.83%) | 44 (25.43%) | 1625 (31.26%) |
| Europe | 1,613,580 (4.74%) | 44 (25.43%) | 875 (16.84%) |
| Latin America | 21,032,465 (61.81%) | 55 (31.79%) | 1829 (35.19%) |
| Northern America | 981,043 (2.88%) | 20 (11.56%) | 627 (12.06%) |
| Oceania | 436,200 (1.28%) | 5 (2.89%) | 109 (2.09%) |

The benefits of a typical BRT system consist of dedicated lanes and proper vehicles and stations. Such a layout guarantees a significant advantage in terms of intermodality and interoperability. If such features are accessible to other specific vehicles, like emergency ones, then, due to reserved lanes, the congestion phenomena could be avoided for the public transport system and ordinary traffic, for instance, when users attracted by the efficiency of BRT give up using their private vehicles. Commonly BRT is considered an upgrade of existing bus mass transit systems that emulate rail systems but with reduced costs and construction times. For example, the construction costs for a single kilometer of BRT are only 52% of the costs of a light rail system and 8% of those of massive rail system construction [2]. A strategy that is commonly used to appeal to citizens consists in building stations or creating reserved lanes in places where there are parking areas for private vehicles. In this way, private vehicle users are more likely to find themselves caught up in congestion and less likely to find a parking place, thereby encouraging people to prefer the use of public transport systems. Some comparative data between BRT systems and more traditional transport systems are shown in Table 2.

**Table 2.** Comparison of the public transport systems parameters.

| Type of Transit Mode | Capital Costs (Million US$/km) | Capacity (pphpd) | Operating Speed (km/h) |
|---|---|---|---|
| Standard bus | - | 3180–6373 | 10–30 |
| BRT | Up to 15 | Up to 55,710 | 18–40+ |
| LRT | 13–40 | Up to 30,760 | 18–40 |
| Heavy rail system | 40–350 | 52,500–89,950 | 20–60 |

Generally, when a new mass transit system has been implemented, the area where it is located must be subjected to requalification works, producing a relevant cost increase. Such a case appears conveniently when the local administration decides to create so-called transit-oriented development (TOD) areas to maximize public transport use. These places are characterized by people living near transit hubs, so there would be the need to invest in activities close to these areas [3], making an essential requalification with significant consequences in terms of property value increase.

The main aim of this paper was to review some of the BRT systems operating worldwide. The following subsections will present the background, general technical features, and the correlation with autonomous vehicles. This last section represents a viable distinguishing trait of the review carried out in this paper. The discussion examines the perspectives concerning autonomous vehicles and how they can enhance and influence mass transit and, mainly, BRT systems, in a positive way, creating meaningful profits for communities.

## 2. General Technical Aspects

To achieve the high efficiency of a BRT system, regardless of new construction or existing mass transit upgrades, several aspects must be taken into account to minimize future interventions. As for any other infrastructure, the design phase represents the central part of the implementation of a public transport system. This is why, before drawing the physical elements of a BRT system, it is necessary to carry out in-depth studies about city urban assets, a demand analysis of potential users, the identification of critical points, analysis of existing mass transit systems, and corridor selection [4,5]. Once the design phase has been concluded, it is possible to begin building and installing the following main elements that characterize a BRT system:

- Running lanes;
- Vehicles;
- Stations;
- ITS, passenger information, and control systems.

Running lanes represent the main characteristic of BRT systems, for economic reasons. Their construction generally amounts to 50% of infrastructure costs; concerning their asset and dimensions that strongly affect the efficiency of the BRT service, usually the standard width of a BRT runway is 3.5 m, as shown in Figure 1. However, this width is reduced to 3 m to guarantee a lower speed, decreasing accident risks for safety reasons. Regarding the lane's position in a road section, it is preferable to locate them at the edges. In this way, passengers do not need to cross the street to reach the station. This is why lanes are often located in the middle of the road section only when that part of the itinerary is without stops. The construction of barriers at the edges of the lanes is a solution that guarantees only public service vehicles. However, the absence of barriers proves useful when, in the case of accidents or dangerous situations, other vehicles need a recovery place, or to facilitate access to ambulances that need to avoid congested areas. Nevertheless, in that case, the lane must maintain a correct width that allows the presence of more than one vehicle.

**Figure 1.** General Bus Rapid Transit (BRT) corridor section, u.m. = meters.

For these reasons, running lane dimensions are strongly affected by vehicle characteristics that mainly depend on two parameters: size and propulsion. The first is related to driver labor costs per passenger, user comfort, service capacity, and frequency. In contrast, the second has consequences concerning emissions and environmental impact. In lower-demand corridors, it is suggested that large buses are avoided to reduce waiting times for users. It has been noted that typical BRT efficiency is attributed to vehicles, but the operation quality is significantly affected by stations. Such infrastructures may be configurated in several different ways according to their role. Generally, it is possible to distinguish open stations (preferred for stops) or closed stations, and their size depends on lines and user quantity. Stations are positioned in relation to the adjacent urban layout, but the system is optimized if they are close to pedestrian areas due to safety reasons. The processing speed does not depend only on vehicles, stations, or runways, because it is the exchange of information that guarantees a correct and timely operation. Such characteristics relate mainly to two contexts: user information and operators and systems information. The first is fundamental to allow passengers to choose between the BRT system's services concerning their needs. The second one affects the operation of the entire system, so it essential to communicate accidents, vehicles, and route data. The public transport system is equipped with high efficiency IT and electronic telecommunication devices, the so-called intelligent transport systems (ITS), to ensure such capabilities. These devices allow real-time traffic data and communication network control. With regard to technological characteristics, there are several types of traffic light systems, satellite navigators, or speed detectors; moreover, thanks to recent innovations, sensor device systems have been implemented that can be installed both in vehicles and in infrastructure (stations, lanes). Nonetheless, the accuracy and precision of all the decisions in the design phase and concerning the aspects above-mentioned can be complicated to avoid delays at 100%, which for users represent the most significant inconvenience. Such events occur for several reasons, and not always attributable to public transport systems. These depend on variable parameters that are impossible to predict. The case of a BRT system that bases its efficiency on reserved lane intersections represents the most critical point. For safety reasons, BRT vehicles are constrained to operate maneuvers (valid also for non-public transport vehicles) of deceleration, braking, and acceleration, respectively, before, in correspondence, and after the intersection. The aggregation times for such maneuvers create the delay, as shown in Figure 2.

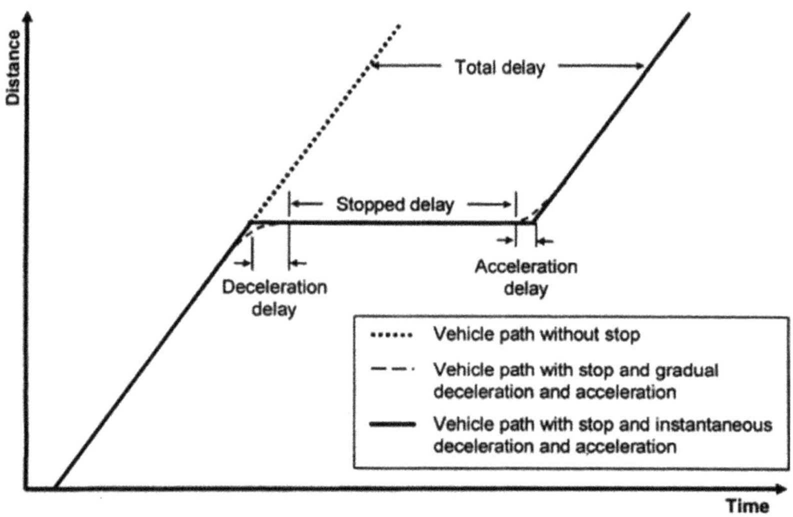


**Figure 2.** Vehicle delay at intersection.

Strategies to manage and maximize such discomfort are various, so the prioritization of BRT vehicles at intersections can be managed passively, with the absence of signal priority and operating according to a pre-defined schedule. Consequently, it is possible to achieve a vehicle detection strategy both in an active and adaptive way with the aim to detect in real-time BRT and traffic vehicles. However, it is commonly preferred to use transit signal priority due to its efficiency. With recent innovations, many other solutions have been studied. One of them consists of implementing an algorithm named TSPAT (Transit Signal Priority for Actuated Timing), which was tested on a real scenario (intersection in Isfahan, Iran) with Verkehr In Städten-SIMulationsmodell (VISSIM) traffic simulation. Such study objects were the "Freiburg intersection" in Isfahan, where there is a BRT station, and in the street, where it is wider, there are two BRT runways positioned at the edges that carry buses in opposite directions. The results of the algorithm above-mentioned showed a more positive trend regarding off-peak hours. For off-peak hours in both for BRT system operation and environmental-economic impact, outputs were all positive. In these cases, delays were reduced by 51% with a reduction in air pollutants and fuel consumption, respectively, by 6.9% and 6.5%, and average speed increased by 78%. In contrast, peak hours of positive outcomes saw a 21% reduction in delays, the average speed increased by 26%, average fuel consumption increased by 2%, and air pollutants by 2.9% [6]. In conclusion, it has to be underlined that among the several parameters that affect the BRT system configuration, the demand analysis is the most significant. This planning phase provides the number of users, so, according to these data, the BRT system will assume various assets. The BRT configuration solutions referring to the number of passengers are shown in Table 3.

**Table 3.** Typical BRT configuration according to demand level.

| Transit Passengers per Hour per Direction | Type of BRT Solution |
|---|---|
| Less than 2000 | Simple bus priority, normally without physical segregation, possible part-time bus lane. |
| 2000 to 8000 | Segregated median busway used by direct services reducing the need to transfer. |
| 8000 to 15,000 | Segregated median busway used by trunk services requiring transfers but benefiting from fast boarding and operating speeds. Transit priority at intersections. |
| 15,000 to 45,000 | Segregated median busway, with overtaking at stops; possible use of express and stopping services. Use of grade separation at some intersections and some form of signal priority at others. |
| Over 45,000 | This level of demand is very rare on existing bus systems. It is possible, however, to design a BRT system that would serve up to even 50,000 passengers per hour per direction. This can be achieved with full segregation, double busway, a high proportion of express services and multiple stops. This capacity could also be handled by spreading the load through two or more close corridors. |

## 3. Bus Rapid Transit (BRT) and Autonomous Vehicles

The most important innovations that affect the transport and automotive sectors nowadays are represented by autonomous vehicles whose equipment can replace driver intervention. To highlight several autonomous vehicle types that have been implemented, it is possible to refer to the classification, depicted in Figure 3, established by SAE (Society of Automotive Engineers). There are six levels of classification: from level zero to level two, there are vehicles with full manual control (level zero) and those with some features that allow driver assistance and partial automation (level one and level two); then level three to level five indicates vehicles that are equipped with the so-called ADAS (Advanced Driver-Assistance System) that permits autonomous performances. In these cases for a third and fourth level, a driver is required. The vehicles operate autonomously only in some circumstances, while, for level five, the vehicle can achieve full autonomy [7]. Among several benefits that would be provided by autonomous vehicles, the main ones are related to safety, considering that a high-tech system would manage driving maneuvers with shorter reaction times compared to human drivers, but also to public transport services that would achieve high efficiency due to the accuracy of the IT systems. With regard to public transport, it has to be pointed out how the ADAS operation would be more relevant for road vehicles such as buses instead of rail vehicles (trains, trams) because while this one is hooked to a platform (predetermined trajectory), the trajectory of autonomous road vehicles would be utterly dependent on ADAS.

**Figure 3.** Vehicle automation levels.

Taking into account the advantages that autonomous vehicles could give to a BRT system, many companies have launched tests with autonomous buses like, for instance, the East Japan Railway Company's (JR East's) Bus Rapid Transit (BRT) lines [8], aiming to analyze self-driving technologies when applied to bus transit primarily focusing on aspects such as keeping in lane and speed control, which strongly affect BRT efficiency or the buses' decision capabilities when managing several scenarios. The cooperation of an efficient system like BRT and the technological capability of ADAS would provide an ultimate low-cost solution for critical traffic issues and emissions reduction in cities, especially considering that it is expected that in 2050, more than two-thirds of the world's population will live in cities [9]. Examples of autonomous bus services consist mainly of autonomous minibuses with a capacity of a maximum of 15 people. They operate in several contexts like hospitals, parks, universities, airports, and public roads. However, with such reduced capacity, it would be complicated to implement a BRT system that is mainly valued for its high capacity buses. Therefore, to guarantee a high capacity system, the solution would be to use a high number of minibuses that are already able to drive on a public road, and to operate them in reserved lanes, thus ensuring a significant efficiency considering that with a high quantity of vehicles, the waiting time would be decreased due to the high frequency and flexibility. Crucially, to ensure the correct operation of an autonomous BRT system, the infrastructures will need to be upgraded with ITS and sensors able to allow the following types of communications: V2I (vehicles to infrastructure), V2V (vehicle to vehicle), and V2X (vehicle to everything) [10]. In Figure 4, it is possible to see an autonomous bus that works on a street in California.

**Figure 4.** Example of an autonomous minibus.

The fact that autonomous minibuses are already operating, despite the higher capacity of autonomous buses, can be attributed to their dimensions, safety, maintenance, and other complex reasons. Moreover, there are several tests of high capacity and articulated buses equipped with ITS and sensors that allow them to operate autonomously. A test of this kind was carried out with a Volvo B10M-ART-RA-IN articulated bus [11]. One such 18 m long bus was fully equipped and tested on a 385 m long private road in Arganda del Rey (Spain). To control speed and brakes, an electronically connected I/O board was used. At the same time, the steering was equipped with a 24-volt DC motor (150 watts) that also had an incremental optical encoder (2000 ppr) and a gear reduction box (74:1). Finally, obstacle detection was allowed, thanks to two Laser Imaging Detection and Ranging (LIDAR) systems (LMS-221 and LMS-291). The average speed during the test was between 10 km/h and 25 km/h. In comparison, 60 km/h was reached only in a straight section. It has been observed that the main challenge for autonomous systems in such cases is represented by the high mass and, consequently, the greater inertia, which is why the main observations showed longitudinal and lateral maneuvers of breaking and acceleration. Test results showed that the maximum error that exceeded trajectory tracking was at least 35 cm on curves with a reduced radius, while the all trajectory error was at least 10 cm. It can be assumed that such errors are considered acceptable, taking into account the bus's elevated dimensions [12] (Figure 5).

Beyond performance, another essential benefit linked to a potential BRT autonomous system is with regard to capacity increase. This achievement is a consequence of the headway reduction between buses, which is allowed thanks to the CACC (cooperative adaptive cruise control). This system can perceive sudden changes in the speed of adjacent vehicles faster than a human driver. In this way, taking into account that vehicles will be able to brake promptly, the required safety distance while they are moving will be shorter compared to that of the human-driven vehicles. Together with shorter headway, this will form the so-called platooning, and with this asset, the BRT system will increase its capacity, emulating that of rail transit systems [13].

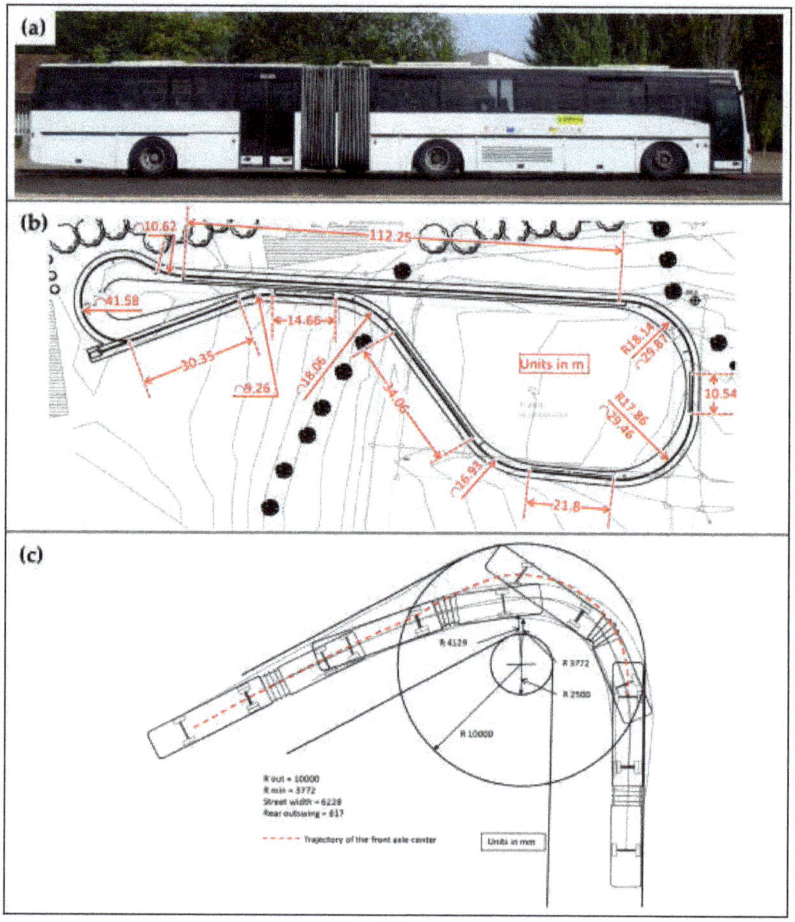


**Figure 5.** (**a**) Tested articulated bus, (**b**) inner road dimensions, (**c**) bus trajectory analysis.

## 4. BRT Systems Applications

The reduced cost–benefit ratio of implementing BRT systems represents a significant turning point for several communities, not only in terms of livability, but also economic gain, since cities also consider the urban redevelopment brought by BRT systems to increase their international attractiveness with consequent positive implications from a tourist point of view. A typical example of BRT's benefits in a developing country is represented by the Lahore case in Pakistan, a city of at least eleven million inhabitants where a BRT system was activated in 2013. It operates in a reserved lane located on a 27 km long corridor with an operational speed of 26 km/h and 25 stations, and manages a quantity of 180,000 daily passengers [14,15]. With regard to performance, due to a fleet of sixty-four buses, there is a headway of three minutes. In terms of Lahore's benefits, the population density passed from 268 persons/acre to 299 persons/acre due to the increase in new construction in areas close to stations.

In conclusion, from an economic point of view, there were investments of almost $140 million, creating 800 new employees [16,17]. In Pakistan, the city of Lahore (Figure 6) is not the only case where BRT has provided significant benefits from an economic point of view and an environmental one. For instance, Multan's BRT system was studied to evaluate the skills and performances of hybrid energy-based buses. Based on DEA (data envelopment analysis), the efficiency range of 21 stations (except one for the hybrid bus system) was almost equal to 1, where the only exception was at a stop where the value was 0.77 [18].

**Figure 6.** Lahore BRT system.

Taking into account the data about South America, considering that it is the continent where the BRT system was first established, it is still the one in which there are more significant examples of such travel networks; moreover, it hosts and is also the often-cited system that acts as a model at an international level, for instance, the "TransMilenio" of Bogotà (Colombia) [19]. The success of TransMilenio is related to the optimal outcomes in terms of profits during the first years that covered the expenses of planning and service provision easily with privately-operated buses. Such advantages led to the implementation of other interesting BRT systems in Colombia, like the one in Barranquilla [20,21]. This metropolitan area had significant urban segregation and inequality that also affected the transportation systems (Figure 7). Due to the rapid economic and urban growth, there was a relevant increase in congestion phenomena attributed to the quantity of private vehicles. A trunk-feeder BRT service was activated to manage such a situation, connecting Barranquilla and Soledad along a 14 km corridor with exclusive right-of-way. This system, named "Transmetro", was also characterized by several feeder routes (190 km). One of the advantages of Transmetro is the free service offered for vehicles moving from the feeder to trunk route. To demonstrate how BRT systems attract private investment, this type of BRT system is characterized by a public-private partnership where the public part deals with operational and organizational aspects while private companies manage delivery service [22].

**Figure 7.** Baranquilla's BRT system.

North America has one of the most recently inaugurated BRT, for example, Albuquerque (USA), which is a city with 560,218 inhabitants. It is characterized by two priority lanes 20.2 km and 21.97 km long, respectively, each one with twenty stations and serves 8100 daily passengers. It is not the most comprehensive system in the USA. It is useful to note that its peak frequency reaches eight bus/hour [23]. Moreover, the highest use of BRT systems is not always linked to the size of continents. North America has several cities with significantly lower passenger numbers than European ones. In Europe, BRT is most widespread in France, being active in 21 cities and with a total extension of 342 km, respectively 47.72% and 39.09% of all Europe. France's most comprehensive system is in Lille (67 km), while the most recent is in Le Mans [23]. Considering its extension in Africa, BRT was not taken up as much as in other countries since it is only established in five cities. However, in Dar-es-Salaam, the most recently inaugurated system dates from 2016 and consists of just one corridor that is 21 km long, but with the highest number of daily passengers in Africa, equal to 180,000. In Oceania, BRT is mainly used in Australia, where it has an extension of 90 km and operates in three cities: Adelaide, Brisbane, and the metropolitan area of Sydney. The BRT system in Adelaide (Figure 8) is the smallest one with just one 12 km corridor. However, it is one of the first to be implemented globally, and its line is mainly characterized by the track-guided bus, a system composed of a specific platform where only the bus can drive. This type of intervention has been used to avoid the introduction of private vehicles altogether [24].

**Figure 8.** Adelaide's BRT system.

## 5. Discussion

Considering what has been discussed in previous sections, it is valuable to note that the combination of autonomous vehicles and BRT public transport systems would bring many benefits. The mere application of driverless vehicles would guarantee every citizen the ability to move freely in the city, reducing the number of vehicles by at least 80%. The potential success of this strategy is based on the concept of vehicle sharing by users, which must be promoted and facilitated mainly from an economic point of view, and subsequently, with intermodal platform implementation. It is well known that automation is not a new concept in metropolitan public transport operation. Therefore, their application to potential BRT systems with autonomous vehicles would not require lengthy delays, considering that globally, in 2016, there were already 37 cities with automated metro systems [25]. Furthermore, it is estimated that the spread of autonomous vehicles will occur quickly, facilitated by existing automation systems and technological innovations. Nowadays, the same thing cannot be assumed for BRT systems. This situation can be thoroughly explained with a comparison between case studies in Istanbul and Cairo. In Cairo, the BRT system was proposed as a solution to redevelop the inner city that was characterized by a high population density of at least 21,700 persons/sq.km, thus heavily inclined to congestion. It also aimed to provide an efficient connection with growing communities settled in the periphery. BRT was regarded as an additional solution achievable in three years and with low costs. However, the project was not realized due to a lack of user trust in the bus sector and skepticism regarding the placement of reserved lanes in an area subject to congestion. In Istanbul, due to a demographic increase of 38.3% and a high number of private vehicles in circulation (4.17 million private vehicles registered), there was a serious problem linked to congestion phenomena. Accordingly, a BRT system was developed by dedicating two lanes of the city's main highway to buses, thus ensuring a considerable daily capacity (30,000 passengers per hour in peak hours) with headways of 20 s. It is important to remark that the first 18.5 km long stretch of the BRT line was implemented in 2007 in just 77 days. Analyzing such cases, considering that both cities are similar in terms of demographics and urban planning, it appears that, while for Cairo the lack of user trust has blocked development, in Istanbul, where the BRT system was implemented in a context of innovation and significantly as a solution to the continuous deferrals of the realization of LRT systems, BRT has achieved excellent results. For these reasons, taking into account that in some communities such as Cairo, BRT was not successful, the application of driverless systems would make it more attractive, especially considering that there are already autonomous vehicles (level 4) capable of operating in mixed traffic. Thus, the BRT system's operational context with reserved lanes and right-of-way would be perfectly suitable [26–30].

## 6. Conclusions

This paper has offered an examination of some BRT systems developed worldwide, summarizing the background, general technical peculiarities, and the relationship with autonomous vehicles. Considering that, in infrastructure and civil engineering, efficiency is not the only requirement but is necessary to guarantee economic advantages, minimal environmental impacts and flexibility must be taken into account carefully. The BRT is a public transport system that reflects the requirements above-mentioned. It has developed mainly in South America, where it was implemented for the first time. Taking into account the positive implications, it has spread globally, especially in Europe. Among the innovations that have most strongly characterized BRT systems as part of the automotive sector is undoubtedly the advent of autonomous vehicles, which would amplify the already efficient and robust performance of the aforementioned public transport systems, even if only in relation to the precisions of maneuvers, and the consequent possibility to reduce the safety distances between vehicles while traveling, thus increasing their frequency. ADAS systems are now used more often for minibuses with a maximum capacity of around 15 people. Therefore, it is possible to use them in a BRT system, the advantage of which is also its high capacity. This implication could be relevant even for small communities. Nevertheless, ADAS systems have been tested with excellent results, even in high capacity and bi-articulated buses. BRT can be an upgrading solution for existing bus line systems that allow contexts with limited economic means to guarantee high-efficiency services, with significant positive implications both in economic and livability terms.

**Author Contributions:** The authors contributed equally to this work. All authors have read and agreed to the published version of the manuscript.

**Funding:** This research received no external funding.

**Acknowledgments:** This work was related to the D.D. 407 of 27 February 2018 "AIM—Attrazione e Mobilitaà Internazionale" issued by the Italian Ministry of Education, University, and Research in the implementation of Action I.2 "Mobilitaà dei Ricercatori" Asse I—PON R&I 2014–2020, taking into account the written amendment procedure of the PON R&I 2014–2020, pursuant to articles 30 and 90 of Regulation (EU) 1303/2013 started on 21 February 2018 as well as the relevant implementation regulations.

**Conflicts of Interest:** The authors declare no conflict of interest.

## References


1. Global BRTData. Available online: brtdata.org (accessed on 27 August 2020).
2. Chatman, D.; Rayle, L.; Palacios, M.S.; Cervero, R. *Sustainable and Equitable Transportation in Latin America, Asia and Africa: The Challenges of Integrating BRT and Private Transit Services*; UC Berkeley Center for Future Urban Transport Institute of Transportation Studies Institute for Urban and Regional Development Department of City and Regional Planning University of California: Berkeley, CA, USA, 2019.
3. Prayogi, L.; Sari, Y. The Approaches on Assessing the Influence of a Bus Rapid Transit System on Urban Development. *Int. J. Built Environ. Sci. Res.* **2019**, *3*, 105–110. [CrossRef]
4. The Online BRT Planning Guide. Available online: https://brtguide.itdp.org/branch/master/guide/ (accessed on 27 August 2020).
5. Dion, F.; Rakha, H.A.; Kang, Y.-S. Comparison of delay estimates at under-saturated and over-saturated pre-timed signalized intersections. *Transp. Res. Part B Methodol.* **2004**, *38*, 99–122. [CrossRef]
6. Tamannaei, M.; Fazeli, M.; Dana, A.C.F.; Mansourianfar, H. Transit Signal Priority: Proposing a Novel Algorithm to Decrease Delay and Environmental Impacts in BRT Route Intersections. *Int. J. Transp. Eng.* **2019**, *7*, 153–169.
7. Society of Automotive Engineers. Available online: www.sae.org (accessed on 27 August 2020).
8. Intelligent Transport. Available online: www.intelligenttransport.com (accessed on 27 August 2020).
9. Forbes. Available online: www.forbes.com (accessed on 27 August 2020).
10. Arena, F.; Pau, G.; Severino, A. An Overview on the Current Status and Future Perspectives of Smart Cars. *Infrastructures* **2020**, *5*, 53. [CrossRef]
11. Navya: Self-Driving Made Real. Available online: navya.tech (accessed on 27 August 2020).
12. Montes, H.; Salinas, C.; Fernández, R.; Armada, M. An Experimental Platform for Autonomous Bus Development. *Appl. Sci.* **2017**, *7*, 1131. [CrossRef]
13. Lutin, J.; Consultant, I. Not If, but When: Autonomous Driving and the Future of Transit. *J. Public Transp.* **2018**, *21*, 92–103. [CrossRef]
14. Shah, S.A.R.; Shahzad, M.; Ahmad, N.; Zamad, A.; Hussan, S.; Aslam, M.A.; Khan, A.R.; Asif, M.A.; Shahzadi, G.; Waseem, M. Performance Evaluation of Bus Rapid Transit System: A Comparative Analysis of Alternative Approaches for Energy Efficient Eco-Friendly Public Transport System. *Energies* **2020**, *13*, 1377. [CrossRef]
15. Far Est Mobility—BRT & Urban Transport Planning. Available online: www.fareast.mobi (accessed on 27 August 2020).
16. Wirasinghe, S.C.; Kattan, L.; Rahman, M.M.; Hubbell, J.; Thilakaratne, R.; Anowar, S. Bus rapid transit—A review. *Int. J. Urban Sci.* **2013**, *17*, 1–31. [CrossRef]
17. Prayogi, L.; Jakarta, U.M. Bus Rapid Transit-oriented Development: A Review of Built Environment Qualities Potentially Triggering Bus Rapid Transit Passengers' Modal Shift. *Int. J. Eng. Res.* **2018**, *7*, 302–305.
18. Bogumil, V. Quantitative Assessment of the Bus Rapid Transit Efficiency in Solving the Problems of Motorization of Modern Cities. *Glob. J. Manag. Bus. Res.* **2019**. Available online: https://journalofbusiness.org/index.php/GJMBR/article/view/2718 (accessed on 27 August 2020).
19. Nikitas, A.; Kougias, I.; Alyavina, E.; Njoya Tchouamou, E. How Can Autonomous and Connected Vehicles, Electromobility, BRT, Hyperloop, Shared Use Mobility and Mobility-As-A-Service Shape Transport Futures for the Context of Smart Cities? *Urban Sci.* **2017**, *1*, 36. [CrossRef]
20. Basheer, M.A.; Boelens, L.; Bijl, R. Bus Rapid Transit System: A Study of Sustainable Land-Use Transformation, Urban Density and Economic Impacts. *Sustainability* **2020**, *12*, 3376. [CrossRef]
21. Ardila, D.S. Global policies for moving cities: The role of think tanks in the proliferation of Bus Rapid Transit systems in Latin America and worldwide. *Policy Soc.* **2020**, *39*, 70–90. [CrossRef]
22. National Academies of Sciences, Engineering, and Medicine. *Analysis of Recent Public Transit Ridership Trends*; The National Academies Press: Washington, DC, USA, 2020. [CrossRef]
23. Arena, F.; Ticali, D. The development of autonomous driving vehicles in tomorrow's smart cities mobility. *AIP Conf. Proc.* **2018**, *2040*, 140007. [CrossRef]
24. Arena, F.; Pau, G.; Severino, A. V2X Communications Applied to Safety of Pedestrians and Vehicles. *J. Sens. Actuator Netw.* **2020**, *9*, 3. [CrossRef]

25. *UITP-Advancing Public Transport, Policy Brief-Autonomous Vehicles: A Potential Game Changer for Urban Mobility*; UITP: Brussels, Belgium, 2017.
26. *UITP-Advancing Public Transport-Transforming Cities with Bus Rapid Transit (BRT) Systems*; UITP: Brussels, Belgium, 2019.
27. Lindau, L.A.; Hidalgo, D.; Lobo, A.D.A. Barriers to planning and implementing Bus Rapid Transit systems. *Res. Transp. Econ.* **2014**, *48*, 9–15. [CrossRef]
28. Nguyen, M.H.; Pojani, D. *Chapter Two—Why Do Some BRT Systems in the Global South Fail to Perform or Expand?* Elsevier: Amsterdam, The Netherlands, 2018.
29. TCRP. Report 90-Volume 1: Case Studies in Bus Rapid Transit. Available online: https://nacto.org/docs/usdg/tcrp_rpt_90_case_studies_volume_1_levinson.pdf (accessed on 27 August 2020).
30. Hidalgo, D.; Graftieaus, P. Bus Rapid Transit Systems in Latin America and Asia: Results and Difficulties in 11 Cities. *Transp. Res. Rec. J. Transp. Res. Board* **2008**, *2072*, 77–88. [CrossRef]

*infrastructures*

MDPI

*Article*

# A Piecewise-Defined Function for Modelling Traffic Noise on Urban Roads

**Mariano Gallo**

Department of Engineering, University of Sannio, 82100 Benevento, Italy; gallo@unisannio.it

Received: 3 July 2020; Accepted: 28 July 2020; Published: 29 July 2020

**Abstract:** In this paper, a piecewise-defined function is proposed to estimate traffic noise in urban areas. The proposed approach allows the use of the model even in the case of very low or zero flows for which the classical logarithmic form is not suitable. A model based on the proposed approach is calibrated for a real case and compared with the results obtained with a model based only on the logarithmic form. The results obtained show how the proposed piecewise-defined function, linear for low traffic flows and logarithmic for medium-high volumes, is able to better represent real noise pollution levels in all conditions. The proposed approach is particularly useful when comparing two plan scenarios from the point of view of noise effects.

**Keywords:** noise models; traffic noise; urban roads; sustainable mobility

## 1. Introduction

In urban areas, road traffic contributes significantly to environmental noise and is its main source. As is evident to anyone living in congested cities, noise causes annoyance, sleep disturbance and damage to human health, reducing the quality of life.

The World Health Organisation [1] has estimated that at least one million years of life are lost every year due to road traffic noise in Western Europe. Impacts on human health have been widely studied. Muzet [2] and Pirrera et al. [3] studied the effects of environmental noise on sleep and, consequently, on health. Some studies [4–8] focused on cardiovascular problems related to noise. Sakhvidi et al. [9] studied the association between noise exposure and diabetes. Jafari et al. [10] evaluated if noise exposure can accelerate cognitive impairment and Alzheimer's disease. Noise and annoyance were studied in [11–15]. Other general studies can be found in [16–18], while the effects of noise on property prices were studied in [19–21].

There is extensive literature on models for estimating noise pollution. Some reviews can be found in [22–24]. Most of the proposed models relate road traffic noise to vehicle flows; some also consider other variables such as average speed or certain characteristics of the road infrastructure (slope, type of pavement, distance and height of buildings, etc.); here, we just mention [25–43].

The analysis of the literature allows us to identify two main types of models:

- *general*, i.e., applicable to different situations and case studies;
- *specific*, calibrated in correspondence with a specific case study and applicable only in the reference context or in very similar contexts.

General models relate noise to vehicle flow and/or average speed, but also take into account other context-specific characteristics (traffic type, gradient, road surface, barrier geometry, mean wind speed, traffic composition, local topography, etc.). Some examples are the models FHWA [44], CoRTN [45], RLS (see [46,47]), ASJ RTN [48], Harmonoise [49,50], Son Road [51], Nord 2000 [52], NMPB-2008 [53] and CNOSSOS-EU [43]. A comparison of these models and more details can be found in [23].

On the other hand, specific models are calibrated for specific situations, such as urban roads with similar characteristics, or sometimes for single infrastructures. These models estimate the noise emissions, for that specific case study, as a function of the traffic flow and sometimes the average speed of that traffic. Most models are based only on traffic flows; the simplest functional form is the following:

$$L_{eq}(f) = \beta_0 + \beta_1 \cdot \log_{10} f \tag{1}$$

where:

$L_{eq}$ is the equivalent noise level at a specific distance from the centre of the road, in dB(A);
$\beta_0$ and $\beta_1$ are the coefficients of the model to be calibrated;
$f$ is the homogenised traffic flow (veh/h).

Other models include the distance of the receiver from the source within the formula, or other features such as the percentage of heavy vehicles or the average flow speed, trying to extend the use of the model to other contexts as much as possible. In almost all formulations, the term $\log_{10} f$, or its functional transformation, is present and plays the main role in the calculation. Some papers that use the approach (1) or similar are [26,27,46,54–59].

Model (1) surely cannot be easily generalised but it is very easy to calibrate in specific contexts. A specific model, once calibrated in correspondence of some roads of a city, can be used to estimate noise pollution levels also in other roads of the same city, in order to estimate the exposed population, identify the most critical areas to intervene on and assess the overall effects of interventions on traffic circulation [60].

In this paper, the calibration of a specific model based on a piecewise-defined function is proposed, to avoid the use of the logarithmic form that can create problems for zero or very low flow, which can occur in simulation models of a whole road network.

The paper is organised as follows. Section 2 introduces the proposed approach. Section 3 calibrates a specific model based on the proposed approach and compares it with other models. Section 4 concludes and discusses the research prospects.

## 2. The Proposed Approach

Model (1) and most models based on the logarithm of traffic flows work very well when traffic flows are not extremely low or zero. It is well known that power and sound pressure levels vary with a logarithmic law. Indeed, the intensity of auditory sensations is in first approximation proportional to the logarithm of the stimulus and not to its absolute value.

For example, if we use the model calibrated in [59], below:

$$L_{eq}(f) = 17.594 + 17.377 \cdot \log_{10} f \tag{2}$$

we can see that it is not applicable in case of null flow (the second term would tend to less infinite) and would give a value equal to 17.594 dB(a) in case of 1 veh/h and 34.971 in case of 10 veh/h. As also written in [59], the model is valid only if the flow is greater than about 50 veh/h, at which the equivalent noise level is equal to 47.1 dB(A).

In most cases, this underestimation of equivalent noise levels for very low flows is not a problem, because roads with low traffic, or periods with low traffic, do not receive attention in noise analysis. The problem arises when we want to analyse the overall noise level of a city, perhaps by comparing pre- and post-intervention scenarios. For example, in Urban Traffic Plans, it is useful to check with simulation whether changes in traffic patterns may or may not have a positive impact on noise pollution. The approximations included in the simulation models, such for example the discretisation of the study area into traffic zones (zoning), may lead to estimate zero or very low traffic flows on some links of the network and any comparative analysis would be compromised in these cases.

To avoid this problem, in this paper we propose the use of a piecewise-defined function, in order to calibrate specific models, which has a first linear part (for low traffic values) and a second logarithmic part (for high traffic values). In any case, the function must be continuous and derivable; therefore, we propose to extend linearly model (1), with an inclination equal to the first derivative of the model, for flows lower than a minimum value, $f_{min}$. This way, we can formulate a model that is valid for all traffic conditions. Under these assumptions, the model can be formulated as follows:

$$L_{eq}(f) = [\beta_0 + \beta_1 \cdot \log_{10} f_{min} - f_{min} \cdot (1/(f_{min} \cdot \ln(10))) \cdot \beta_1] + [(1/(f_{min} \cdot \ln(10))) \cdot \beta_1] \cdot f \text{ if } f < f_{min} \quad (3)$$

$$L_{eq}(f) = \beta_0 + \beta_1 \cdot \log_{10} f \text{ if } f \geq f_{min} \quad (4)$$

The calibration of models (3)–(4) requires the calculation of three values, in contrast to model (1) for which it was sufficient to calibrate two coefficients ($\beta_0$ and $\beta_1$); indeed, in addition to the $\beta_0$ and $\beta_1$ coefficients, it is necessary to calibrate the value of $f_{min}$.

## 3. Model Calibration

The calibration of the model is performed using the same data collected in the testing campaign reported in [59] in the city of Benevento. These data refer to four road sections (see Figure 1) representative of the prevailing type of roads in the urban network; the pavement was bituminous in all cases.

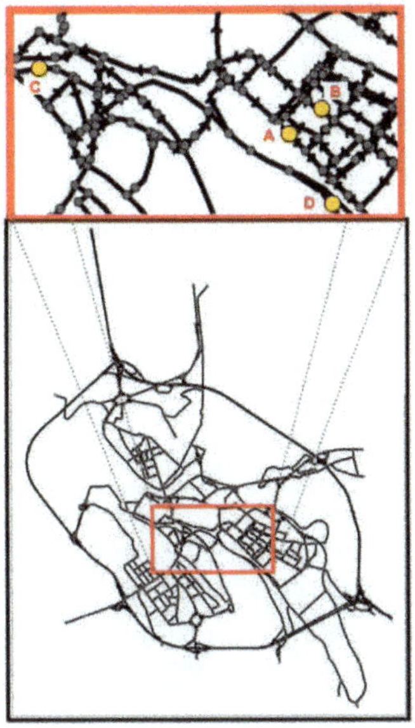


**Figure 1.** Survey locations.

The phonometric surveys were conducted by a specialised technician using a Svantek 949 sound level meter, with the periodic certification, equipped with a preamplifier Svantek SV 12L and a pre-polarised microphone Svantek SV22. Before and after the measurements, the tuning of the system was verified with a precision calibrator DELTA OHM. A microclimatic station for measuring temperature and wind speed and direction was used; indeed, the phonometric measures must be recorded in absence of rain, snow or fog and the maximum wind speed must be lower than 5 m/s. The phonometer is disposed to 1.5 m in height from the road level and on the side of the road. The traffic surveys were obtained with a manual procedure, counting cars, light-duty vehicles (LDV) and heavy-duty vehicles (HDV) every 15 min (motorcycle flows are negligible in Benevento), and assuming the following equivalence coefficients: LDV = 2 cars; HDV = 8 cars. Overall, 32 measures were conducted; in Table 1 the main data are summarised.

**Table 1.** Survey measures.

| Location | Hom. Flow [veh/h] | $L_{eq}$ [dB(A)] | $L_{eq}{}^{c}$ [dB(A)] |
|---|---|---|---|
| A | 500 | 62.3 | 64.4 |
| | 648 | 67.1 | 69.2 |
| | 496 | 61.9 | 64.0 |
| | 368 | 58.6 | 60.7 |
| | 168 | 54.2 | 56.3 |
| | 48 | 49.9 | 52.0 |
| | 1260 | 70.2 | 72.3 |
| | 1040 | 71.0 | 73.1 |
| | 704 | 69.8 | 71.9 |
| B | 528 | 63.5 | 65.6 |
| | 628 | 65.9 | 68.0 |
| | 436 | 60.9 | 63.0 |
| | 312 | 57.9 | 60.0 |
| | 120 | 52.1 | 54.2 |
| | 856 | 66.3 | 68.4 |
| | 828 | 67.7 | 69.8 |
| | 792 | 65.9 | 68.0 |
| C | 648 | 61.8 | 61.8 |
| | 568 | 63.1 | 63.1 |
| | 436 | 60.0 | 60.0 |
| | 228 | 56.9 | 56.9 |
| | 80 | 50.1 | 50.1 |
| | 1184 | 70.0 | 70.0 |
| | 544 | 69.4 | 69.4 |
| D | 552 | 62.0 | 62.0 |
| | 568 | 63.4 | 63.4 |
| | 364 | 58.8 | 58.8 |
| | 208 | 56.2 | 56.2 |
| | 104 | 51.0 | 51.0 |
| | 772 | 65.2 | 65.2 |
| | 680 | 70.0 | 70.0 |
| | 536 | 68.1 | 68.1 |

The phonometric measures have to be corrected for the locations A and B according to the distance from the centre of the road; indeed, as reported in Figure 2, the distances are different in these locations since there are parking lots (the measures were, anyway, performed where no cars were parked). Assuming a linear noise source, the sound in locations A and B arrives to the receptor attenuated by the following factor:

$$\Delta L_{eq} = 10 \cdot \log_{10}(6.18/3.81) = 2.1 \text{ dB(A)}$$

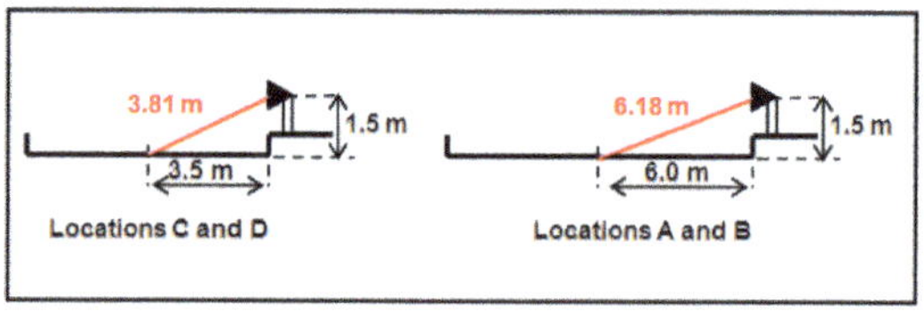


**Figure 2.** Distances of phonometer from the centre of the road.

Therefore, the measures on locations A and B are incremented of 2.1 dB(A); these corrected values, $L_{eq}{}^{c}$, are reported in the third column of Table 1.

The model was calibrated using the generalized least squares method and the following values were obtained: $\beta_0 = 4.427$; $\beta_1 = 22.109$; $f_{min} = 287$ veh/h. With these values, models (3)–(4) become:

$$L_{eq}\,(f) = 49.160 + 0.0335 \cdot f \text{ if } f < 287 \tag{5}$$

$$L_{eq}\,(f) = 4.427 + 22.109 \cdot \log_{10} f \text{ if } f \geq 287 \tag{6}$$

The value of the coefficient of determination, $R^2$, is significantly high (0.878); Figure 3 reports the comparison between measured and estimated data and the comparison between the model curve and the experimental data. This model improves model (2) for which $R^2$ was equal to 0.847. The RMSE value also improved, decreasing from 2.48 to 2.22.

It is interesting to compare the results obtained between the two models for low traffic flow values. It is noted that the proposed model can provide plausible results in all flow ranges, while the logarithmic model provides acceptable values only for sufficiently high flow values (see Table 2 and Figure 4).

**Table 2.** Comparison of models.

| Flow [veh/h] | $L_{eq}$ Model (2) | $L_{eq}$ Model (5)–(6) | $L_{eq}$ Model (7) |
|---|---|---|---|
| 0 | N/A | 49.16 | N/A |
| 1 | 17.59 | 49.19 | 47.29 |
| 5 | 29.74 | 49.33 | 54.42 |
| 10 | 34.97 | 49.50 | 57.49 |
| 20 | 40.20 | 49.83 | 60.56 |
| 30 | 43.26 | 50.17 | 62.35 |
| 40 | 45.43 | 50.50 | 63.63 |
| 50 | 47.12 | 50.84 | 64.62 |
| 60 | 48.49 | 51.17 | 65.43 |
| 100 | 52.35 | 52.51 | 67.69 |
| 150 | 55.41 | 54.19 | 69.48 |
| 200 | 57.58 | 55.86 | 70.76 |
| 250 | 59.26 | 57.54 | 71.75 |
| 300 | 60.64 | 59.19 | 72.55 |
| 350 | 61.80 | 60.70 | 73.24 |
| 400 | 62.81 | 61.96 | 73.83 |
| 500 | 64.49 | 64.10 | 74.82 |
| 600 | 65.87 | 65.85 | 75.63 |
| 700 | 67.03 | 67.33 | 76.31 |
| 800 | 68.04 | 68.61 | 76.90 |
| 900 | 68.93 | 69.74 | 77.42 |
| 1000 | 69.75 | 70.75 | 77.89 |
| 1500 | 72.78 | 74.64 | 79.68 |

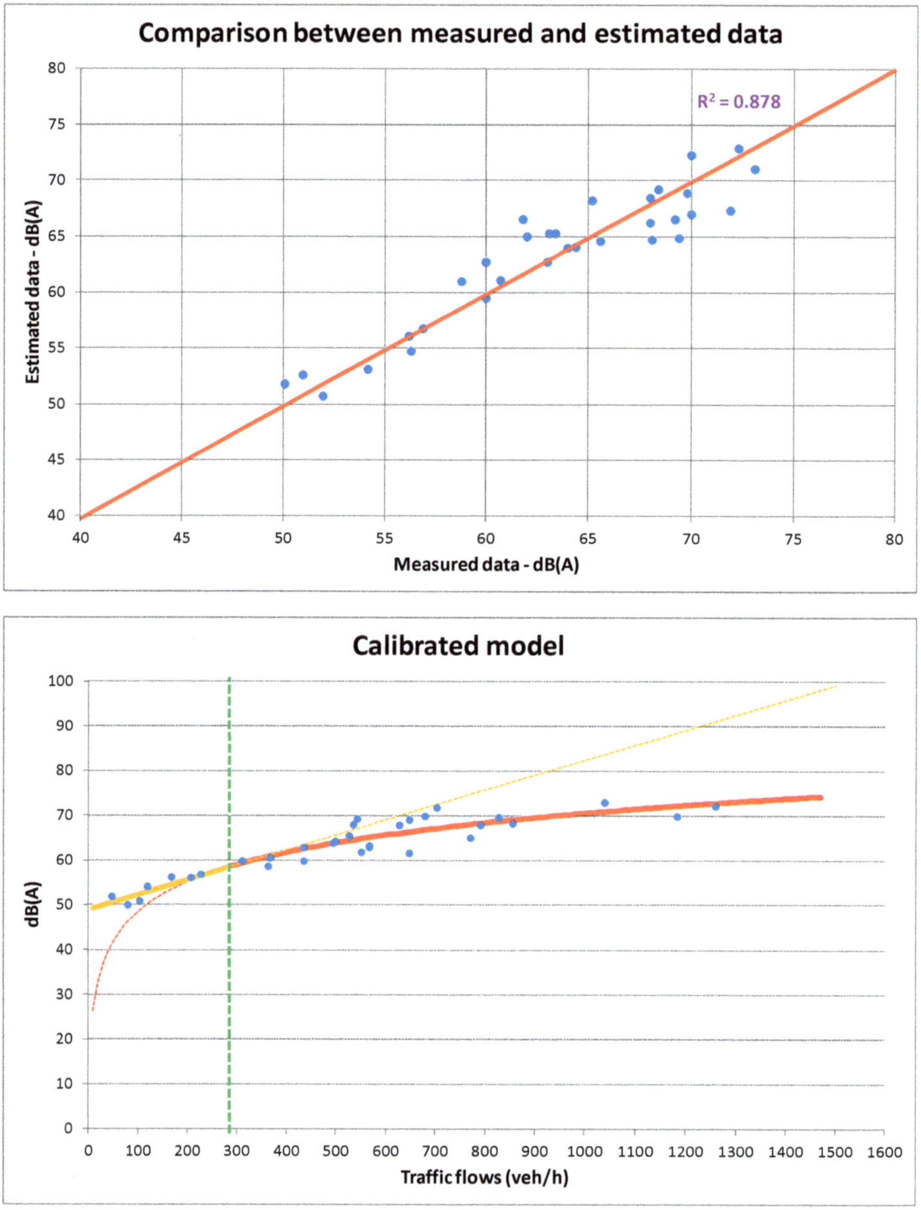


**Figure 3.** Comparison between measured and estimated data.

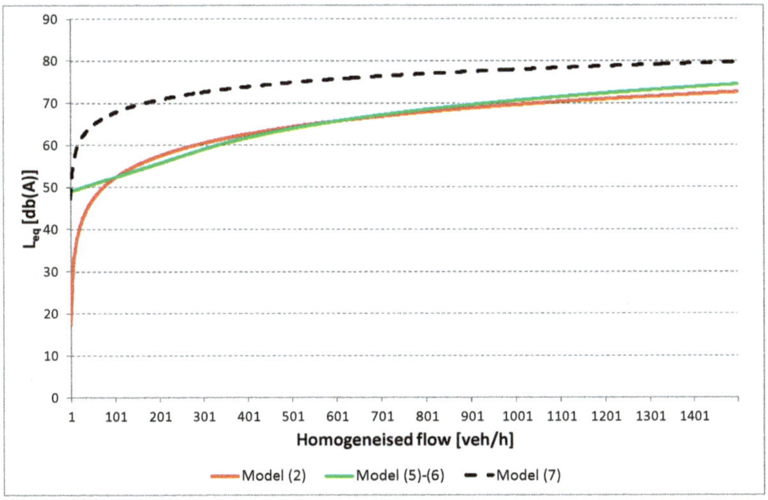


**Figure 4.** Comparison of models.

Moreover, the proposed model was also compared with the model proposed in [54], which has been widely used:

$$L_{eq}(f) = 55.5 + 10.2 \cdot \log_{10} f + 0.3\,P - 19.3 \log_{10} d \tag{7}$$

where:

$P$ is the percentage of heavy vehicles;
$d$ is the distance from the source.

For the comparison, we assume a percentage of heavy vehicles of 10% and a distance from the source equal to 3.81 m.

It should be noted that model (7) was not calibrated for the case study, so it is possible to compare only the trend of the function, which is similar to that of model (2); model (7) overestimates the noise levels for the case study examined, but, from the trend of the function, it presents the same problems as model (2).

## 4. Conclusions

Noise pollution is one of the main external impacts of the road transport system. Numerous models have been proposed in the literature, some more general, others more specific, for its estimation. In almost all models, equivalent noise levels are assumed to be a function of the logarithm of traffic flows; this theoretically correct hypothesis does not, however, allow the use of such models for very low or zero flows.

On the other hand, in practice, in particular for urban roads, there is always background noise to which the noise emitted by vehicular traffic is added. The approach proposed in this paper, based on the use of a piecewise-defined function to be calibrated for the specific context, makes it possible to use the calibrated model even on roads with very low or no traffic.

Comparison with a logarithmic model calibrated with the same data shows the robustness of the proposed approach.

In the literature, the need to estimate noise emissions at low traffic values has always been considered unimportant, because noise pollution is usually a real problem in case of high traffic flows. Often, models have been calibrated and used only on high traffic roads and at peak times.

The need to have a model that is also valid for low (or no) traffic flows occurs when we want to examine, in simulation, the situation of an overall city network, also before and after interventions on traffic schemes. In these cases, it may occur that on some road sections, the level of traffic is very low or zero, even for the approximations of the model. The proposed approach makes it possible to use a unique model to estimate all traffic conditions and, consequently, to compare the intervention scenarios.

The proposed approach can be used to calibrate specific models in other contexts; the calibrated models (5)–(6), on the other hand, have uses limited to the case study or very similar situations.

The research prospects can be directed to test the proposed approach on other urban contexts and to generalise the model based on this type of function so that it can also be used in contexts other than the one in which it has been calibrated.

**Funding:** This research received no external funding.

**Acknowledgments:** The author is very grateful to Giuseppe Mazza (Artea Srl) and Orazio Mascolino for having supported the survey activities.

**Conflicts of Interest:** The author declares no conflict of interest.

## References

1. World Health Organization. *Environmental Noise Guidelines for the European Region*; WHO Regional Office for Europe: Copenhagen, Denmark, 2018.
2. Muzet, A. Environmental noise, sleep and health. *Sleep Med. Rev.* **2007**, *11*, 135–142. [CrossRef]
3. Pirrera, S.; De Valck, E.; Cluydts, R. Nocturnal road traffic noise: A review on its assessment and consequences on sleep and health. *Environ. Int.* **2010**, *36*, 492–498. [CrossRef]
4. Fyhri, A.; Aasvang, G.M. Noise, sleep and poor health: Modeling the relationship between road traffic noise and cardiovascular problems. *Sci. Total Environ.* **2010**, *408*, 4935–4942. [CrossRef]
5. Paunovic, K.; Stansfeld, S.; Clark, C.; Belojevic, G. Epidemiological studies on noise and blood pressure in children: Observations and suggestions. *Environ. Int.* **2011**, *37*, 1030–1041. [CrossRef] [PubMed]
6. Recio, A.; Linares, C.; Banegas, J.R.; Diaz, J. Road traffic noise effects on cardiovascular, respiratory, and metabolic health: An integrative model of biological mechanisms. *Environ. Res.* **2016**, *146*, 359–370. [CrossRef] [PubMed]
7. Munzel, T.; Schmidt, F.P.; Steven, S.; Herzog, J.; Daibner, A.; Sorensen, M. Environmental Noise and the Cardiovascular System. *J. Am. Coll. Cardiol.* **2018**, *71*, 688–697. [CrossRef] [PubMed]
8. Khosravipour, M.; Khanlari, P. The association between road traffic noise and myocardial infarction: A systematic review and meta-analysis. *Sci. Total Environ.* **2020**, *731*, 139226. [CrossRef] [PubMed]
9. Sakhvidi, M.J.Z.; Sakhvidi, F.Z.; Mehrparvar, A.H.; Foraster, M.; Dadvand, P. Association between noise exposure and diabetes: A systematic review and meta-analysis. *Environ. Res.* **2018**, *166*, 647–657. [CrossRef] [PubMed]
10. Jafari, Z.; Kolb, B.E.; Mohajerani, M.H. Noise exposure accelerates the risk of cognitive impairment and Alzheimer's disease: Adulthood, gestational, and prenatal mechanistic evidence from animal studies. *Neurosci. Biobehav. R.* **2019**, in press. [CrossRef] [PubMed]
11. Heinonen-Guzejev, M.; Vuorinen, H.S.; Kaprio, J.; Heikkilag, K.; Mussalo-Rauhamaa, H. Self Report of Transportation noise exposure, annoyance and noise sensitivity in relation to noise map information. *J. Sound Vib.* **2000**, *234*, 191–206. [CrossRef]
12. Ouis, D. Annoyance from Road Traffic Noise: A Review. *J. Environ. Psychol.* **2001**, *21*, 101–120. [CrossRef]
13. Klæboe, R.; Amundsen, A.H.; Fyhri, A.; Solberg, S. Road traffic noise–the relationship between noise exposure and noise annoyance in Norway. *Appl. Acoust.* **2004**, *65*, 893–912. [CrossRef]
14. Klæboe, R.; Kolbenstvedt, M.; Clench-Aas, J.; Bartonova, A. Oslo traffic study part 1: An integrated approach to assess the combined effects of noise and air pollution on annoyance. *Atmos. Environ.* **2000**, *34*, 4727–4736. [CrossRef]
15. Di, C.; Liu, X.; Lin, Q.; Zheng, Y.; He, L. The relationship between urban combined traffic noise and annoyance: An investigation in Dalian, north of China. *Sci. Total Environ.* **2012**, *432*, 189–194. [CrossRef] [PubMed]
16. Ohrstrom, E. Effects of low levels of road traffic noise during the night a laboratory study on number of events maximum noise levels and noise sensitivity. *J. Sound Vib.* **1995**, *179*, 603–615. [CrossRef]

17. Franco, V.; Garraín, D.; Vidal, R. Methodological proposals for improved assessments of the impact of traffic noise upon human health. *Int. J. Life Cycle Assess.* **2010**, *15*, 869–882. [CrossRef]
18. Lekaviciute, J.; Kephalopoulos, S.; Stanfeld, S.; Clark, C. *ENNAH-European Network on Noise and Health*; EU Project no. 226442; Publications Office of the European Union: Luxembourg, 2013.
19. Theebe, M.A.J. Planes, Trains, and Automobiles: The impact of traffic noise on houses prices. *J. Real Estate Financ.* **2004**, *28*, 209–234. [CrossRef]
20. Kim, K.S.; Park, S.J.; Kweon, Y.J. Highway traffic noise effects on land price in an urban area. *Transport. Res. D* **2007**, *12*, 275–280.
21. Chang, J.S.; Kim, D.-J. Hedonic estimates of rail noise in Seoul. *Transport. Res. D* **2013**, *19*, 1–4. [CrossRef]
22. Steele, C. A critical review of some traffic noise prediction models. *Appl. Acoust.* **2001**, *62*, 271–287. [CrossRef]
23. Garg, N.; Maji, S. A critical review of principal traffic noise models: Strategies and implications. *Environ. Impact Asses.* **2014**, *46*, 68–81. [CrossRef]
24. Khan, J.; Ketzel, M.; Kakosimos, K.; Sorensen, M.; Jensen, S.S. Road traffic air and noise pollution exposure assessment–A review of tools and techniques. *Sci. Total Environ.* **2018**, *634*, 661–676. [CrossRef] [PubMed]
25. Pamanikabud, P.; Vivitjinda, P. Noise prediction for highways in Thailand. *Transport. Res. D* **2002**, *7*, 441–449. [CrossRef]
26. Calixto, A.; Diniz, F.B.; Zannin, P.H.T. The statistical modeling of road traffic noise in an urban setting. *Cities* **2003**, *20*, 23–29. [CrossRef]
27. Piccolo, A.; Plutino, D.; Cannistraro, G. Evaluation and analysis of the environmental noise of Messina, Italy. *Appl. Acoust.* **2005**, *66*, 447–465. [CrossRef]
28. Tansatcha, M.; Pamanikabud, P.; Brown, A.L.; Affum, J.K. Motorway noise modelling based on perpendicular propagation analysis of traffic noise. *Appl. Acoust.* **2005**, *66*, 1135–1150. [CrossRef]
29. Gundogdu, O.; Gokdagb, M.; Yuksel, F. A traffic noise prediction method based on vehicle composition using genetic algorithms. *Appl. Acoust.* **2005**, *66*, 799–809. [CrossRef]
30. Can, A.; Leclercq, L.; Lelong, J. Dynamic estimation of urban traffic noise: Influence of traffic and noise source representations. *Appl. Acoust.* **2008**, *69*, 858–867. [CrossRef]
31. Cho, D.S.; Mun, S. Development of a highway traffic noise prediction model that considers various road surface types. *Appl. Acoust.* **2008**, *69*, 1120–1128. [CrossRef]
32. Pamanikabud, P.; Tansatcha, M.; Brown, A.L. Development of a highway noise prediction model using an Leq20 s measure of basic vehicular noise. *J. Sound Vib.* **2008**, *316*, 317–330. [CrossRef]
33. Rajakumara, H.N.; Gowda, R.M.M. Road Traffic Noise Prediction Model under Interrupted Traffic Flow Condition. *Environ. Model. Assess.* **2009**, *14*, 251–257. [CrossRef]
34. Hamet, J.F.; Besnard, F.; Doisy, S.; Lelong, J.; le Duc, E. New vehicle noise emission for French traffic noise prediction. *Appl. Acoust.* **2010**, *71*, 861–869. [CrossRef]
35. Oyedepo, O.S.; Abdullahi, A.S. Evaluation and analysis of noise levels in Ilorin metropolis, Nigeria. *Environ. Monit. Assess.* **2010**, *160*, 563–577. [CrossRef] [PubMed]
36. Pamanikabud, P.; Tansatcha, M. 3D analysis and investigation of traffic noise impact from a new motorway on building and surrounding area. *Appl. Acoust.* **2010**, *71*, 1185–1193. [CrossRef]
37. Phan, H.Y.T.; Yano, T.; Sato, T.; Nishimura, T. Characteristics of road traffic noise in Hanoi and Ho Chi Minh City, Vietnam. *Appl. Acoust.* **2010**, *71*, 479–485. [CrossRef]
38. Agarwal, S.; Swami, B.L. Comprehensive approach for the development of traffic noise prediction model for Jaipur city. *Environ. Monit. Assess.* **2011**, *172*, 113–120. [CrossRef]
39. Makarewicz, R.; Gałuszka, M. Road traffic noise prediction based on speed-flow diagram. *Appl. Acoust.* **2011**, *72*, 190–195. [CrossRef]
40. Rahmani, S.; Mousavi, S.M.; Kamali, M.J. Modeling of road-traffic noise with the use of genetic algorithm. *Appl. Soft Comput.* **2011**, *11*, 1008–1013. [CrossRef]
41. Seong, J.C.; Park, T.H.; Ko, J.H.; Chang, S.I.; Kim, M.; Holt, J.B.; Mehdi, M.R. Modeling of road traffic noise and estimated human exposure in Fulton County, Georgia, USA. *Environ. Int.* **2011**, *37*, 1336–1341. [CrossRef]
42. Cirianni, F.; Leonardi, G. Environmental modeling for traffic noise in urban area. *Am. J. Environm. Sci.* **2012**, *8*, 345–351.
43. Kephalopoulos, S.; Paviotti, M.; Anfosso-Lédée, F. *Common Noise Assessment Methods in Europe (CNOSSOS-EU)*; EUR 25379 EN; Publications Office of the European Union: Luxembourg, 2012.

44. Barry, T.M.; Reagan, J.A. *FHWA Highway Traffic Noise Prediction Model., FHWA-RD-77-108*; US Department of Transportation, Federal Highway Administration, Office of Research, Office of Environmental Policy, US Department of Transportation, Federal Highway Administration, Office of Research, Office of Environmental Policy: Washington, DC, USA, 1978.
45. Department of Transport. *Calculation of Road Traffic Noise*; Department of Transport Welsh office: Cardiff, UK; HMSO: Richmond, UK, 1998.
46. Quartieri, J.; Mastorakis, N.E.; Iannone, G.; Guarnaccia, C.; Ambrosio, S.D.; Troisi, A.; Lenza, T.L.L. A review of traffic noise predictive models. In Proceedings of the 5th WSEAS International Conference on "Applied and Theoretical Mechanics" (MECHANICS'09), Puerto De La Cruz, Canary Islands, Spain, 14–16 December 2009; pp. 72–80, ISBN 978-960-474-140-3.
47. Alam, P.; Ahmad, K.; Afsar, S.S.; Akhtar, N. Validation of the Road Traffic Noise Prediction Model RLS-90 in an Urban Area. In Proceedings of the 3rd International Conference on Emerging Technologies in Computer Engineering: Machine Learning and Internet of Things (ICETCE-2020), Jaipur, India, 7–8 February 2020.
48. Yamamoto, K. Road traffic noise prediction model "ASJ RTN-Model 2008": Report of research committee on road traffic noise. *Acoust. Sci. Technol.* **2010**, *31*, 1–55. [CrossRef]
49. Watts, G. *Harmonoise Prediction Model for Road Traffic Noise, PPR 034*; TRL Limited: Wokingham, UK, 2005.
50. Jonasson, H.G. Acoustical source modeling of road vehicles. *Acta Acust. United Acust.* **2007**, *93*, 173–184.
51. Heutschi, K. Son Road: New Swiss road traffic noise model. *Acta Acust. United Acust.* **2007**, *90*, 548–554.
52. Kragh, J.; Svein, Å.; Jonasson, H.G. *Nordic Environmental Noise Prediction Methods*; Nord 2000, Summary Report; DELTAAcoustics & Vibration: Kogens Lyngby, Denmark, 2002.
53. Dutilleux, G.; Defrance, J.; Ecotière, D.; Gauvreau, B.; Bèrengier, M.; Besnard, F.; Duc, E.L. NMPB-Routes 2008: The revision of the French method for road traffic noise prediction. *Acta Acust. United Acust.* **2010**, *96*, 1–11. [CrossRef]
54. Burgess, M.A. Noise prediction for urban traffic conditions-related to measurements in the Sydney Metropolitan Area. *Appl. Acoust.* **1977**, *10*, 1–7. [CrossRef]
55. Canelli, G.B.; Gluck, K.; Santoboni, S.A. A mathematical model for evaluation and prediction of mean energy level of traffic noise in Italian towns. *Acustica* **1983**, *53*, 31–36.
56. García, A.; Bernal, D. The prediction of traffic noise levels in urban areas. In Proceedings of the International Conference on Noise Control Engineering, (NCE' 85), Munich, Germany, 18–24 September 1985; pp. 843–846.
57. Fagotti, C.; Poggi, A. Traffic Noise Abatement Strategies. The Analysis of Real Case not Really Effective. In Proceedings of the 18th International Congress for Noise Abatement, Bologna, Italy, 10–12 July 1995.
58. Lam, W.K.H.; Tam, M.L. Reliability analysis of traffic estimates in Hong Kong. *Transport. Res. D* **1998**, *3*, 239–248. [CrossRef]
59. Gallo, M.; Mascolino, O.; Mazza, G. A model for estimating road traffic noise in urban areas. In Proceedings of the IEEE EEEIC 2016–16th International Conference on Environment and Electrical Engineering, Florence, Italy, 7–10 June 2016; pp. 374–378.
60. Gallo, M.; De Luca, G. A methodology for evaluating urban traffic plan scenarios from the point of view of traffic noise. *Wseas Trans. Circuits Syst.* **2016**, *15*, 187–197.

MDPI
St. Alban-Anlage 66
4052 Basel
Switzerland
Tel. +41 61 683 77 34
Fax +41 61 302 89 18
www.mdpi.com

*Infrastructures* Editorial Office
E-mail: infrastructures@mdpi.com
www.mdpi.com/journal/infrastructures

CPSIA information can be obtained
at www.ICGtesting.com
Printed in the USA
LVHW071155130422
716078LV00009B/297

9 783036 537269